Books published by
Professional Management Spectrum, Inc.
PO Box 30330
Pensacola, Florida 32504
(800) 346-6114
Web: servicebooks.com

Check our web site for the latest information on:

Navy Eval & Fitrep Writing Guide
Navy & Marine Corps Performance Writing Guide
The Definitive Performance Writing Guide
Successful Leadership Today
U.S. Navy Dictionary: Terms, Abbreviations &
Acronyms
Navy-Wide Exam Advancement Guide for E-4/E-7
    (Book & tapes)
Enlisted Surface Warfare Specialist (ESWS)
    (Book & tapes)
The Naval Officer's Manual
The Chief Petty Officer's Manual
The Navy Petty Officer's Manual
Fitness Report Writing Guide for Marines
Writing Guide for Air Force Efficiency Reports
Writing Guide for Army Efficiency Reports
Performance Appraisal Phrases
Positive Performance Paragraphs & Phrases

THE DEFINITIVE PERFORMANCE WRITING GUIDE

THIRD EDITION

ISBN Number: 0-9623673-0-3

Published by Professional Management Spectrum, Inc.
Pensacola, Florida

PRINTED IN THE UNITED STATES OF AMERICA

THE DEFINITIVE

PERFORMANCE

WRITING GUIDE

THIRD EDITION

THE *DEFINITIVE PERFORMANCE WRITING GUIDE* can be used by anyone who writes on the **performance, behavior**, or **character** of others.

Primary uses of this book include writing:

* PERFORMANCE APPRAISALS

* LETTERS OF INTRODUCTION

* LETTERS OF REFERENCE

* LETTERS OF RECOMMENDATION

* Any other writings on an individual's performance, behavior, or character.

THE *DEFINITIVE PERFORMANCE WRITING GUIDE* contains:
* 5,500 + **BULLET PHRASES** (from SUPERIOR to UNSATISFACTORY)

* 2,300 + WORDS grouped in convenient **WORD BANKS** covering SUPERIOR through UNSATISFACTORY PERFORMANCE and PERSONAL TRAITS

Major sections of the book include **FAVORABLE** through **UNSATISFACTORY** chapters on:
* PERSONAL PERFORMANCE (in 5 levels of performance)

* PERSONALITY & WORK RELATIONSHIPS

* PROBLEM SOLVING, MENTAL FACULTY, & JUDGMENT

* LEADERSHIP, SUPERVISION, & MANAGEMENT

* SELF EXPRESSION & COMMUNICATION SKILLS

* PLUS, SPECIAL SECTIONS ON COUNSELING & "BRAG SHEETS"

TABLE OF CONTENTS

CHAPTER 1

PERFORMANCE APPRAISAL INFORMATION

PERFORMANCE APPRAISAL

INTRODUCTION
Every organization has some method of evaluating its members. Administrators call this evaluation process "performance appraisal."

PRIMARY OBJECTIVES OF GIVING PERFORMANCE APPRAISALS:
1. Identify an individual's potential, retention and future assignments.
2. Provide feedback to the evaluee.

PERFORMANCES MEASURED:

1. **PERSONAL TRAITS** - How something is done (for example, the personal initiative, leadership, etc. used or applied to accomplish something).
2. **JOB PERFORMANCE** - What and how much is accomplished.
3. **JOB BEHAVIOR** - Personal behavior, adaptability, how well someone gets along with others, etc.

OBJECTIVE AND SUBJECTIVE ANALYSIS:

1. **OBJECTIVE ANALYSIS** - Means to quantify performance results. How much was done? What was done? Use hours, time, percent, dollars, etc.
2. **SUBJECTIVE ANALYSIS** - Is the evaluator's perceptions, beliefs, or thoughts on how someone accomplished tasks. This is an evaluation or analysis of a person's "inner" qualities (or personality) and should be based on observations over a period of time. Subjective analysis is used to describe what prompted or caused an individual to do something (personal traits such as leadership, imagination, initiative, etc.). These inner characteristics relate HOW or WHAT POSSESSED a person to accomplish something. These inner qualities help to project a person's POTENTIAL, WORTH and VALUE to an organization.

Performance Appraisal Information

FINDING THE CORRECT WORD MIX

A well written performance appraisal will have a mix of objective job accomplishments and the subjective "inner" quality words. For example:

EXAMPLE #1   (Name) performance has been of the highest caliber. During (period of time) completed (job accomplishment).

THE FIRST SENTENCE IS A SUBJECTIVE ANALYSIS.   THE SECOND SENTENCE IS AN OBJECTIVE ANALYSIS.

EXAMPLE #2   (Name) innovative ideas and suggestions greatly assisted in developing new procedures that led to   (area of improvement).

THE FIRST PART OF THE SENTENCE IS A SUBJECTIVE ANALYSIS AND THE SECOND PART IS THE OBJECTIVE ANALYSIS.

3-STEP APPROACH TO DRAFTING PERFORMANCE APPRAISALS

STEP #1   Make a listing of all objective job accomplishment particulars. A list of WHAT WAS DONE. List all quantifiable areas.

STEP #2   Look through the appropriate sections of this book and make a list of the words and phrases that fit the person and the situation.   Include any appropriate personal or behavioral traits.

STEP #3   Combine the two above lists into the desired mix.

PREPARATION CHECK-LIST

1. Performance appraisals should be handled discretely. They should be worked on in private.
2. Copies of previous appraisals should be reviewed if possible.
3. People being evaluated in comparable or competitive categories should be evaluated at the same time. This will facilitate comparative grading.

4. Try not to gravitate toward either a gratuitously high or rigidly severe policy of evaluating others.

5. Exercise care to evaluate objectively, avoiding any tendency which might allow general impressions, a single incident, or a particular trait, characteristic, or quality to influence the appraisal unduly.

6. Before you begin to write, check over any available information and determine an overall performance placement of the person being evaluated (e.g. HIGHLY FAVORABLE, FAVORABLE, MARGINAL or UNFAVORABLE). When this determination has been made, write a performance appraisal that will support and justify your position.

7. If grading or ranking marks are assigned, and they are significantly higher or lower than previous appraisals, a reason for the change might need to be included in the write-up.

8. Remember, words in a performance appraisal are both valuable and dangerous tools. Choose them carefully.

9. Before submitting a smooth performance appraisal, analyze the narrative to make sure that what is meant to be written, is in fact, actually being written. Give careful thought not only to the words you want to use, but also what the words will mean to others.

10. When the performance appraisal is finished, review it to ensure that:

   a. Any grading or ranking marks agree with the narrative.

   b. Any increasing or decreasing trend in performance is correctly conveyed.

11. When making subsequent performance appraisals on the same individual, guard against repetitive phraseology. Don't write the same thing time after time.

PERFORMANCE APPRAISAL "DO" CHECK-LIST

1. DO submit performance appraisals on time and in the correct format.

2. DO write on HOW someone contributed above or below what is normally expected.

3. DO write to express, NOT impress.

4. DO be fair, honest and objective.

5. DO write using hard, pertinent facts, not "faint praises" without substance.

PERFORMANCE APPRAISAL "DON'T" CHECK-LIST

1. DON'T assign grades or marks that are inconsistent with a narrative write up.
2. DON'T include minor, isolated, or insignificant imperfections which do not affect performance. A person doesn't have to be perfect to receive a good appraisal.
3. DON'T use "glittering generalities" which go on and on without saying anything useful.
4. DON'T use long words when shorter words will do just as well.
5. DON'T be verbose or redundant by writing the same thing over and over. Cover an area or subject adequately and move on to another subject.
6. DON'T start every sentence with the person's name. Reading becomes sluggish and boring, and shows lack of attention or ability on the part of the drafter.
7. DON'T evaluate someone's performance based on a comparison of another person whose job requirements are different.
8. DON'T restrict your evaluation of a new person to the amount of skill or knowledge they have acquired up to a particular point in time. Consider the amount of time it has taken that person to learn the skill or knowledge (e.g. learns at faster than normal pace, slower than normal pace, etc.).

"The pen is mightier than the sword." SHAKESPEARE

"Respect yourself and others
will respect you." CONFUCIUS
From the book: **Successful Leadership Today**

BULLET PHRASES

What is a "bullet phrase?" A bullet phrase is a statement that may or may not have a verb, object or subject.

Bullet phrases are straightforward, matter-of-fact statements. Bullet phrases serve to reduce the amount of space required to make a statement. Thus, using bullet phrases allows more material to be covered in the same space, or the same amount of material to be covered in less space than using formal sentence structure.

HELPFUL HINTS

There are three generally accepted ways to have the most important information in a performance appraisal stand out. It is recommended that some or all of these methods be used, if permitted by your organization.

ONE: Underline what you consider to be the most important parts of the performance appraisal.

EXAMPLE:
(Name) is a <u>self-starter</u> and an <u>inspirational leader.</u> <u>Unequaled ability to obtain maximum results</u> of available material and manpower resources. Strong moral fiber. Responsible for successful completion of (...). <u>Top achiever of boundless potential.</u>

TWO: CAPITALIZE what you consider to be the most important parts of the performance appraisal.

(Name) is a SELF-STARTER and an INSPIRATIONAL LEADER. Unequaled ability to obtain maximum results of available material and manpower resources. STRONG MORAL FIBER. Responsible for successful completion of (...). TOP ACHIEVER of BOUNDLESS POTENTIAL.

> "Either attempt it not, or succeed." OVID
> From the book: **Successful Leadership Today**

THREE: Use a combination of Underlining and CAPITALIZING.

EXAMPLE:
(Name) is a <u>SELF-STARTER</u> and an <u>INSPIRATIONAL LEADER</u>. <u>Unequaled ability to obtain maximum results</u> of available material and manpower resources. <u>STRONG MORAL FIBER</u>. Responsible for successful completion of (...). <u>TOP ACHIEVER</u> <u>of BOUNDLESS POTENTIAL</u>.

If the appraisal write-up is more than a few lines in length, using one of the above methods will ensure that the most important information can he seen at a glance.

CHOOSE YOUR WORDS CAREFULLY

Words are both valuable and dangerous tools. Choose them carefully. Review the following:

POTENTIAL   CAPACITY   ABILITY
To indicate that an individual has one of these qualities without the proper support words isn't saying anything useful. A person can have POTENTIAL, CAPACITY, or ABILITY and yet accomplish nothing. If you use words such as these, go on to write how these qualities were demonstrated.

TRIES   STRIVES   ATTEMPTS
Someone can TRY, STRIVE, or ATTEMPT to do something without accomplishing anything. As above, note how these qualities were demonstrated.

ACCEPTS   ASSIGNED
Simply ACCEPTING a job does not show initiative. Performing an ASSIGNED job does not show initiative.

NORMALLY   GENERALLY   USUALLY
These words mean less than always.

> Don't let a personal passion
> overcome your logic and good sense.
> From the book: **Successful Leadership Today**

7

AVERAGE ABOVE AVERAGE EXCELLENT SUPERIOR

These words have come to have "CANNED" meanings. ABOVE AVERAGE is generally assumed to mean less than EXCELLENT. And, EXCELLENT is good, but it is less than SUPERIOR. If you are going to place someone's performance in one of these categories, be sure to choose the correct word(s).

AGGRESSIVE

Careful how you use this one. If the word AGGRESSIVE is linked to a person's personality, it may be understood by the reader that that person is overbearing. But, to write that a person is JOB AGGRESSIVE gives the reader a completely different impression.

"A leader is a dealer
in hope." NAPOLEON
From the book: **Successful Leadership Today**

The key to good writing is to
know your subject matter well.

"Success is a journey,
not a destination." H.T. COLLARD
From the book: **Successful Leadership Today**

KEY WORDS

The "KEY WORDS" listed on the following pages serve as general guidance for: (1) determining which grading category an individual's performance might fit;
and, (2) words that would be appropriate to use to justify grading in that particular category. Remember, however, that many of the key words--just like the WORD BANK in the various chapters--could be used appropriately in a category higher or lower than the category in which it is listed. Each word used along would fit in the category where it is listed. However, when you add other words to the original word, the overall meaning of the sentence or phrase might better fit in another grading category. For example, take the word "ACCURATE" in the EFFECTIVE CHAPTER. By writing "HIGHLY ACCURATE," this phrase could then fit in the ABOVE AVERAGE CHAPTER. And, by writing "NOT ACCURATE," this phrase could fit in one of the unfavorable chapters.

"Never promise more than you
can perform." PUBLILIUS SYRUS
From the book: **Successful Leadership Today**

"It is tedious to tell tales already told." HOMER

"We confide in our strength, without
boasting of it; we respect that of others,
without fearing it." THOMAS JEFFERSON
From the book: **Successful Leadership Today**

SUPERIOR (PERFORMANCE LEVEL 10-9)	ABOVE AVERAGE (PERFORMANCE LEVEL 8-7)	EFFECTIVE (PERFORMANCE LEVEL 6-5)
ARTICULATE	ABOVE AVERAGE	ABILITY
BEST	ACHIEVER	ABLE
BOUNDLESS	AGGRESSIVE	ACCEPTS
CONSUMMATE	BETTER	ACCURATE
DISTINGUISHED	CAREFUL	AMPLE
EPITOME	COMPETITIVE	ASSISTS
EXCELLENCE	CONTRIBUTES	AVERAGE
EXCEPTIONAL	CREDIBLE	BENEFICIAL
FAULTLESS	DEDICATED	CAPABLE
IMPECCABLE	EAGER	COMPETENT
INCOMPARABLE	EARNEST	CONFIDENT
MASTERFUL	EXCEEDS	CORRECT
MATCHLESS	FRUITFUL	COOPERATIVE
METICULOUS	GOOD	DEPENDABLE
OUTSTANDING	HIGH	EFFECTIVE
PARAGON	INDUSTRIOUS	EFFICIENT
PEERLESS	PRODUCTIVE	FAVORABLE
PERFECTION	PRUDENT	HELPFUL
PINNACLE	QUALITY	KNOWLEDGEABLE
PREEMINENT	RESOURCEFUL	NORMAL
SUPERIOR	SKILLED	ORDERLY
SUPREME	SUCCESSFUL	POSITIVE
UNEQUALED	TALENTED	PREPARED
UNPARALLELED	THOROUGH	PROPER
UNSURPASSED	VOLUNTEERS	RELIABLE

Performance Appraisal Information

BELOW AVERAGE (PERFORMANCE LEVEL 4-3)	UNSATISFACTORY (PERFORMANCE (LEVEL 2-1)
ABNORMAL	BLUNDER
AMBIGUOUS	CARELESS
AWRY	DEPLORABLE
BELOW-PAR	DEROGATORY
COMPLACENT	DISASTROUS
CONFUSED	FAIL
DEFICIENT	FUTILE
DISSATISFIED	HORRENDOUS
ERODE	IMPOTENT
ERRATIC	INABILITY
FALTER	INAPT
FLAWED	INCAPABLE
FLIMSY	INCOMPETENT
FORGETFUL	NEGLECTFUL
FRUITLESS	NEGLIGENT
HAMPER	PATHETIC
HINDER	SLOPPY
IMPAIR	STAGNANT
INADEQUATE	UNDEPENDABLE
INCONSISTENT	UNRELIABLE
INEFFECTIVE	UNSATISFACTORY
INFERIOR	USELESS
LACKING	VALUELESS
RELAPSE	WASTED
SHABBY	WORTHLESS

"People who fly into a rage always make
a bad landing." WILL ROGERS
From the book: **Successful Leadership Today**

THE BELL CURVE

The below bell curve showing grading, or ranking, within a "typical" organization has been around for a number of years. The curve is based on the theory that the typical organization would have 5% of its personnel with the highest performance appraisal write-up and grading, another 20% with above average write-ups, etc. In reality, however, no organization considers itself as "typical." Therefore, the bell curve should serve only as a reference point for individual organizations.

PERFORMANCE DISTRIBUTION	TOP 5%	TOP 20%	MIDDLE 50%	BOTTOM 20%	BOT. 5%
GRADING SCALE ** 10-to-1	10-9	8-7	6-5	4-3	2-1
GRADING SCALE 5-to-1	5	4	3	2	1
GRADING SCALE 3-to-1		3	2	1	

** NOTE: This book uses a 10-to-1 grading scale. Individual organizations may use a different grading scale. As indicated above, regardless of the grading scale used, the bell curve for grading distribution should be effective in dividing performance levels on any scale.

12

Performance Appraisal Information

WORDS OF WISDOM

The single most difficult task in constructing this writing guide was the placing of the words and bullet phrases in the "correct" chapter of the book. In fact, it was an impossible task. One day a phrase would seem to "fit" nicely into one particular chapter. A week later, however, it was obvious that that phrase was out of place. I decided that I could work on into infinity and never have every word and phrase fit nicely--and absolutely without question--into any specific chapter. Eventually, I discovered that the proper placement of the words and bullet phrases depended upon my particular mental frame of reference at a particular time. This hard-earned wisdom I pass along to you. As noted earlier in this chapter, to author a valid and correct performance appraisal narrative on an individual, you must use both objective and subjective analysis. This book covers only subjective analysis. You, the drafter, must supply the objective analysis information (qualify, quantify, measure, etc.) for a narrative. If you go to a particular chapter of this book after having mentally placed an individual's performance at one level and the words don't seem to be appropriate, then you have come face to face with the problem I noted above. In this case, you may be able to go to a chapter "higher" or "lower" in this book and find the word mix that fits in with your mental frame of reference. Again, it's a matter of finding the correct subjective information in this book that matches the objective information that you, the drafter, have on any particular individual.

For example, the subjective words "AMPLE ABILITY" mean little in and of themselves. Consider the following examples:

AMPLE ABILITY to do menial tasks
AMPLE ABILITY for routine assignments
AMPLE ABILITY to produce favorable output
AMPLE ABILITY for top quality work
AMPLE ABILITY in even most difficult activities

In the final analysis, YOU must decide which words and bullet phrases are most appropriate for the particular performance appraisal you are drafting.

> If you don't know the true meaning
> of a word, don't use it.

13

PERFORMANCE/PROGRESS REPORTS (PPRs)

Writing performance appraisals, Letters of Appreciation, or any other report on an individual's performance is a difficult task in itself. When long periods of time separate written records of performance, the job becomes even more difficult. You can't expect to sit down one day and conveniently recall all pertinent facts of an individual's performance for an extended period of time. This difficulty is multiplied by the number of individuals on whom performance documents are written. Additionally, an individual's job may change, and, more than one person may be involved in keeping track of performance. These are just a few of the reasons organizations are turning to some means of documenting work performance at times other than at the end of a specific reporting period.

Almost any "as occurring" report is better than no documentation. The key is to have a form that is simple and convenient to use. This form can carry any title. A sample Performance Progress Report (PPR) form is provided on the following page. This sample form can be modified to fit any organizational structure or need.

The PPR can be either formal or informal. Completed PPRs are normally accumulated and held for use at the appropriate reporting period.

A PPR, or equivalent, is an excellent means of offering immediate feedback to an individual who has demonstrated superior or below acceptable action. For superior performance, a PPR provides an immediate "pat on the back" to a deserving individual. Conversely, receiving a PPR for unacceptable work serves as an immediate warning signal to an individual.

When can the PPR be used? PPRs can be used by any superior to report on any junior. The more often PPRs are used the better they serve as a management tool and the easier it becomes to grade individuals and write performance appraisals.

> "Destiny is not a matter of chance,
> it is a matter of choice...it is a thing
> to be achieved." WILLIAM JENNINGS BRYAN
> From the book: **Successful Leadership Today**

Performance Appraisal Information

PERFORMANCE/PROGRESS REPORT (PPR)

ORGANIZATION:_____   DATE:_____

NAME:_____
      JOB:_____

PERFORMANCE:
    ☐ MERITORIOUS   ☐ DEROGATORY   ☐ OTHER
_____

REMARKS

      (ENTER REMARKS & COMMENTS HERE)

_____

_____   _____
SIGNATURE OF   SIGNATURE OF
PERSON REPORTING   INDIVIDUAL

SAMPLE PERFORMANCE/PROGRESS REPORT (PPR)

ORGANIZATION: ADMINISTRATION   **DATE**: 4 August (year)

NAME: JOHN DOE   **JOB:** FILE CLERK

PERFORMANCE:
☐ MERITORIOUS   ■ DEROGATORY   ☐ OTHER

REMARKS

10-15 Minutes late for work 3 days in a row. Must make better effort to be on time

_

SIGNATURE OF
PERSON REPORTING

SIGNATURE OF
INDIVIDUAL

SAMPLE PERFORMANCE/PROGRESS REPORT (PPR)

ORGANIZATION:ADMINISTRATION   **DATE**: 4 August (date)

NAME: JOHN DOE   **JOB**: FILE CLERK

PERFORMANCE:
■ MERITORIOUS   ☐ DEROGATORY   ☐ OTHER

REMARKS

Always offers beneficial suggestions.   One such suggestion should save ($xxx) over the next year alone. KEEP UP THE GOOD WORK.

_

SIGNATURE OF
PERSON REPORTING

SIGNATURE OF
INDIVIDUAL

PERFORMANCE COUNSELING SHEET

When an individual develops a serious problem that cannot be adequately covered by a Performance/Progress Report, a form such as a Performance Counseling Sheet (PCS) is suggested.

The PCS is a more formal, official document. A sample PCS form is provided on the following page.

> Win the heart and the body will follow.
> From the book: **Successful Leadership Today**

> "Once a word has been allowed to escape,
> it cannot be recalled." HOMER

> "Reason and judgment are the
> qualities of a leader." TACITUS
> From the book: **Successful Leadership Today**

PERFORMANCE COUNSELING SHEET

NAME   ORGANIZATION   DATE

AREA OF COUNSELING

☐ Performance   ☐ Dress-Appearance
☐ Behavior   ☐ Tardiness
☐ Training Progress   ☐ Duties-Responsibilities
☐ Other (Specify)

REASONS WHICH BROUGHT ABOUT COUNSELING SESSION
(Give details, facts, specific dates, names, sequence of events, etc.)

SOLUTION THAT COUNSELOR AND COUNSELEE DEVELOP AND DISCUSSED TO OVERCOME THE PROBLEM(S) AND PRECLUDE FUTURE INVOLVEMENT
(Outline all solutions and indicate which one(s) individual freely elected.)

18

Performance Appraisal Information

COUNSELEE'S COMMENTS

_____   _____
Signature/Supervisor   Date

REMARKS/FOLLOW-UP ACTION
(To be completed ONE MONTH following counseling session. Outline
all efforts indicating dates, names, progress, etc.)

OUTCOME: Problem Resolved   Problem Persists

COMMENTS:

_____   _____
Signature/Supervisor   Date

KEY COUNSELING POINTS

* Point out to counselee that serious flaws in performance/behavior
  must be corrected.
* Counseling is performed to solve a problem or to fulfill a need.
* Determine interview objective prior to meeting, review available
  records, and arrange office seating for best results.
* It may be advisable for the counselee's immediate supervisor to be
  in attendance during the counseling session so that each will know
  exactly what is expected.
* Give the individual the facts, whether pleasant or unpleasant.
* Be a good listener-Be fair.
* Refer individual to more professional personnel if the problem can
  be better resolved.
* Follow-up on any new information brought to light during interview.
* Keep personal problems CONFIDENTIAL.
* Help the person to grow in self-understanding.

DO NOT lose self control. The results could be disastrous.
DO NOT make promises you cannot keep.
DO NOT make snap decisions.
DO NOT forget to document the counseling and have counselee
           sign this sheet.

19

Performance Appraisal Information

INTERCHANGEABLE WORDS

Throughout this book words such as INDIVIDUAL, PERSON, PERFORMER, WORKER, etc. appear. These words are interchangeable. If you do not desire to use one of these words in the phrase in which it appears, simply exchange that word for one of your choice. ADDITIONALLY, any of these words may be replaced by using a person's job title or professional title (e.g. MANAGER, OFFICER, FILE CLERK, etc.).

"Great souls have wills,
feeble ones have only wishes." PROVERB
From the book: **Successful Leadership Today**

"No meritorious act of a subordinate should
escape attention or be left to pass without
reward, even if the reward be only one
word of approval." JOHN PAUL JONES

"The best morale exists when you never hear
the word mentioned. When you hear a lot of
talk about it, it's usually lousy." DWIGHT D. EISENHOWER
From the book: **Successful Leadership Today**

CHAPTER 2

SUPERIOR PERSONAL PERFORMANCE
(LEVELS 10-9)

PERSONAL PERFORMANCE

LEVELS 10-9
* Contributes GREATLY to organization mission
* CONTINUALLY seeks additional responsibility
* THOROUGHLY understands all job components
* Works well independent of supervision

LEVELS 8-7
* Contributes HIGH LEVEL to organization mission
* Seeks additional responsibility
* Exhibits drive for self-improvement
* Proposes good solutions to difficult problems

LEVELS 6-5
* Contributes SOME to organization mission
* ACCEPTS additional responsibility
* Requires LIMITED supervision
* Good understanding of major jobs

LEVELS 4-3
* DOES NOT contribute to organization mission
* DOES NOT desire additional responsibility
* Requires ROUTINE supervision
* Satisfied with less than quality work

LEVELS 2-1
* HINDERS organization mission
* AVOIDS added responsibility
* Requires CONSTANT supervision
* DOES NOT or CAN NOT understand job

SAMPLE WRITE-UPS

(FAVORABLE)

Industrious & versatile. Approaches any task enthusiastically and with dispatch.

Skillful manager. Proven ability to attain high standard of performance. Ready for positions of increased responsibility.

Superior leader, manager, and organizer. Mature, articulate, and dedicated.

Enjoys my complete confidence and support. Asset to high morale.

Unequaled ability to obtain maximum results. "Head and shoulders" above contemporaries.

Strong moral fiber, respected by everyone.

Top achiever of boundless potential and ability.

Industrious, meticulous, and accurate. Aggressively tackles any job.

Maximizes strengths of subordinates. Positive influence in achieving organization goals.

Proven leader, manager, and organizer. Good potential.

Most productive and versatile (peer group) in (organization).

Proven top quality organizer and administrator.

Possesses great deal of energy, highly industrious. Establishes and maintains atmosphere of pride and professionalism.

Capable of making independent judgments and decisions.

Poised and mature with thirst for knowledge and desire for challenge.

22

Self-starter with great personal initiative and leadership skills. Far above contemporaries.

Sets standards by which excellence is measured.
Proven manager and leader. Displays the character, initiative, and resourcefulness to accept and accomplish most demanding tasks.

Energetic and conscientious. Especially adept in dealing with people.

Dedicated professional who thrives on new challenges.

Dynamic leader and superb manager. Ideally suited for top leadership positions.

Dress and grooming impeccable. Calm, affable manner prime assets. Potential for positions of higher authority..

Completely self-reliant. Consistent top performer. Unbound potential. Excellent candidate for increased and more demanding duties.

Exceptional manager and organizer whose demonstrated expertise as a leader has measurably improved the overall performance and readiness of (organization).

Commands fullest respect and support. An original thinker.

Self-starter whose work is marked by integrity and initiative.

Meticulously accurate. Great sense of responsibility for quality of work.

Tireless worker. True professional in every sense of the word.

Courage of conviction and strong moral character.

Fosters high morale, esprit de corps, and total winning attitude.

Consistently executed the weighty responsibilities of (job) with fervor, determination, and overall superb success. Very talented.

Superior Personal Performance (Levels 10-9)

Good sense of organization. Spontaneous propensity to leadership. Reputation for dependable & timely work.

Infused (organization) with enthusiasm and dedication.

Astute management of personnel and equipment.

Markedly improved operation, working conditions, & physical appearance of (organization).

Tactful, yet strong leader by instilling desire to excel.

Truly an exceptional (peer group). Ready for increased responsibility now. A "front runner."

Discharges all responsibilities with complete professionalism and tireless dedication. Conscientious and persevering.

Sound leadership and management techniques.

Receives maximum support from subordinates because of ability to generate enthusiasm through "follow me" approach.

Appearance and personal behavior on par with other exceptional qualities.

Proven leader and accomplished specialist in professional field.

Top performer. Totally professional, poised, mature, and dedicated. Self-starter.

Neat, trim, and fit. Articulate in speech, polite in manner.

Enjoys loyalty, cooperation, and support of subordinates.

Highly qualified and recommended for any demanding and challenging job.

Possesses managerial and organizational expertise rarely observed in contemporaries.

Performance nothing short of outstanding.

Potential to fill positions of greater trust and responsibility not normally available.

Superior Personal Performance (Levels 10-9)

Keen interest in work, sets and maintains a high standard of performance.

Methodical and extremely conscientious, actions well planned, smoothly executed, in the best interest of job well done.

Team consistently produces quality results while being sensitive to needs of (organization).

Can be relied upon to see that all tasks are completed expeditiously and efficiently. High level of expertise.
A dedicated leader whose standards of integrity are of finest quality.

encourages every subordinate to set highest possible goals.

One of our finest (peer group) in (organization).

Played vital role in achievement of (organization) mission and goals.

Cornerstone of technical knowledge and management skill.

Vast experience enhanced by intelligence, sincerity, and ability to communicate effectively at all levels.

Personal sacrifice, and uncompromising standards of conduct provided impetus for growth and development of (organization).

Most highly respected (peer group) in this organization.

Support of organization and leadership have significantly enhanced work within (organization).

Efficient procurement and management of operational and administrative assets saved ... dollars in sorely needed financial assets.

Sets exceptional example as leader and manager.

Attained professional and technical knowledge and competence rarely observed within peer group.

Ability to obtain quality results in any environment.

Superior Personal Performance (Levels 10-9)

Always finds time to help those in need. Emphatic demeanor and timely responsiveness. a model.

Consistently performed all duties in outstanding manner.

Strong abilities; excellent manager of material and equipment.

Displays tact and compassion with innovative and intelligent view of future.

Innovative approach displayed in day-to-day work, as well as special programs, consistently above expected norm.

Intelligent, energetic manager and organizer. Enjoys fast-paced work environment.

Quick thinker, makes positive decisions that are easily supported.

Completely dependable, performs all tasks with accuracy and dispatch.

Professional attitude radiates to others, causing them to respond in kind with full effort and cooperation.

Instituted many procedures that simplified and streamlined (organization) operations and administrative effort.

Has knack for getting job done where others fail.

Top notch manager and organizer. Energetic and resourceful, plans ahead.

Impressively managed (organization) transition from (.......) to (......). Structured organization met or exceeded all tasking.

Self-starter with desire for challenge.

Firm, fair unbiased leader. Demands high standards of performance from self and others. . Highly talented, a front runner.

26

Excels wherever assigned. Invaluable manager and counselor, a source of knowledge and inspiration in every area of responsibility.

Tact, coordination, and ability to get to heart of any problem increased efficiency and effectiveness of (organization).

Extremely intelligent and dynamic leader with limitless potential.

Solid, proven leadership and management principles.

Structured organization dynamic in nature and allowed for self-evaluation and internal correction. All deadlines met.

Morale very high. Displayed compassion and concern. Inspired unequaled loyalty. Asset to this (organization).

Performance continues to be underscored by pride, self-improvement, and accomplishment.

Organized monumental task of ... Successful efforts met all tasking.

Working with others in a unified and cohesive manner a particularly strong asset.

An achiever possessed with imagination and initiative.

Superior ability and performance. Totally professional and dedicated.

Performance underscored by pride, personal involvement, and accomplishment.

Industrious and creative. Likes to get into "nuts and bolts" of problems regardless of complexity or magnitude.

Outstanding technical knowledge and managerial ability.

Unbound initiative and extremely conscientious.

Actions well planned, organized, and smoothly executed.

Team player, fosters cooperation and harmony throughout (organization).

27

Successful, dynamic, and compassionate leader, knows how to motivate others. Great potential.

Sustained superior performance has been inspiration to each member of this (organization).

Deep respect and sincere affection received result of superlative qualities of leadership, integrity, and professional knowledge.

Fostered unparalleled productivity with ability to anticipate potential problem areas.

(Organization) received high marks in...... due, in large part, to (name) active involvement.

Unparalleled ability to manage money, material, and personnel.

Instills high-performance motivation and creativity. Stimulates individual growth and responsibility.

Performance, across the board, nothing less than outstanding.

Truly outstanding individual. Demonstrates unfailing diligence, job-aggressiveness, and total dedication to excellence.

Self-starter. Personal initiative and leadership skills guarantee exceptional results of all tasks assigned or assumed.

Top shelf organizer, manager, and administrator. Unique ability to assimilate myriad of diverse inputs.

Poised and mature with matchless thirst for knowledge and increased responsibility.

Earned my complete trust and confidence, most capable of making independent judgments and decisions. Proven top achiever.

Demonstrates specific talents and character traits required for ascent to positions of high responsibility.

Extremely knowledgeable, industrious, completely resourceful. Performance of all duties singularly outstanding.

Personally selected to assume   .. Selected because of demonstrated superior management and leadership abilities.

Superb ability to write clear, concise, and accurate material. Continually striving for personal growth.

Plans ahead, stays on top of every project or assignment until quality results achieved.

Takes rapid, effective action without guidance from above.

Excellent counselor, particularly adept in solving problems encountered by other personnel.

Unlimited potential for responsibility and challenge. Without reservation (name) has my highest recommendation for ....

Industrious, conscientious, and highly motivated (peer group). Exhibits highest degree of professionalism in accomplishing all tasks.

Contributed personally to (organization) during critical periods that lead to...... Designed and completed major upgrade of (......). Task completed in half allowed time.

Accomplished leader, manager, and organizer. Convincing speaker. Keen judgment.

Self-starter who has implemented many programs within organization which have served to upgrade capability and increase morale.

Advice actively sought by others. Bold, imaginative (leader/supervisor), ready for promotion now.

Efficient and highly knowledgeable. Performance, singularly and collectively, outstanding.

Demonstrated unbound ability and capacity to successfully assume positions of greater authority and jurisdiction.

Firm, earnest, exacting, and flexible. Highest degree of support while maintaining extraordinarily high morale.

Superior Personal Performance (Levels 10-9)

Provided outstanding (.....) support as well as continued superior...... skills.

Adaptable, polished, and receptive, the person to see when a job needs completed with dispatch and efficiency.

Confident of abilities and work. Volunteers to tackle any assignment without doubt or hesitation.

Works zealously to complete each task as perfectly as possible.

Sound management background. Analytical mind and ability to adapt to changing situations.

Highly effective in any situation. (name) should be assigned to most demanding and challenging jobs.

(name) enjoys my complete trust and confidence.

Absolute top performer in every respect. Outstanding leadership, superb management techniques. Total dedication to (organization).

Complete confidence to represent (organization) in any circumstance.

Quiet manner, commanding presence. Total consideration for others in all endeavors, whether a professional or personal matter.

Earned genuine respect of seniors, juniors, peers.
Extremely well-rounded individual. Demonstrated potential for greater responsibilities through uncompromising performance.

Self-starting individual needed in order to meet tomorrow's challenges.

Model (peer group). Inquisitive, creative, and foresighted. Consistently makes sound management decisions.

Energetic personality, positive "can do" attitude.

SUPERIOR PERSONAL PERFORMANCE

WORD BANK

NOTE: The words in this word bank, USED ALONE, describe SUPERIOR PERFORMANCE. When combined with other "qualifying" words, many of these words can be used to describe lower performance.

EXAMPLE: POTENT (SUPERIOR)
            SOMETIMES POTENT (ABOVE AVERAGE)
            NOT POTENT (UNSATISFACTORY)

* When writing on SUPERIOR PERFORMANCE, try not to use a negative word in conjunction with a positive "qualifying" word (**"NEVER INCORRECT"**). An appropriate SUPERIOR PERFORMANCE bullet to the above could be **"ALWAYS CORRECT**."

Words listed in other word banks can similarly be used to describe higher or lower performance.

ACCOMPLISHED	ADEPT	ADMIRABLE
ADROIT	ADROITNESS	ALACRITY
ALL-AROUND	ALL-STAR	ARTFUL
ARTICULATE	ARTISTIC	BEST
BOUNDLESS	CHAMPION	CONSUMMATE
COURAGEOUS	DEVOTED	DISTINGUISHED
EAGER BEAVER	ENERGIZE	ENERGY
EPITOME	ERUDITE	ERUDITION
EXACTING	EXCELLENCE	EXCELLENT
EXCEPTIONAL	EXEMPLARY	EXEMPLIFY
EXPERT	FABULOUS	FANTASTIC
FAULTLESS	FIRST	FIRST CLASS
FIRST-RATE	FIRST-STRING	FOREMOST
GREAT	GREATER	GREATEST
GIFTED	HARD CHARGER	IMPECCABLE
INCOMPARABLE	INVENTIVE	INVENTOR
JOURNEYMAN	LAUDABLE	LAUDATORY
MASTER	MASTERFUL	MASTERY

31

MATCHLESS	MERITORIOUS	METICULOUS
OUTCLASS	OUTDO	OUTMATCH
OUTSHINE	OUTSTANDING	PARAGON
PARAMOUNT	PATHFINDER	PEERLESS
PERFECT	PERFECTION	
PERSONIFICATION		
PERSONIFY	PINNACLE	PLAUDIT
POTENT	PRAISE	PRAISEWORTHY
PREDOMINANT	PREDOMINATE	PREEMINENT
PREMIER	PROMINENCE	PROMINENT
PROWESS	RENOWN	RENOWNED
SPARTAN	STANDARD-BEARER	STANDOUT
STAR	STERLING	SUPERB
SUPERFINE	SUPERIOR	SUPERLATIVE
SUPREMACY	SUPREME	SURPASS
TIRELESS	TOP-LEVEL	TOP-NOTCH
TOP QUALITY	TRAILBLAZER	UNBEATABLE
UNBLEMISHED	UNERRING	UNEQUALED
UNFAILING	UNPARALLELED	UNRIVALED
UNSURPASSED	UNTIRING	UTMOST
VIRTUOSO	WHIZ	WINNER
WONDERWORK	ZEALOT	ZENITH

Written words live longer than memory.

"No power is strong enough to be
lasting if it labors under the
weight of fear." CICERO
From the book: **Successful Leadership Today**

BULLET PHRASES

Select a word in COLUMN #1 to go with a word in COLUMN #2.

EXAMPLE: OUTSTANDING MANAGER

COLUMN #1	**COLUMN #2**
BEST	INDIVIDUAL
CONSUMMATE	OFFICER
EXCEPTIONAL	MANAGER
EXEMPLARY	PERSON
EXTRAORDINARY	SUPERVISOR
FAULTLESS	TECHNICIAN
FOREMOST	TYPIST
GIFTED	WORKER
IMPECCABLE	(or, use
MASTERFUL	Professional
MATCHLESS	title)
OUTSTANDING	
PEERLESS	
PREEMINENT	
REMARKABLE	
STERLING	
SUPERIOR	
SUPREME	
UNBEATABLE	
UNEQUALED	
UNPARALLELED	
UNRIVALED	
UNSURPASSED	

"Write to EXPRESS,
not IMPRESS."
From the book:
**Successful Leadership
Today**

"TACT: The ability to describe
others as they see themselves."
ABRAHAM LINCOLN
From the book: **Successful Leadership Today**

BULLET PHRASE STATEMENTS

...Masterful innovator

...Relentless dedication

...Strong initiative

...Exceedingly articulate

...Completely dependable

...Boundless ability

...Ultimate professional

...Unparalleled success

...Unblemished record

...Great foresight

...Sterling performer

...Exceedingly accurate

...Considerable talent

...Unrelenting effort

...Completely competent

...Exceptional ability

...Unfailing performance

...Boundless energy

...Always volunteers

...Exacting work

...Tireless worker

...Success oriented

...Advanced knowledge

...Highly motivated

...Exacting nature

...Matchless desire

...Unwavering dedication

...Exceptional results

...Expert technician

...Steadfast dedication

...Strongly motivated

...Results oriented

...Tireless dedication

...Unparalleled credentials

...Praiseworthy accomplishments

...Inexhaustible energy

...Endless drive

...Intense dedication

...A self-starter

...Forward thinking

...Dominating force

...Enviable performance

...Brilliant future

...Relentless dedication

34

...Without equal

...Banner performer

...Top professional

...Highly respected

...Completely competent

...Creatively inclined

...Outstanding worker

...Tremendous ability

...Impressive credentials

...Great enthusiasm

...Unsurpassed work

...Unlimited potential

...Unending contributions

...Unequaled ability

...Thoroughly proficient

...Extremely zealous

...Impressive individual

...Tremendous success

...Exemplary performer

...Quality performer

...Relentless drive

...Overcomes adversity

...Hard charger

...Abundant energy

...Always accurate

...Technically advanced

...Commands respect

...High achiever

...Self sacrificing

...Prolific performer

...Tough competitor

...No mistakes

...Remarkable abilities

...Valuable accomplishments

...Great initiative

...Matchless productivity

...Stellar performer

...Abundantly productive

...Ace technician

...Highly industrious

...Superior work

...Extremely productive

...Flawless performer

...Model worker

35

Superior Personal Performance (Levels 10-9)

...Uncommon excellence

...Skillful undertaking

...Multi-disciplined individual

...Meticulously accurate

...Top performer

...Uncommon workmanship

...Always resourceful

...Impressive abilities

...Inspires confidence

...Impressive ability

...Industrious nature

...Unparalleled potential

...Contributes maximum effort

...Resilient and energetic

...Hurdles over obstacles

...Enormous professional abilities

...Displays selfless devotion

...Exceeds highest expectations

...A well-rounded professional

...Forward looking individual

...Exhibits technical excellence

...Highly industrious individual

...Always productively employed

...Competitive spirit

...Highly self-motivated

...Unmatched efficiency

...Endless energy

...Irreplaceable performance

...Intense dedication

...Unending energy

...Insatiable curiosity

...Exceptional talent

...Significant contributions

...Impressive accomplishments

...A take-charge individual

...Astute, quality performer

...Always gives 100%

...Top quality performer

36

Superior Personal Performance (Levels 10-9)

...Knows job completely

...Exceptionally well organized

...A real competitor

...Persevering and enduring

...Never caught unprepared

...Results always impressive

...Proficient and industrious

...Anticipates problem areas

...Contributes to excellence

...Meticulous in manner

...Intense, eager performer

...Great personal industry

...Resolute in action

...Steadfast, loyal dedication

...Unhesitant in action

...Resourceful and energetic

...Solid professional competence

...Highly motivated achiever

...Composed under pressure

...Versatile and multi-disciplined

...Self-motivated and resourceful

...Stands above others

Superior Personal Performance (Levels 10-9)

...True team player

...Adds extra dimension

...A role model

...Smooth and flawless

...Accustomed to success

...A top professional

...Enterprising, intense performer

...Great technical curiosity

...Strong professional pride

...Proficient and industrious

...Benchmark of excellence

...Sets superior example

...Overcomes all obstacles

...A standard bearer

...Delivers wholehearted support

...In-depth technical knowledge

...Thrives on diversity

...Decisive in action

...Superior to others

...Gives extra effort

...Highest caliber performance

...A driving force

...Unrelenting work habits

38

...Enjoys stressful situations

...Meets diverse challenges

...Captures the imagination

...Keen technical abilities

...Reaches new heights

...Decisive, action oriented

...Total, complete professional

...Springs into action

...Exerts total effort

...Quick to respond

...Promoted new ideas

...Comprehensive technical skill

...Great self control

...Organized and industrious

...Always highly motivated

...Firm and resolute

...Never gives up

...Rich technical expertise

...Uncommon professional insight

...Extremely well organized

...Great personal drive

...Sustained superior performance

Superior Personal Performance (Levels 10-9)

...Poised and mature

...Sound professional judgment

...Maintains highest standards

...Seeks challenging assignments

...Responsibilities discharged superbly

...Consistently outstanding results

...Skillfully performs job

...Exceptional professional competence

...Unusually accurate and effective

...Successfully meets any challenge

...Reputation for dependable results

...Actively seeks additional responsibility

...Aggressively tackles demanding assignments

...Performance routinely exceeds standards

...Provides whatever assistance required

...Intense desire to succeed

...Performance always exceeds expectations

...Aggressively pursues difficult challenges

...Remarkable capability and versatility

...Routinely resolves difficult problems

...Consistently gives quality performance

...Ability to overcome obstacles

...Seeks additional professional knowledge

40

Superior Personal Performance (Levels 10-9)

...Achieves uniformly outstanding results

...Completely self-reliant and dependable

...Unending appetite for self-improvement

...Meticulous attention to detail

...Long-standing record of creditability

...Extremely well rounded individual

...Job-aggressive, demonstrates unfailing diligence

...Total commitment to job

...Enjoys fast-paced work environment

...Maintains composure under pressure

...Inexhaustible drive and initiative

...Competent in any situation

...Relentless energy and drive

...Ingrained pursuit of excellence

...Great initiative and persistence

...Confident, composed under pressure

...A "take charge" individual

...High ambition. High achiever

...Creative and decisive nature

...Thrives under adverse conditions

...Endless zeal and enthusiasm

...Responsive in stressful situations

41

...Utmost degree of accuracy

...Responsive to all tasking

...Always produces quality results

...Strong sense of purpose

...Reputation for top performance

...Impressive motivation and ability

...Adapts with uncommon ease

...Has pride and self-assurance

...Admirable courage of conviction

...Unyielding dedication and loyalty

...Alert, quick and responsive

...Strong desire to excel

...Unlimited ability and potential

...Achieves uniformly outstanding results

...Succeeds despite any adversity

...Achieves more than others

...Always prepared and ready

...Seeks opportunities to grow

...Vigorously tackles any assignment

...Great strength of character

...Eagerly accepts work assignments

...Intense dedication and enthusiasm

...Extremely energetic and helpful

42

...Long-standing record of credibility

...Almost infinite growth potential

...Adamantly supports all rules

...Always achieves positive results

...Complete understanding of specialty

...Superlative dedication and self-sacrifice

...Persevering in all tasking

...Promptly executes all jobs

...Unselfish devotion to organization

...Superior knowledge of job

...Keen appreciation of responsibilities

...Highly motivated. Enjoys challenge

...Acts decisively on own

...Remarkable ability to adapt

...Achieves highest performance levels

...Very quick but thorough

...Readily tackles any assignment

...Proven performer under pressure

...Careful, exacting work practices

...Productive worker, overcomes obstacles

...Ignites enthusiasm of others

...Goal oriented. Stays ahead

43

Superior Personal Performance (Levels 10-9)

...Totally committed to excellence

...Finds and fixes problems

...Work free of mistakes

...Acts decisively under pressure

...Makes positive things happen

...Bright, on the ball

...Emerging as premier performer

...Totally reliable and dependable

...Perceptive and hard working

...Proficient in all ventures

...Performs at peak intensity

...Makes good things happen

...Enthusiastically tackles any assignment

...Superlative contributions and achievements

...Highly competent and dedicated

...Exemplary support of organization

...Produces only quality results

...Impressive record of accomplishment

...Successfully faced all challenges

...Superlative contributions and actions

...Energetic, highly motivated achiever

...Recognizes opportunities to excel

...Superior performance routinely displayed

44

Superior Personal Performance (Levels 10-9)

...Thrives on important responsibilities

...Enjoys maximum effort environment

...Intense and highly capable

...Accomplishes most difficult tasking

...Finest technical skill available

...Trains for the unexpected

...A true team player

...Steadfast performance and dedication

...Excels in every endeavor

...Epitomizes the highest standards

...Great sense of responsibility

...Irreplaceable source of knowledge

...Skillful and refined workmanship

...Unsurpassed devotion to job

...Always sets the example

...Dedicated to highest standards

...Introduces sound new ideas

...Delivers with uncommon accuracy

...Surmounts problems. Gets results

...Intolerant of mediocre performance

...Accepts challenges with conviction

...Enjoys total job diversity

45

Superior Personal Performance (Levels 10-9)

...Puts forth unrelenting effort

...Highly respected technical specialist

...Professional contributions are noteworthy

...Carries out demanding responsibilities

...Forward-minded, aggressive performance

...Uncompromising high work standards

...Performance of the highest caliber

...Enjoys deep respect of others

...Performance regularly exceeds job requirements

...Accomplishes tasks in superior fashion

...Intense desire for self improvement

...Tireless in efforts to excel

...Technical qualifications absolutely first rate

...Great amount of personal industry

...Well-rounded person of many interests

...Cheerful, creative and industrious individual

...Volunteers to accept any assignment

...Top achiever of boundless potential

...Dedicated, thrives on new challenges

...Energetic and resourceful. Plans ahead

...Unafraid of accepting challenging jobs

...Discharges duties with complete confidence

...Displays continued excellence and enthusiasm

Superior Personal Performance (Levels 10-9)

...Continually puts forth maximum effort

...Unusually high standard of work

...A self-starter who plans ahead

...Takes exceptional pride in job

...Abundance of zeal and enthusiasm

...Full of vigor and vitality

...Keen, enthusiastic desire for success

...Renders quick and decisive action

...Diversity of talents and strengths

...Unsurpassed talent and self-discipline

...Thrives on pressures of immediacy

...Wide diversity of personal talent

...Converts ideas into positive action

...Faces demanding challenges without failure

...Self motivated. Driven to success

...At ease in any situation

...Never shows despair or resignation

...Always ahead of the action

...Great amount of innate talent

...Endless zeal and personal resourcefulness

...Full of energy and vitality

...Particularly adept working with others

47

Superior Personal Performance (Levels 10-9)

...Exemplary character and outstanding ability

...Completes all tasks on time

...Strong personal desire to excel

...Dedicated to job-improvement. Works hard

...Possesses invigorating, unending work habits

...Sets the example for others

...An expert in technical field

...Unwavering support for organization objectives

...Quick to offer constructive, positive improvements

...Unstinting commitment to job accomplishment

...Demonstrates unwavering support and loyalty

...Unfailing devotion to job accomplishment

...Enjoys challenging and demanding situations

...Never loses sight of responsibilities

...Takes wise courses of action

...Energetic and persevering by nature

...Head and shoulders above others

...Decisive in action and deed

...Follows organization policy without fail

...Unending ability to accomplish diverse tasking

...Totally dedicated and highly competent

...Possesses a great natural talent

...Contributed greatly to organization success

Superior Personal Performance (Levels 10-9)

...Provides timely advise and guidance

...Abundance of inspiration and energy

...Strong abilities across the board

...Unusually high level of expertise

...Highly motivated and hard working

...Quality performer with bright future

...Always gets the job done

...Work performed with exacting quality

...Exhibits skill of true professional

...Excels in every job facet

...Commendable job aggressiveness and dedication

...Can always be relied upon

...Deeply devoted to chosen profession

...Long list of impressive accomplishments

...Possesses rare degree of excellence

...Intense emotional drive and determination

...Places a premium on punctuality

...Accepts all challenges without wavering

...Unswerving allegiance to job accomplishment

...Highly skilled and well trained

...Sets highest standards of excellence

...Vigorous in pursuit of excellence

Superior Personal Performance (Levels 10-9)

...Established reputation for meeting challenges

...A winning spirit of excellence

...Great personal commitment to quality

...Meets all new challenges head-on

...Aggressive in assuming new responsibilities

...Loyalty and dedication above question

...No wasted effort or energy

...Attains results regardless of complexity

...Rates first against all competition

...Succeeds under stress and pressure

...Decisive response to any tasking

...Unblemished record of proven performance

...Maintains punishing and productive schedule

...Successfully meets long range tasking

...A hard charger. Job aggressive

...Thrives on pressures of immediacy

...Good touch of common sense

...Earns complete support of others

...A front-runner in every category

...Performs well in all situations

...Meets or exceeds all requirements

...Considers no job too difficult

...Completes assignments with remarkable reliability

50

Superior Personal Performance (Levels 10-9)

...Always ahead of the action

...Made substantial and quality contributions

...Unsurpassed devotion to job accomplishment

...Takes advantage of every opportunity

...Superior performance in difficult assignments

...Delivers wholehearted cooperation and support

...Attention to detail most impressive

...Executes tasks expediently and correctly

...Exhibits exceptional degree of accuracy

...Pursues excellence with boundless energy

...Enjoys the most challenging positions

...Energetic personality and work habits

...Performs beyond abilities of others

...At the pinnacle of excellence

...Vast experience and technical knowledge

...Makes contributions of lasting value

...Totally reliable. Completes any tasking

...Gives complete energy and support

...Introduces progressive ideas that work

...Routinely contributes to high standards

...Top performer in every category

...Performance regularly exceeds job requirements

Superior Personal Performance (Levels 10-9)

...Exceptionally high level of performance

...Quick to provide personal effort

...Plans and completes ambitious workload

...Great individual vitality and "can do" spirit

...Achieves unusually high level of performance

...Responds to any situation with considerable effort

...Achieves performance levels that exceed others' abilities

...Work accomplishment merits special praise and gratitude

...Earned admiration and respect of others

...Admirable blend of technical expertise and personal reliability

...Many personal accomplishments are truly impressive

...Provides valuable solutions to complex problems

...Sets standards for superior performance

...Achieved commendable results in many stressful situations

...Attains positive results regardless of tasking difficulty

...Demonstrates superior knowledge in technical specialty

...Impressive ability to get the job done correctly

...The standard bearer in specialty area

...Motivated individual. Productive output of highest quality

...Compiled an impressive job accomplishment record

...Sets and achieves long rang goals and objectives

...Commands fullest respect and support of others

...Enriches team spirit and pride in accomplishment

Superior Personal Performance (Levels 10-9)

...Puts job accomplishment ahead of personal interests

...Unflagging zeal and dedication to job at hand

...Complete, thorough performer. Leaves nothing to chance

...Extremely well liked and respected by others

...Sparks a spirit of job excitement in others

...Own radiant energy and zeal quickly picked up by others

...A unifying presence to any organization

...Improves professional development at every opportunity

...Individual productivity has been a significant contribution

...Infectious positive attitude and devotion are without equal

...Great competence. Always knows what to do

...Mentally alert. Always on top of job

...Possesses all the special qualities it takes to succeed

...Great personal initiative. Always achieves success

...The best trained and most productive

...Initiative and drive have proven to be without equal

...Superb performance under stressful and trying situations

...Rare individual. Possesses maturity and intellect

...Industrious manner and proven ability to get the job done

...Extremely accurate. Places great emphasis on detail

...Intense individual whose paramount interest is efficiency

...Moves toward clear-cut goals with initiative and purpose

Superior Personal Performance (Levels 10-9)

...Possesses direction of vision and economy of effort

...Results of work always exceptionally effective

...On top of things. Does not need to wait for direction

...Always on the ball and ahead of the others

...Individual drive and motivation are refreshing

...Sets high standards. Achieves high goals

...Job accomplishment always number one priority

...Time-tested ability to perform above others

...Wide range and scope of capabilities

...Sets the course and speed for others

...Every facet of responsibilities completed with dispatch

...Uncanny ability to find and fix problem areas

...High achiever. Always attains desired results

...Takes corrective action while others ponder and discuss

...Relentless drive and motivation without peer

...A "hot runner" with unlimited potential

...Routinely hand-picked to handle difficult assignments

...Ready now to assume much more responsible positions

...Continues to improve already high level of expertise

...Always proper performance in dynamic and critical events

...Completely reliable and thorough in all assignments

...Consistently asks for more challenging assignments

...Menial and complex tasking completed with ease

Superior Personal Performance (Levels 10-9)

...Achieved exceptional results across the board

...Works hard to make jobs of others easier

...Demonstrated rare blend of effectiveness and reliability

...At the forefront of peer group

...Realizes success requires sacrifice and dedication

...Especially good in executing demanding tasks

...Personal talent and commitment rivaled by few

...Exemplary ability to get things done on time

...A continuing source of new, workable ideas

...Extremely proficient in all aspects of job

...Meets unusual and taxing situations without becoming rattled

...Totally mastered each aspect of job

...Maintains unusually high standard of personal performance

...Intense dedication to the task at hand

...Rare ability to attain quality results in any environment

...Completes all jobs with accuracy and dispatch

...Unique ability to get to heart of any problem

...Thrives on new challenge and responsibility

...Remarkably poised and confident in trying situations

...A high achiever with imagination and initiative

...Performs demanding and challenging tasks with ease

...Performance a definite "cut above" typical "good" performer

Superior Personal Performance (Levels 10-9)

...The person to see when a job needs completing with dispatch

...Works zealously to complete each job as perfectly as possible

...Ability to get the job done regardless of circumstances

...Always adds more to the job than expected

...Attains quality results at any tasking level

...Possesses a great deal of creative energy

...Always contributes full measure to any job

...A rising star of unlimited potential

...Completes large volume of work each day

...Always meets or exceeds all job requirements

...Stands above others in ability to get things done

...Performs with uncommon vision and vigor

...Decisions and efforts contributed markedly to success

...Not satisfied with anything less than perfection

...Totally reliable in execution of responsibilities

...Relentless drive and energy won plaudits of many

...Invariable leader in conference and group discussion

...Bold and practical in attacking complex situations

...Puts responsibilities ahead of own interests

...Unafraid of setting, steering new course of thought or action

...Applies vast and varied personal skills extremely effectively

...Absolute quality performer in any tasking

...Exhibits excellence in all aspects of job

Superior Personal Performance (Levels 10-9)

...Long history of devotion and pride in work

...Extremely beneficial example for others to follow

...Exemplifies true meaning of pride in work

...Always a step ahead of the others

...Has vim, vigor and strong desire to succeed

...A straight line of dedication and inspiration

...Duties performed with uncommon quality and timeliness

...A real mainstay to the organization

...Flawless support of policies and goals

...Satisfied with nothing less than full personal effort

...Performs extremely well under stress and pressure

...Work highlighted by profusion and variety

...Possesses abundance of skill and self resource

...Insatiable appetite and ability for increased responsibility

...Always gives total dedication and effort

...High sense of personal responsibility for quality of work

...Unending urge and ability to succeed

...Energetic with no wasted motions or actions

...Strength of character and ability to meet any challenge

...Utmost degree of accuracy and attentiveness

...Work underscored by initiative and excellence

...Highly respected for point of view

57

Superior Personal Performance (Levels 10-9)

...Unending drive and urge for success

...Makes best use of available resources

...Puts abundant energy to good use

...Ability to succeed in any endeavor. Proves it daily

...Takes pride in exceeding accomplishments of others

...Self sacrificing. A real team player

...Pursues, with success, ultimate standards of excellence

...Aspiring performer. Sets and achieves highest goals

...Completes each job with accuracy and dispatch

...Exemplifies highest standards of dedication and determination

...Routinely receives high acclaim and praise

...Frequently sought out for expert opinion

...A model for all to emulate

...Actions and deeds of the highest measure

...Consistently puts forth extra degree of effort

...Will not retreat in face of adversity

...Abilities and skills know virtually no bounds

...Actions well planned and smoothly executed

...No magnitude of tasking too difficult

...At the zenith of technical specialty

...Routinely able to overcome seemingly insurmountable odds

...Never caught off guard of loses sight of important issues

...Displays exceptional degree of personal initiative

...Continual source of good, innovative ideas

...Always volunteers for more than fair share of work

...Infuses organization with enthusiasm and dedication

...Ability to accept & complete any job regardless of scope or complexity

...Resourcefulness to accomplish most demanding tasks

...Great sense of responsibility for quality of work

...Attacks each task with zeal and enthusiasm. Gets results

...Not content until every detail successfully completed

...Superior results in progressively more challenging jobs

...Can be relied upon to complete any task successfully

...Great ability to adapt to any assignment

...Proven superior performer with high personal integrity

...A high achiever in every sense of the word

...Consistently performs in enthusiastic and outstanding manner

...Performance far exceeds that of others of comparable experience

...A zealot in performing and completing any assignment

...Sets standards by which excellence is measured

...Great resource for coping with difficult jobs

...Compiled impressive list of individual accomplishments

...Clearly exceeds all established standards of excellence

...Sets and achieves highest work standards

Superior Personal Performance (Levels 10-9)

...Aggressive in seeking, finding answers to complex problems

...Takes initiative. Gets the job done

...Unyielding drive and desire for success

...Top achiever in any task assigned or assumed

...Invariably submits timely solutions to complex problem areas

...Has considerable talent. Gives considerable effort

COMPLETE THE PHRASE

Select a word in COLUMN 1 to go with a word in COLUMN 2 and use a word in COLUMN 3 and provide the appropriate ending in COLUMN 4.

COLUMN #1	COLUMN #2	COLUMN #3	COLUMN #4
COURAGEOUS			
DISTINGUISHED			
EXCELLENT	ABILITY		
EXCEPTIONAL	APTITUDE		
FABULOUS	CAPABILITY		
FANTASTIC	PERFORMER		
FAULTLESS	RECORD	AS/IN/TO	(ADD
FIRST-RATE	TALENT		ENDING)
GIFTED	WORKER		
IMPECCABLE			
MASTERFUL			
MATCHLESS			
OUTSTANDING			
PERFECT			
PRAISEWORTHY			
PREMIER			
STERLING			
SUPERIOR			
SUPREME			
TOP-NOTCH			
UNBEATABLE			
UNFAILING			
UNPARALLELED			
UNSURPASSED			
UNTIRING			

"The wise are instructed by reason; ordinary minds experience; the stupid by necessity; and brutes by instinct." CICERO

"It is better to have one person working WITH you than to have three people working FOR you."
DWIGHT D. EISENHOWER
From the book: **Successful Leadership Today**

BULLET PHRASE STATEMENTS
(COMPLETE THE PHRASE)

...A model of (...)

...Particularly effective in (...)

...Strongly motivated toward (...)

...Highly respected for (...)

...Proven top quality (...)

...Unblemished record of (...)

...Inspires confidence by (...)

...Unlimited capacity to/for (...)

...Truly an exceptional (...)

...Thoroughly prepared for (...)

...Excellent talent for/in (...)

...Uniquely skilled to (...)

...Highly specialized in (...)

...Successfully carried out (...)

...Thoroughly understands the (...)

...Unswerving dedication to (...)

...Developed a landmark (...)

...A remarkably skilled (...)

...Inexhaustible source of (...)

...Impressive accomplishments include (...)

...Praiseworthy characteristics include (...)

...Remarkable ability to (...)

...Amazing talent for (...)

...Highly respected by (...)

...Successfully carried out(...)

...Masterful ability to (...)

...Indispensable performance in/as (...)

...Skilled innovator in (...)

...Matchless ingenuity for (...)

...Boundless ability to (...)

...Inexhaustible creativity in (...)

...Unmatched capacity for (...)

...The epitome of (...)

...Highly versatile as/in (...)

...Easily the best (...)

...Our most valuable (...)

...Single handily completed (...)

...Provided the expertise to (...)

...An unequaled ability to/for (...)

...Made extensive improvements in (...)

...Continuing enthusiastic approach to (...)

...Extremely well prepared for (...)

...Developed and implemented comprehensive (...)

...Highly productive and versatile (...)

63

...Earned strongest endorsement for (...)

...A dominating force in (...)

...Achieved total success in/by (...)

...Gives others enthusiasm and (...)

...Has natural curiosity for (...)

...Most impressive performer in (...)

...Earned individual distinction by/for (...)

...Made significant contribution to/in (...)

...Sets exceptional example as/for (...)

...Performed exceptionally well in/as (...)

...Established procedures which strengthened (...)

...Fostered unparalleled productivity in (...)

...A matchless thirst for (...)

...Made marked improvement in (...)

...An indispensable member of (...)

...Has veracious appetite for (...)

...Articulate in ability to (...)

...Maintains high standards in/of (...)

...Possesses overwhelming capacity to/for (...)

...Maintains sharp edge in (...)

...Has extensive knowledge in/of (...)

...An absolute master at (...)

Superior Personal Performance (Levels 10-9)

...Displays intense dedication in/to (...)

...Has special talent for (...)

...Skilled in art of (...)

...Maintains highest standards in (...)

...The driving force behind (...)

...Has natural aptitude for (...)

...Provided masterful insight into (...)

...Created perfect foundation for/to (...)

...An accomplished and proficient (...)

...An acknowledged expert in (...)

...Has substantial knowledge of (...)

...Played vital role in (...)

...Represents the embodiment of (...)

...Spearheaded a project that (...)

...Takes exceptional pride in (...)

...Routinely hand picked to (...)

...Produced commendable results in/as (...)

...Demonstrated exceptional skills in (...)

...Exceptionally well qualified to/for (...)

...A valuable asset to (...)

...A sterling example of (...)

...Demonstrates uncommon perceptiveness in (...)

...Has diverse knowledge in/of (...)

Superior Personal Performance (Levels 10-9)

...Has performed flawlessly in/while (...)

...Actively supports and encourages (...)

...A strong advocate of (...)

...A perfect example of (...)

...Has mastered art of (...)

...Rare, extraordinary ability to (...)

...Gives wholehearted support in/to (...)

...Achieved impressive results in/by (...)

...The foremost authority in/on (...)

...Excels in ability to (...)

...Great mental aptitude for (...)

...Furthers technical specialty by (...)

...Personal enthusiasm infiltrated throughout (...)

...Successfully faced extremely complex (...)

...Achieved resounding success in/by (...)

...Ever-energetic, looks forward to (...)

...Capitalizes on strengths of (...)

...No one better at (...)

...A tremendous success in/at (...)

...Embodies the spirit of (...)

...Gives added dimension to (...)

...Takes the lead in (...)

Superior Personal Performance (Levels 10-9)

...Offers so much to (...)

...Takes full advantage of (...)

...Paved the way for (...)

...Gave unforgettable performance in/as (...)

...Enjoys getting involved in (...)

...Introduces productive ideas in (...)

...Always well prepared for (...)

...Achievements in (...) are truly impressive

...Demonstrates in-depth technical knowledge In (...)

...Has a natural flare for (...)

...Continually exhibits high degree of (...)

...Applies correct mental approach to/in (...)

...No end to potential for/to (...)

...Despite ever increasing difficulty, accomplished (...)

...Responded positively and correctly to (...)

...Inspires and encourages others by (...)

...Has comprehensive technical knowledge in/of (...)

...A proven (...) with unbound ability

...Ideally suited for positions of (...)

...Demonstrated expertise has measurably improved (...)

...Has complete, in-depth knowledge of/in (...)

...Contributed an innovative approach to (...)

...Punctuality and (...) highlight daily performance

67

Superior Personal Performance (Levels 10-9)

...Possesses solid, proven abilities in/to (...)

...Organized the monumental task of (...)

...Demonstrates versatility and exceptional (...) skills

...Particularly adept at solving (...) problems

...Widely recognized for ability to (...)

...Conforms to exacting standards of (...)

...Possesses overabundance of energy and (...)

...Singularly responsible for improvement in/of (...)

...Successfully accepted the challenge of (...)

...Charismatic personality has greatly enhanced (...)

...Instrumental in developing a new (...)

...Unlimited potential with capacity to/for (...)

...Firmly established as the top (...)

...Routinely prevails over others at (...)

...Did a masterful job in/as (...)

...Without equal in ability to (...)

...Advanced education and skill in (...)

...Has tremendous natural ability for/in (...)

...Widely respected for ability to (...)

...Transformed below average organization into (...)

...Performance goes beyond limits of (...)

...Has a fine touch for (...)

...Direct personal involvement instrumental in/to (...)

...Skillful employment of manpower enabled (...)

...Established stability and integrity in (...)

...Especially effective in management of (...)

...Contributed to vital interests by (...)

...Quality performer. Knows value of (...)

...Has positive, clear view of (...)

...Unquenchable thirst for knowledge in (...)

...Assumed greatly expanded responsibilities when/with (...)

...Simplified and streamlined procedures for (...)

...Impressively managed diverse and complex (...)

...Demonstrates the skillful direction to (...)

...Instrumental in the successful completion of (...)

...Maintained a high percentage of (...)

...Thoughtful and concerned dealing with (...)

...Exceptional (...) abilities led to (...)

...Developed new procedures which led to (...)

...Significantly contributed to the improvement of (...)

...Became an immediate and positive impact on (...)

...A top specialist in the field of (...)

...Diligent efforts and unending resourcefulness led to (...)

...Made valuable and lasting contributions to (...)

...Epitomizes those rare qualities most sought in (...)

69

Superior Personal Performance (Levels 10-9)

...Ability to comprehend and master complex (...)

...Highly motivated with a particular desire to/for (...)

...Gained the respect and confidence of others by (...)

...Exhibits high personal initiative and superb (...)

...Performance has established new standards in (...)

...Displays an ideal mix of (...) and (...)

...Possesses the mental dexterity and competence to (...)

...A major source of innovative contributions in/of (...)

...A proven (...) who always attains positive results

...The leading force and influence in (...)

...Gives full spirit and support to (...)

...Extremely high degree of excellence in (...)

...Exhibits all essential features of a (...)

...Made significant progress and gain on/when (...)

...A fundamental, essential ingredient to the successful (...)

...Routinely receives high compliment and praise when (...)

...Enjoys the especially difficult and complex job of (...)

...Has the natural ability and flair for/to (...)

...Has acquired the necessary attributes to (...)

...Top performer. Merits serious consideration for (...)

...Displays special skill and knowledge in field of (...)

...Surpasses others in sheer ability to (...)

Superior Personal Performance (Levels 10-9)

...Has full insight and understanding of (...)

...Has the knowledge and competence to (...)

...Rejuvenated and put new life into (...)

...Established new standards of excellence in (...)

...A champion in the field of (...)

...Rapidly established dynamic & motivating leader image by (...)

...Exceptionally talented and well qualified in/for (...)

...Foresight and planning abilities led to (...)

...Thoroughly exhibited the potential to excel in/as (...)

...Continually takes positive steps to improve (...)

...Work habits have won the respect of (...)

...An acknowledged expert in the field of (...)

...A "hard charger," exceptionally talented in/as (...)

...Eminently qualified and prepared to accept (...)

...Directly responsible for the outstanding performance of (...)

...An accomplished (...) who has demonstrated exceptional skill in/as (...)

...Demonstrated unbound ability and capacity to successfully assume (...)

...Adaptable and receptive, the person to see when (...)

...Runs an orderly and highly productive (...)

...Already a quality performer, has not yet reached full potential in/for (...)

...Has advanced knowledge and skill in (...)

71

Superior Personal Performance (Levels 10-9)

...Takes maximum advantage of opportunities to (...)

...A major contributing factor in the success of (...)

...Technical knowledge and curiosity led to (...)

...Does not necessarily stay in beaten path of others when (...)

...Enjoys unparalleled success. Recently emerged as (...)

...Personal vision and courage led to (...)

...Possesses a wealth of information in/on (...)

...Good mental capacity. Quick to grasp significance of (...)

...A person on the move, can adjust readily to changes in (...)

...Successfully (...) despite severe limitations of personnel resources

...Carefully monitored diverse component demands of/on (...)

...Stimulated improved harmony and attitudes on/toward (...)

...Industrious manner and positive attitude resulted in (...)

...Successfully overcame potentially serious impediment to (...)

...Places proper and heavy emphasis on (...)

...Developed superb plan of action and milestones in/for (...)

...Superb academic credentials. A prime candidate for (...)

...Rendered outstanding support and service to (...)

...Superb common sense and professional knowledge led to (...)

...Played leading and aggressive role in establishing (...)

...Proved more than equal to the task of (...)

...Implemented necessary management techniques and concepts to (...)

72

Superior Personal Performance (Levels 10-9)

...Met goals across a diverse spectrum by (...)

...Won wide acclaim for promptness in responding to (...)

...Demonstrates untiring dedication and an ability to (...)

...Has a superb working knowledge of (...)

...Ideas and suggestions contributed directly to (...)

...Personally assisted in developing new procedures for/to (...)

...Fully exploits the information and tools available to (...)

...Constantly seeking new and more effective methods in/for (...)

...An original thinker who has demonstrated ability to/for (...)

...Consistently executed the weighty responsibilities of (...)

...Possesses (...) expertise rarely observed in others

...Responsible, in large measure, for the success(ful) (...)

...Instituted procedures that simplified and streamlined (...)

...Well versed in all facets of (...)

...A source of knowledge in every area of (...)

...Has increased the efficiency and effectiveness of (...)

...Stays abreast of the latest changes in (...)

...Exceptionally skilled in all facets of (...)

...Sustained superior performance has been an inspiration to (...)

...Stimulates individual growth and responsibility of/in (...)

...Possesses a high level of expertise in (...)

...Personal initiative and dedication directly responsible for (...)

Superior Personal Performance (Levels 10-9)

...Demonstrated creative intelligence and wisdom by (...)

...Personal liaison efforts particularly effective in (...)

...Possesses concise knowledge and understanding of (...)

...One of the most accomplished experts/specialists in (...)

...Contributions both substantial and significant in (...)

...Carefully planned, organized, and executed successful (...)

...Personal example has been a positive influence on (...)

...Especially strong & effective executing demanding job of (...)

...Using foresight and exceptional planning ability, put together a complicated and comprehensive (...)

...Flexibility and initiative responsible for upgrade in/of (...)

...Personal concern and initiative directly responsible for (...)

...Ability to elicit maximum effort from (...)

...Innovative ideas and close personal supervision led to (...)

...A motivating force in achieving significant improvement in (...)

...Enjoys excitement of devising new ways to (...)

...Combined innate sense of leadership & keen foresight led to (...)

...Use of sound & prudent judgment was instrumental in/to (...)

...Strong spirit of inquiry and drive led to (...)

...Awareness of people's strengths and capabilities led to (...)

...Held in high esteem for ability to (...)

...Possesses requisite competence and aptitude to/for (...)

Superior Personal Performance (Levels 10-9)

...Stands above peers in ability to (...)

...Succeeded in reaching new heights in (...)

...Thoroughly diligent effort and patience led to proficient (...)

...Has decisive advantage over others in ability to (...)

...Earned high praise and acclaim by/for (...)

...Open minded. Can accommodate wide variety of (...)

...Has natural gift and ability to/for (...)

...Quickly surged ahead of contemporaries by/in (...)

...Fully experienced in practical application of (...)

...Successfully fused together all elements of (...)

...Performance reached a peak of intensity when (...)

...Great deductive power. Insatiable appetite for (...)

...Prompt and proper in response to (...)

...Became a moving force in ability to (...)

...Devised procedures that carefully weighed time, personnel,
   and financial procedures that resulted in (...)

...Personal sacrifice and uncompromising standards provided
   impetus to/for (...)

...Strong leadership, acute management acumen, and technical
   competence resulted in (...)

...Totally mastered each and every aspect of (...)

...Established and enforced strict controls of/on (...)

...Through acute awareness and personal diligence (...)

...Successfully managed wide and varied programs in/on (...)

75

Superior Personal Performance (Levels 10-9)

...Personal drive and ambition hastened progress and development of (...)

...Through foresight and outstanding knowledge, played vital role in (...)

...Aggressively responded to significantly increased responsibilities of (...)

..."Follow me " leadership won respect of (...)

...Sound manager with proven ability to (...)

...Receives maximum effort of others because (...)

...Remarkable ability to work with people and effectively organize tasks and priorities enhanced (...)

...Personally molded cohesive and dedicated team that (...)

...Constant personal examples earned respect & admiration of (...)

...Personal initiative and skills overcame (...)

...Unselfishly contributed time and talent to (...)

...Demonstrated clearly a superior ability to (...)

...Professional knowledge and zeal significantly improved (...)

...Consistently met or exceeded demanding job of (...)

...Invariably submits well thought and detailed plans for (...)

...Dogged determination and relentless pursuit of excellence paved the way to a successful (...)

...Brilliant execution of duties brought highest praise from (...)

...Devised highly effective management control system that/to (...)

Superior Personal Performance (Levels 10-9)

"There is no security on this
earth. Only opportunity."
GENERAL DOUGLAS MACARTHUR
From the book: **Successful Leadership Today**

Writing without thinking isn't much different
than shooting without aiming.

"The best ideas are common property."
LUCIUS ANNAEUS SENECA
From the book: **Successful Leadership Today**

77

CHAPTER 3

ABOVE AVERAGE PERFORMANCE
(LEVELS 8-7)

PERSONAL PERFORMANCE LEVELS

LEVELS 10-9
* Contributes GREATLY to organization mission
* CONTINUALLY seeks additional responsibility
* THOROUGHLY understands all job components
* Works well independent of supervision

LEVELS 8-7
* Contributes HIGH LEVEL to organization mission
* Seeks additional responsibility
* Exhibits drive for self-improvement
* Proposes good solutions to difficult problems

LEVELS 6-5
* Contributes SOME to organization mission
* ACCEPTS additional responsibility
* Requires LIMITED supervision
* Good understanding of major jobs

LEVELS 4-3
* DOES NOT contribute to organization mission
* DOES NOT desire additional responsibility
* Requires ROUTINE supervision
* Satisfied with less than quality work

LEVELS 2-1
* HINDERS organization mission
* AVOIDS added responsibility
* Requires CONSTANT supervision
* DOES NOT or CAN NOT understand job

ABOVE AVERAGE PERSONAL PERFORMANCE

WORD BANK

NOTE: The words in this word bank, USED ALONE, describe ABOVE AVERAGE PERFORMANCE. When combined with other "qualifying" words, many of these words can be used to describe higher or lower performance.

EXAMPLE: PROFICIENT (ABOVE AVERAGE)
EXTREMELY PROFICIENT (SUPERIOR)
USUALLY   PROFICIENT (EFFECTIVE)
NOT   PROFICIENT (UNSATISFACTORY)

Words listed in other word banks can similarly be used to describe higher or lower performance.

ABOVE AVERAGE	ACHIEVER	AGGRESSIVE
ALERT	ANALYTICAL	ATTENTIVE
BETTER	BUSY	CARE
CAREFUL	COMPETITIVE	COMPETITOR
CONTRIBUTE(S)	CONTRIBUTION	CREDIBLE
CREDITABLE	DEDICATED	DETERMINATION
DETERMINED	DEXTERITY	DILIGENT
DILIGENTLY	EAGER	EARNEST
ENERGETIC	ENHANCE(S)	EXCEED(S)
EXCEL(S)	EXPERIENCED	FAITHFUL
FINE	FLEXIBLE	FRUITFUL
GOOD	HIGH	HIGHER
INDUSTRIOUS	LOGICAL	LOYAL
LOYALTY	MATURE	MERIT
NO-NONSENSE	ORGANIZED	PERSISTENT
POSITIVE	PRODUCTIVE	PROFESSIONAL
PROFESSIONALISM	PROFICIENCY	PROFICIENT
PRUDENT	QUALITY	RESOURCEFUL

Above Average Performance (Levels 8-7)

RESPONSIVE	SELF-STARTER	SKILL(ED)
SKILLFUL	SPECIALIST	SUCCEED(S)
SUCCESSFUL	TALENT	TALENTED
THOROUGH	TRUSTWORTHY	VERSATILE
VOLUNTEER(S)	WELL-DONE	WELL-ROUNDED

BULLET PHRASE STATEMENTS

Select a word in COLUMN #1 to go with a word in COLUMN #2

EXAMPLE: FRUITFUL INDIVIDUAL

COLUMN #1	COLUMN #2
ABOVE AVERAGE	INDIVIDUAL
ADEPT	OFFICER
COMPETENT	MANAGER
CREDIBLE	PERSON
DEDICATED	SUPERVISOR
ENERGETIC	TECHNICIAN
FRUITFUL	TYPIST
GOOD	WORKER
INDUSTRIOUS	(or, use
PROFICIENT	professional
QUALITY	title)
RESOURCEFUL	
SKILLFUL	
SUCCESSFUL	
TALENTED	

"Formula for success:
Keep an ACTIVE MIND.
Have a FERTILE IMAGINATION."
From the book: **Successful Leadership Today**

...Quality performance

...Practical individual

...Enjoys responsibility

...Always busy

...Good determination

...Quality worker

...Tries hard

...Good accomplishments

...Great job

...Full effort

...Performs well

...Faithful worker

...Positive outlook

...Favorable record

...Self motivated

...Works diligently

...Experienced worker

...Industrious nature

...Proficient action

...Gets results

...Acts responsibly

...Keeps busy

...Quality abilities

...Positive results

...Great performance

...Sincere effort

...Technically capable

...Alert individual

...Energetic personality

...Always improving

...Methodical person

...Earnest performer

...Great production

...Likes responsibility

...Helpful dedication

...Likes challenges

...Mature individual

...Developing quickly

...Exceeds requirements

...High performance

...Loyal individual

...Credible talent

...Accurate work

...Supports superiors

...Performs well

...Confident worker

81

Above Average Performance (Levels 8-7)

...Adept performance

...Smooth worker

...Stays organized

...Obedient personality

...Enthusiastic individual

...Quality work

...Skilled worker

...Routinely volunteers

...Eager performer

...High achiever

...Meaningful work

...Vigorous worker

...Steadfast determination

...Skillful individual

...Enjoys competition

...Few mistakes

...Very productive

...Skilled worker

...Credible record

...Exceeds requirements

...Completes assignments

...Pursues excellence

...Quality results

...Aspiring newcomer

...Persistent efforts

...Good technician

...Prudent action

...Resourceful individual

...Always trustworthy

...Positive attitude

...Good performance

...Proven ability

...Readily adaptable

...Technically competent

...Good ability

...Hard worker

...Has initiative

...Industrious individual

...Overcomes obstacles

...Much energy

...Gets results

...Enthusiastic desire

...Diverse talent

...Personal resourcefulness

Above Average Performance (Levels 8-7)

...Makes contributions	...Accepts challenges
...Action oriented	...Generates enthusiasm
...Promising newcomer	...Vigorous individual
...Welcomes responsibility	...Achieves goals
...Progressive outlook	...Intense worker
...Career potential	..Proper action
...Thorough worker	...Good ability
...A competitor	...Expedient individual
...Ample ability	...Good apprentice
...Very dedicated	...Good credentials
...Promising future	...Productive individual
...Good work habits	...An enterprising newcomer
...Efficient and effective	...Always accurate work
...Nearly perfect work	...Obeys all rules
...A promising future	...Gives quality effort
...Takes proper action	...Aggressive work performance
...Careful about detail	...A competitive spirit
...Dedicated to work	...Determined and dedicated
...Diligent, steady effort	...Eager to work
...Works in earnest	...Excels at job
...Flexible and experienced	...Always fruitful effort
...Shows good loyalty	...Mature and dedicated
...Reliable work habits	...A prudent individual

83

Above Average Performance (Levels 8-7)

...Deliberate work habits

...Gives productive effort

...Gets quality results

...Cooperative and helpful

...Pursues tasks diligently

...Gives credible performance

...Gives encouraging effort

...Dedicated, mature individual

...Mostly error-free work

...Has great competence

...Does fruitful work

...Enhances team spirit

...Does thorough work

...A no-nonsense worker

...Work has merit

...Organized and productive

...Contributes positive effort

...Responsible to job

...Skillfully attacks work

...Thorough and skillful

...Versatile and energetic

...Shows good determination

...Well rounded skills

...Gets positive results

...A persevering individual

...An active individual

...Does quality work

...Has good desire

...Takes desired actions

...Has high capabilities

...Confident of abilities

...Always positive results

...Positive, fruitful career

...Performs above many

...Exhibits professional accuracy

...Strives for success

...Prompt in response

...Has technical curiosity

...Uses time wisely

...Takes positive action

...Sets good example

...Prompt and responsive

...Aggressive work habits

...Overcomes most obstacles

84

Above Average Performance (Levels 8-7)

...Hard working individual ...Reliable and thorough

...Quality, steady performer ...Better than many

...Sound technical background ...Beneficial work habits

...Tackles difficult tasking ...Clear cut goals

..."Can do" attitude ...Submits new ideas

...Methodical and conscientious ...Contributes good effort

...Good professional judgment ...Varied professional abilities

...Always good results ...Maintains high standards

...Meets all challenges ...Has practical ideas

...Takes proper action ...Accurate about detail

...Achieves positive results ...Gets quality results

...Prompt in response ...Desire for self-improvement

...Quick and effective ...A thorough worker

...Quick and thorough ...Enjoys a challenge

...High work standard ...Confident of abilities

...Performs under pressure ...Makes positive contributions

...Committed to excellence ...Takes correct action

...Benefit to organization ...Sets high standards

...Good job accomplishment ...Provides own motivation

...High work standards ...Enjoys difficult jobs

...Provides timely results ...Enthusiastic about job

...Determined and dedicated ...Enjoys challenging jobs

...Energetic and helpful ...Above standard performance

85

Above Average Performance (Levels 8-7)

...Eager to learn

...Gives determined effort

...Responsive to tasking

...Has positive attitude

...Accepts any assignment

...Above average performer

...Makes gallant effort

...Above normal ability

...Works for self-improvement

...Likes job diversity

...Provides faithful service

...Makes good effort

...Produces notable results

...A successful worker

...Generates great enthusiasm

...A thorough worker

...Completes difficult assignments

...Performance exceeds requirements

...Prudent, careful worker

...Makes positive contributions

...Performance above many

...Good personal initiative

...Good daily work

...Acts correctly under pressure

...Successfully faces new challenges

...Good performance routinely displayed

...Good sense of responsibility

...Stays prepared and ready

...Always energetic and helpful

...Perceptive and alert individual

Above Average Performance (Levels 8-7)

...Accomplishes meaningful work assignments

...Plans carefully and wisely

...Industrious and willing individual

...Prompt, proper in action

...Responsive to changing conditions

...Good record of accomplishment

...Works well without supervision

...Pursues tasks with spirit

...Takes pride in work

...Meets all stated objectives

...Responsive to special tasking

...Plunges into all work

...A fruitful future ahead

...Good capacity for growth

...Steady, highly productive worker

...Works quickly and efficiently

...Enjoys high visibility jobs

...Positive attitude and outlook

...Adaptable to changing situations

...Competent in most situations

...Works well under pressure

...Dedicated, results-oriented individual

...Job aggressive and industrious

87

Above Average Performance (Levels 8-7)

...Exhibits initiative and resourcefulness

...Determined to get ahead

...Flexible, able to adapt

...Has loyalty to organization

...Succeeds where others fail

...Work worthy of mention

...Offers valid new ideas

...Always does favorable work

...Adapts readily to change

...Quality of workmanship good

...Contributes to team effort

...Likes to stay busy

...Ample drive and determination

...Well skilled in job

...Puts forth quality effort

...Has pride in job

...Does not tire easily

...Accepts all work assignments

...Accurate in detailed matters

...Completes heavy work assignment

...Always gives good effort

...Has pep and energy

88

Above Average Performance (Levels 8-7)

...Good level of reliability

...Performance is above average

...Good ability and effort

...Has desire to excel

...Enhances high team spirit

...Ability to create enthusiasm

...Enjoys giving good effort

...Anxious to get ahead

...Completes all work successfully

...A benefit to organization

...An almost flawless worker

...Has some good talents

...Shows attention to detail

...Puts forth good effort

...High level of performance

...Keen interest in work

...Contributes to work effort

...Meets all job requirements

...Gives good work effort

...Will volunteer for assignments

...Good dedication to job

...Routinely gives error-free work

...Technical knowledge above average

89

Above Average Performance (Levels 8-7)

...Believes in being prepared

...Developed productive work habits

...Gives support and loyalty

...Contributed to organization success

...High level of expertise

...Takes advantage of opportunities

...High degree of accuracy

...Can be relied upon

...Well trained and productive

...Seeks solutions to problems

...Meets all job requirements

...Takes pride in work

...Enjoys demanding work pace

...Copes with difficult situations

...High record of accomplishment

...Works well without supervision

...Good level of experience

...Takes pride in work

...Continues to make improvement

...Seeks solutions to problems

...A mostly productive individual

...Gives above normal effort

90

Above Average Performance (Levels 8-7)

...Performs well in stressful situations

...Believes in quality of workmanship

...Correctly balances and prioritizes workload

...Ability to get things done

...Diligent effort and good resourcefulness

...Dedicated to job at hand

...Has a desire for challenge

...Punctuality and productivity always evident

...Works with vigor and enthusiasm

...Possesses attributes needed to excel

...Determined to achieve high goals

...Calm and cool under pressure

...Demonstrates keen understanding of responsibilities

...Efficient effort highlights daily actions

...Works without prompting or prodding

...Deliberate actions. Attention to detail

...Doesn't believe in idle time

...Unafraid of long, hard work

...Well defined plans and goals

...Goals met correctly and timely

...Work efficiently planned and executed

...Quick to lend helping hand

...Volunteers to shoulder additional responsibility

91

Above Average Performance (Levels 8-7)

...Ability to perform under pressure

...Performance characterized by positive actions

...Adapts quickly to changing situations

...Not satisfied with status quo

...A no-nonsense approach to jobs

...Does not get discouraged easily

...Takes favorable courses of action

...Little wasted time or effort

...Responds favorable to new situations

...Takes right courses of action

...Responsive to needs of superiors

...Record of accomplishment above average

...Positive approach to problem solving

...Mainly timely and accurate results

...Not afraid of hard work

...Works without prompting or prodding

...Likes to meet new challenges

...Stays on top of job

...Performs most jobs without assistance

...Has good sense of loyalty

...Works hard to please others

...Earned the trust of others

Above Average Performance (Levels 8-7)

...Works for approval of superiors

...A diligent and persistent worker

...Able to foresee problem areas

...Makes genuine effort to excel

...Does not sacrifice quality for quantity

...Fully capable of meeting new situations

...Has will and desire to do good job

...Knows how to get the job done

...Takes pride in doing best job possible

...Work underscored by pride and accomplishment

...Aggressive and meticulous in completion of work

...Never in doubt or confused about job

...Willing to forge ahead into new areas

...Gives quality results in most any job

...Enjoys demanding pace and heavy workload

...Energetic and methodical with ability to excel

...Performs will good skill, eagerness and ingenuity

...Well organized. Plans for the future

...Discharges responsibilities with accuracy and dispatch

...Carries out jobs in usually successful manner

...Adapts to varying job conditions with ease

...Keen interest and ability in all tasking

...Readily takes initiative for additional work

93

Above Average Performance (Levels 8-7)

...Well rounded individual of many talents

...Eager and interested in professional matters

...Brings pertinent parts of any tasking into proper focus

...Punctuality and effectiveness highlight daily performance

...Can adjust or adapt to most any job situation

...Takes action when necessary without waiting for guidance

...Continually seeks to broaden own experience

...Thoroughly familiar with all phases of job

...Takes difficult jobs in full stride

...Prompt, quick and correct in action

...Always willing to share time and talent with others

...Professional competence enhanced by ability to get along with others

...Active. Never too busy to help others

...Abundant energy given in each undertaking

...Highly skilled in facets of job

...Keen interest in all work activities

...Strong desire and good ability to get ahead

...Makes good use of available resources

...Natural ability and aptitude for technically oriented jobs

...Eager and ardent interest in all work assignments

...Knows how to handle trying situations

...Unyielding desire to do good job

94

Above Average Performance (Levels 8-7)

...Applies knowledge and skill to situations

...Takes personal interest in each task assigned

...Accepts each job with positive and cooperative spirit

...Balances workload according to required priorities

...Approaches each job with positive attitude

...Likes to get into "nuts and bolts" of problems

...Does not hesitate to provide personal assistance to others

...Willingness and ability to accept added responsibility

...Able to focus sharply on the task at hand

...Strong desire to do good job under any conditions

...Eager and interested in every facet of job

...Contributes good effort to any job

...Works to learn the most from each situation

...Does not merely "follow the pack"

...Capacity to assume broader scope of duties

...Performs well under stress and pressure

...Jobs completed on or ahead of schedule

...Has stamina needed to tackle most difficult jobs

...Gives helpful shot in the arm to new projects

...Contributes full abilities to any project

...Has good deal of drive and persistence

...Energetic personality with a positive attitude

95

...Ready now for positions of increased responsibility

...Excels in working without constant instruction

...Unending dedication and performance to job

...Industrious. Doesn't believe in idle time

...A thirst for knowledge and a desire for challenge

...Quick to take the lead in starting new projects

...Always busy and involved in something helpful

...Adapts to any work environment particularly rapid

...Actively seeks out solutions to problems

...Dedicated with obvious willingness to help

...Approaches even menial tasks with zeal

...Past performance and future ambitions all positive assets

...Finds valuable solutions to pending problems

...Quickly grasps the intricacy of new assignments

...Always knows what's planned and what's happening

...Highly flexible to meet any task at hand

...Works with unusual determination and dedication

...Has a real knack for getting the job done

...A loyal, energetic and conscientious individual

...Displays genuine concern for daily work effort

...Varied background. Good experience. Job oriented

...Always careful and accurate about detail

...Earned the personal trust and confidence of others

96

Above Average Performance (Levels 8-7)

...Good ability to plan own workload

...Natural ability to make the most of a trying situation

...Able to cope with difficult jobs

...Works to find solutions to problem areas

...Tries to excel in any job

...Concerned with good daily work effort

...Always has desire to do good work

...Takes minor setbacks in full stride

...Does not panic in face of obstacles

...Sense of purpose and pride in work

...Strong will and desire to succeed

...Ability to cope with stress-filled situations

...An individual with a promising future

...Always gives serious and determined effort

...Works to get the job done correctly

...Does not need direct supervision to do job

...Willing to lend a helping hand to others

...A cut above the average worker

...Produces accurate work most of the time

...Work usually correct the first time

...Keeps things tidy and in good order

...Makes sincere attempt to do quality work

97

Above Average Performance (Levels 8-7)

...Knows how to get the job done

...Has clear understanding of the job at hand

...Works hard on the job at hand

...Serious about doing good job

...Keeps informed and up to date

...Completes work to best of ability

...Good enthusiasm to get the job done

...Has good insight of job requirements

Unrewarded acts can
result in uninvolved people.
From the book:
Successful Leadership Today

Above Average Performance (Levels 8-7)

COMPLETE THE PHRASE

...Talented in field/art of (...)

...Enjoys success at (...)

...Responds with efficient effort when (...)

...Always tries hard to (...)

...Developing rapidly into a/an (...)

...Submits suggestions to improve (...)

...Makes genuine effort to (...)

...Natural ability to (...)

...Maintains high interest in (...)

...Always correct and (...)

...Devised practical method of/to (...)

...Has promising future as/in (...)

...Maintains high standards in (...)

...Uses time wisely when/to (...)

...Takes positive action when (...)

...Alert and on the ball when (...)

...Very comfortable working around (...)

...Error-free work in (...)

...Has no-nonsense approach to (...)

...Always prepared for (...)

...Skilled in art of (...)

...Takes pride in (...)

99

Above Average Performance (Levels 8-7)

...Has strong desire to (...)

...Enjoys increased responsibilities of (...)

...Highly skilled in (...)

...Always busy and active doing/in (...)

...Above average ability to (...)

...Takes care to/of (...)

...Careful in matters of (...)

...Made valuable contribution to (...)

...Dedicated to improvement of (...)

...Eager to (...)

...Enjoys competition in/of (...)

...Personal industry helped (...)

...Always skillful in (...)

...Succeeds in (...)

...Enjoys success in/at (...)

...Energetic effort in/to (...)

...Faithful service in/as (...)

...High performance in (...)

...Industrious nature led to (...)

...Quality work in/as (...)

...Skilled in (...)

...Responsive to needs of (...)

100

Above Average Performance (Levels 8-7)

...High achiever in area(s) of (...)

...Better than others in (...)

...Careful attention to detail in (...)

...Dedicated effort led to (...)

...Works in earnest to (...)

...Contributes to (...)

...Successful in efforts to (...)

...Personal talent helped (...)

...Volunteered for/to (...)

...Talented in area(s) of (...)

...Enhanced ability to (...)

...Experienced in matters of (...)

...Fruitful work in area of (...)

...Achieved success in/as (...)

...Gave quality effort in (...)

...Improved in area of (...)

...Personal flexibility led to (...)

...Aggressively pursues (...)

...Always alert for (...)

...Stays busy working in/on (...)

...Can be counted on to contribute to (...)

...Diligent and persistent in (...)

...Gave earnest effort to/in (...)

101

Above Average Performance (Levels 8-7)

...Looks for ways to improve (...)

...Exceeds requirements in/of (...)

...Industrious and persistent in (...)

...Proficient in (...)

...Personal resourcefulness led to (...)

...Attentive to needs of (...)

...Always busy doing (...)

...Looks for better ways to (...)

...Correct and careful about (...)

...Contributes full measure in/on (...)

...Determined to improve (...)

...A diligent effort in (...)

...Excels in area(s) of (...)

...Experience led to improvement of/in (...)

...Gave fine effort in (...)

...Fruitful and productive in (...)

...Successfully completed (...)

...Productive effort in (...)

...Resourceful in (...)

...Succeeded in (...)

...Excels in ability to (...)

Above Average Performance (Levels 8-7)

CHAPTER 4

EFFECTIVE PERSONAL PERFORMANCE
(LEVELS 6-5)

PERSONAL PERFORMANCE LEVELS

LEVELS 10-9
* Contributes GREATLY to organization mission
* CONTINUALLY seeks additional responsibility
* THOROUGHLY understands all job components
* Works well independent of supervision

LEVELS 8-7
* Contributes HIGH LEVEL to organization mission
* Seeks additional responsibility
* Exhibits drive for self-improvement
* Proposes good solutions to difficult problems

LEVELS 6-5
* Contributes SOME to organization mission
* ACCEPTS additional responsibility
* Requires LIMITED supervision
* Good understanding of major jobs

LEVELS 4-3
* DOES NOT contribute to organization mission
* DOES NOT desire additional responsibility
* Requires ROUTINE supervision
* Satisfied with less than quality work

LEVELS 2-1
* HINDERS organization mission
* AVOIDS added responsibility
* Requires CONSTANT supervision
* DOES NOT or CAN NOT understand job

103

EFFECTIVE PERSONAL PERFORMANCE

WORD BANK

NOTE: The words in this word bank, USED ALONE, describe EFFECTIVE PERFORMANCE. When combined with other "qualifying" words, many of these words can be used to describe higher or lower performance.

EXAMPLE: CAPABLE (EFFECTIVE)
HIGHLY CAPABLE (ABOVE AVERAGE)
SOMEWHAT CAPABLE (MARGINAL)
NOT CAPABLE (UNSATISFACTORY)

Words listed in other word banks can similarly be used to describe higher or lower performance.

ABIDE(S)	ABIDING	ABILITY
ABLE	ABREAST	ACCEPT(S)
ACCEPTABLE	ACCOMMODATE	ACCOMMODATING
ACCURATE	ADAPTABLE	ADAPTS
ADEQUACY	ADEQUATE(LY)	ADHERE(S)
ADHERENCE	AGREEABLE	AID(S)
ALL RIGHT	AMPLE	ASSIST(S)
AVERAGE	BASIC	BENEFICIAL
BENEFIT(S)	CAPABLE	CAPABILITY
COMMON	COMPATIBLE	COMPETENCE
COMPETENT	COMPLIANCE	COMPLIES
COMPLY	CONFIDENT	CONFORM(S)
CONFORMANCE	CONFORMITY	CORRECT
CONVENTIONAL	COOPERATIVE	CONSISTENT
CONTENT	CREDIBLE	DECENT
DEPENDABLE	DESIRABLE	DURABLE
EASY	EFFECTIVE	EFFICIENT
EFFORT	ENOUGH	EQUALITY
EQUITABLE	EVEN	FAIR
FAVORABLE	FEASIBLE	FUNDAMENTAL
HELP(S)	HELPFUL	IMPROVING IN

104

ACCORD	INTERESTED	KNOWLEDGE
KNOWLEDGEABLE	LEVEL	MEDIUM
MIDDLE	MILD	MODERATE
MODERATELY	MODERATION	MODEST
MOST	MOSTLY	NEWCOMER
NICE	NORM	NORMAL
OBEDIENT	OBEY(S)	ORDERLY
ORDINARY	ORTHODOX	PATIENT
POSITIVE	PRACTICABLE	PRACTICAL
PREPARED	PROMISING	PROPER
PUNCTUAL	QUALIFIED	RATIONAL
REASONABLE	REGULAR	RELIABLE
RESPECTABLE	RESPONSIBLE	RESPONSIBILITY
RIGHT	ROUTINE(LY)	SATISFACTORY
STABLE	STEADY	SUFFICIENT
SUITABLE	SUPPORT(S)	SUPPORTIVE
TIDY	TRIES	TRY
TYPICAL(LY)	UP-AND-COMING	USEFUL
VALID	WILLING	WORKABLE

> Failure is an education in learning.
> From the book: **Successful Leadership Today**

> "The superior man is firm in the
> right way, not merely firm." CONFUCIUS
> From the book: **Successful Leadership Today**

BULLET PHRASE STATEMENTS

Select a word in COLUMN #1 to go with a word in COLUMN #2.

EXAMPLE: EFFECTIVE PERFORMER

COLUMN #1

ABLE
ACCURATE
ADEQUATE
AMPLE
AVERAGE
BENEFICIAL
CAPABLE
COMPETENT
CONFIDENT
DEPENDABLE
EFFECTIVE
EFFICIENT
HELPFUL
PRODUCTIVE
QUALIFIED
RESPECTABLE
RESPONSIBLE
RESPONSIVE
SATISFACTORY
SUITABLE
USEFUL

COLUMN #2

INDIVIDUAL
OFFICER
MANAGER
PERSON
SUPERVISOR
TECHNICIAN
TYPIST
WORKER
(or, use
Professional
title)

> People want to believe they made
> a difference, that they contributed
> something someone else might
> not have contributed.
> From the book:
> **Successful Leadership Today**

Select a word from each column that best describes an individual.

COLUMN #1	COLUMN #2	COLUMN #3
ALWAYS	ACCEPTABLE	
COMMONLY	ADEQUATE	
CONSISTENTLY	AVERAGE	PERFORMANCE
CUSTOMARILY	CAPABLE	
GENERALLY	COMPETENT	RESULTS
NORMALLY	CREDIBLE	
ORDINARILY	DEPENDABLE	WORK
ON AVERAGE	EFFECTIVE	
REGULARLY	EFFICIENT	
STEADY	GOOD	
TYPICAL	HELPFUL	
USUALLY	POSITIVE	
	PRODUCTIVE	
	SATISFACTORY	
	SUCCESSFUL	

Select a word in COLUMN #1 to go with a word in COLUMN #2.

COLUMN #1	COLUMN #2
ACCEPTABLE	
AVERAGE	ACCOMPLISHMENTS
DEPENDABLE	EFFORT
EFFECTIVE	OUTPUT
FAVORABLE	PERFORMANCE
GOOD	RESULTS
MODERATE	WORK HABITS
POSITIVE	
PRODUCTIVE	
RELIABLE	
SATISFACTORY	

"Leadership is the ability to get
men to do what they don't want to do,
and like it." HARRY S. TRUMAN
From the book: **Successful Leadership Today**

Effective Personal Performance (Levels 6-5)

Select a word in COLUMN #1 to go with a word in COLUMN #2.

EXAMPLE: EFFECTIVE EMPLOYEE

COLUMN #1	**COLUMN #2**
ADEQUATE	EMPLOYEE
AVERAGE	INDIVIDUAL
CAPABLE	MANAGER
COMPETENT	PERFORMER
DEPENDABLE	(or, use
EFFECTIVE	professional
EFFICIENT	title:
ENTHUSIASTIC	ACCOUNTANT
GOOD	CASHIER
HELPFUL	NURSE
METHODICAL	POLICEMAN
PRODUCTIVE	SECRETARY
POSITIVE	TEACHER, etc.)
SATISFACTORY	
SUCCESSFUL	
WILLING	

...Sincere effort   ...Adequate performance

...Practical individual   ...Technically capable

...Has determination   ...Alert individual

...Tries hard   ...Is improving

...Good worker   ...Helps others

...Keeps organized   ...Positive attitude

...Always prepared   ...Productive output

...Promising future   ...Always punctual

...Reliable effort   ...Satisfactory work

...Average work   ...Moderately successful

...Capable individual   ...Typically effective

108

Effective Personal Performance (Levels 6-5)

...Acceptable performance

...Favorable work

...Methodical person

...Dependable performance

...Performs well

...Likes responsibility

...Helpful dedication

...Likes challenges

...Steady performer

...Plans ahead

...Developing quickly

...Ample results

...Diligent performance

...Typically effective

...Credible talent

...Keeps busy

...Average abilities

...Satisfactory results

...Aspiring newcomer

...Moderately successful

...Stays organized

...Obedient performance

...Good technician

...Effective performer

...Good accomplishments

...Competent job

...Good production

...Able worker

...Faithful individual

...Positive outlook

...Favorable record

...Careful individual

...Self motivated

...Accepts responsibility

...Competent work

...Supports rules

...Works diligently

...Accurate work

...Favorable workmanship

...Confident individual

...Smooth worker

...Aids others

...Average talent

...Persistent efforts

...Keeps poise

...Hopeful future

109

Effective Personal Performance (Levels 6-5)

...Helpful disposition

...Enthusiastic individual

...Readily adaptable

...Technically competent

...Meets requirements

...Willing individual

...Capable individual

...Ample ability

...Effective performer

...Good work habits

...Orderly work habits

...Gets positive results

...Accommodating to superiors

...Adequately completes tasks

...Does ordinary work

...Usually error-free work

...Patient and understanding

...Takes correct action

...Gives desirable effort

...Pursues tasks diligently

...Does decent job

...Deliberate work habits

...Favorable work

...Meaningful work

...Has initiative

...Few mistakes

...Supports superiors

...Proper action

...Acceptable performance

...Good apprentice

...Mostly good work

...Does accurate work

...Gives good effort

...Helpful and alert

...Delivers accurate work

...Adheres to rules

...Attains routine results

...Common and ordinary

...Gives reasonable effort

...Reliable work habits

...Cooperative and helpful

...Gives credible performance

...A maturing individual

...Adequately completes tasks

110

Effective Personal Performance (Levels 6-5)

...Capable and dependable

...Competent in job

...Cooperative toward others

...Work is commonplace

...Gives ample effort

...Has moderate abilities

...Credible job accomplishment

...Qualified at job

...Effective work habits

...Consistent job performance

...Contributes reliable effort

...Supportive of others

...Usual good performance

...Mostly error-free work

...Does helpful work

...Interested in job

...Neat and orderly

...Orthodox work habits

...Does respectable job

...Has good desire

...Has ample competence

...Conventional work habits

...Gives routine effort

...Careful about detail

...Conventional work habits

...Work is dependable

...Achieves moderate success

...Does respectable job

...Conforms to standards

...Satisfactory work ethics

...Does level work

...Making satisfactory progress

...Dependable and reliable

...Sound, steady effort

...Always tries hard

...Gives encouraging effort

...Has ample competence

...Conscientious about job

...Careful about detail

...Gets positive results

...Knows job well

...Gives proper effort

...Does decent job

...Complies with rules

...Meets job requirements

...A satisfactory effort

111

Effective Personal Performance (Levels 6-5)

...Does nice job

...Shows reasonable effort

...Obedient and trustworthy

...Keeps positive attitude

...Does proper job

...Responsible work output

...Diligent at job

...Interested in job

...Achieves medium success

...Punctual for work

...Successful work habits

...Confident of abilities

...Performs job effectively

...Has practical ideas

...Diligent and careful

...Even, steady performance

...Good and improving

...Gives sufficient support

...Routinely good work

...Provides useful work

...Overcomes some obstacles

...Achieves satisfactory results

...Achieves satisfactory results

...Steady, normal effort

...Patient and understanding

...Gives productive attempt

...Work is punctual

...Responsive to others

...Provides good service

...Loyal to organization

...Takes desired actions

...Benefit to organization

...Supportive of co-workers

...Sets good example

...Conventional work habits

...Qualified in job

...Effective on job

...Produces favorable work

...Knowledgeable of job

...Punctual and reliable

...Willing to learn

...Has positive spirit

...Effective and reliable

...Fair productive output

112

...Does accurate work

...Possesses effective abilities

...Orderly and organized

...An effective performer

...Able and willing

...Attains ordinary output

...Effectively accomplishes jobs

...Efficient on-job work

...Prompt and responsive

...Contributes good effort

...Enjoys work environment

...Gets steady results

...Desire for self-improvement

...Attention to detail

...Responsive to tasking

...Benefit to organization

...Enjoys job diversification

...Enthusiastic about job

...Works for self-improvement

...Accurate in work

...Good work ethics

...Takes proper action

...Gives faithful effort

...Adheres to rules

...Observes the rules

...Follows direction well

...Has required skills

...Gives normal effort

...Work mostly correct

...Continues to improve

...Reasonable work effort

...Reliable and thorough

...Effective job accomplishment

...Good about detail

...Interested in job

...Ability to adapt

...Proper mental attitude

...Has positive spirit

...Has good standards

...Meets job requirements

...Conforms to standards

...Gives determined effort

...Agreeable work habits

...Deliberate work habits

...Work is encouraging

...Does level work

113

Effective Personal Performance (Levels 6-5)

...Makes good effort

...Continues to improve

...Making satisfactory progress

...Smooth, effective results

...Does beneficial work

...Attains desired results

...Steady, methodical work

...Does successful job

...Has normal ability

...An experienced individual

...Desire for self-improvement

...A good asset

...Makes effective effort

...Gets steady results

...Willing to learn

...Works with determination

...Good daily work

...Has good ability

...A competent individual

...Possesses effective abilities

...An effective performer

...Good sense of responsibility

...Competent and dedicated

..Achieves satisfactory results

...Does careful work

...Knowledgeable of job

...Satisfactory competence level

...Flexible and adaptable

...Gives good performance

...Performs job effectively

...Understands job well

...Prudent, careful worker

...Conventional work habits

...Effective job accomplishment

...Easy to motivate

...Shows effective skills

...Can overcome obstacles

...Careful work habits

...Fair productive output

...Making steady progress

...Does accurate work

...Follows direction well

...Work has few mistakes

...Meets the stated objectives

114

Effective Personal Performance (Levels 6-5)

...Flexible, able to adapt

...Useful to have around

...Suitable for many jobs

...Willing to help others

...Pleasant to work with

...Orderly and organized effort

...Abides by the rules

...Well skilled in job

...Takes pride in work

...Good level of competence

...Responsive to changing conditions

...Positive attitude and outlook

...Steady, consistent performance

...Understands responsibilities well

...Effective job accomplishment

...Has medium-range capabilities

...Satisfactory competence level

...Understands procedures well

...Newcomer with good potential

...Adaptable to changing situations

...Adapts to changing requirements

...Agreeable to work time-changes

...Capable of good work

...Ordinarily does good work

...Work worthy of mention

...Neat and tidy person

...Obeys all the rules

...Work area always organized

...Continues to be punctual

...Works without direct supervision

...Puts forth ample effort

...Does not tire easily

...Quality of workmanship good

115

Effective Personal Performance (Levels 6-5)

...Aids others when possible

...Understands basic job requirements

...Contributes to team effort

...Conforms to expected standards

...Works comfortably with others

...Adheres to job requirements

...Usually does good job

...Most work is acceptable

...Usually gets positive results

...Performs routine jobs well

...Desired results routinely achieved

...Work worthy of mention

...Puts forth ample effort

...Sufficient drive and determination

...Good level of competence

...Complies with the rules

...Correct and productive work

...Adaptable to procedural changes

...Diligently pursues job requirements

...Easy to work with

...Flexible to job changes

...Willing to help others

Effective Personal Performance (Levels 6-5)

...Has interest in work

...Tries to improve self

...Believes in giving loyalty

...Gives good, level effort

...Detailed knowledge of job

...Usually does favorable work

...Conforms to expected standards

...Completes ample work assignment

...Has required basic knowledge

...Capable of efficient effort

...Good level of reliability

...Has desire to excel

...Seeks to expand knowledge

...Polite and cordial nature

...Has some good talents

...Keeps a positive attitude

...Responsive to changing situations

...More than adequate worker

...Good dedication to job

...Believes in being prepared

...Gives support and loyalty

...Can be relied upon

...Well trained and productive

117

Effective Personal Performance (Levels 6-5)

...Easy to work with

...Will comply with direction

...Cooperative to work with

...Has required basic knowledge

...Capable of efficient effort

...Average ability and know-how

...Satisfactory level of competence

...Obeys policy and procedure

...Acceptable record of accomplishment

...Adaptable to job changes

...Maturing into job requirements

...Normal work and production

...Suitable for most jobs

...Results of sufficient quality

...In adherence with rules

...Basic understanding of job

...Works well with supervision

...Routinely attains desired results

...Adequate level of performance

...Conforms to job requirements

...Possesses an ample knowledge

...Sound understanding of job

118

...Suitable for most jobs

...Results of sufficient quality

...Good record of performance

...Seeks solutions to problems

...Contributes to organization effectiveness

...Works without prompting or prodding

...Deliberate actions. Attention to detail

...Does not get discouraged easily

...Little wasted time or effort

...Responds favorably to new situations

...A fair amount of talent

...Does sufficient amount of work

...Able to do good job

...Completes average amount of work

...Capable of above average work

...Tries to give good effort

...Able to make steady progress

...In adherence with job requirements

...Stays abreast of changing situations

...Delivers ample amount of work

...Basic knowledge of job content

...Takes care in doing work

...In compliance with job requirements

119

...Contributes good measure of work

...Able to complete all jobs

...Offers positive ideas and suggestions

...Comes to work well prepared

...Has prompt and proper answers

...Responsive to job content changes

...Gives efficient and effective effort

...Does equitable amount of work

...Flexible to new job assignments

...Good fundamental knowledge of job

...Very helpful during busy periods

...Interested in doing good job

...Does most jobs very well

...A fair amount of talent

...Does modest amount of work

...Concerned about doing good job

...Attentive to needs of job

...Easy to get along with

...Likes even, moderate work load

...Does fair amount of work

...Patient in training inexperienced personnel

...Performs most jobs without assistance

120

Effective Personal Performance (Levels 6-5)

...Does most jobs very well

...Does not require constant supervision

...Takes minor setbacks in stride

...Usually accurate and effective

...Tries to do quality work

...Best suited for routine jobs

...Suitable for routine, ordinary jobs

...Does adequate amount of work

...Work is of common variety

...Works well on special projects

...Happiest with routine, uncomplicated jobs

...Makes daily contribution to work effort

...Has practical solutions to problem areas

...Qualified in all aspects of job

...Has fundamental understanding of job requirements

...Eager to do a good job

...Adapts to current conditions of work

...Tries to do best job possible

...Carries out job in usually successful manner

...Down-to-earth individual. Easy to work with

...Works to get the job done correctly

...Gives accurate work most of the time

...Work usually correct the first time

121

Effective Personal Performance (Levels 6-5)

...Does good job when routine and repetitive in nature

...Performs well with only routine supervision

...Most of the time gets job completed on time

...Needs to work in areas adequately covered by instruction

COMPLETE THE PHRASE

...Keeps busy during/when (...)

...Takes positive action when (...)

...Steady effort in (...)

...Accurate in/when (...)

...Stays busy doing (...)

...Capable of (...)

...Good competence in/with (...)

...Always complies with (...)

...Effectively accomplishes (...)

...Made contribution to/in (...)

...Credible work with/in (...)

...Always decent job as/in (...)

...Can be depended upon to (...)

...Diligent in efforts to (...)

...Good, effective work in (...)

...Does enough work to (...)

...Flexible in (...)

...Organized a/an (...)

...Positive attitude in/toward (...)

...Does proper job of (...)

...Satisfactory performance in/as (...)

...Knowledgeable of (...)

123

...Effectively accomplishes (...)

...Makes good effort to (...)

...Has favorable record in/as (...)

...Orderly and organized in (...)

...Productive in (...)

...Performs well in/as (...)

...Punctual for (...)

...Satisfactory results in (...)

...Useful in/as (...)

...Always accurate effort when/in (...)

...Gets acceptable results in/when (...)

...Has ability to (...)

...Willing to accept (...)

...Adapts easily to (...)

...Knows basics of (...)

...Always takes care of (...)

...Very comfortable working in/around (...)

...Gets creditable results in (...)

...Continues to improve in (...)

...Responsibly handles (...)

...Understands need to/for (...)

...Keeps workspace tidy and (...)

124

...Ability to adapt to (...)

...Responsive in (...)

...Flexible and productive in/as (...)

...Knows fundamentals of (...)

...Adequately carries out job of (...)

...Careful to complete (...)

...Cooperative with/in (...)

...Finds it easy to (...)

...Gives favorable effort in (...)

...Has practical ideas to improve (...)

...Able to adapt to (...)

...Does reliable work on/in (...)

...Provides continuity in (...)

...Helpful in areas of (...)

...Adheres to (...)

...Good ability to (...)

...Encourages others to (...)

...Qualified to (...)

...Reliable in (...)

...Good, steady effort in/on (...)

...Does sufficient work in/on (...)

...Supports efforts to (...)

...Tries to (...)

125

Effective Personal Performance (Levels 6-5)

...Agreeable to (...)

...Has good competence in (...)

...Ample ability to (...)

...Confident of abilities to (...)

...Effective in (...)

...Good fundamental ability to (...)

...Helps others in/to (...)

...Improving in (...)

...Shows strong interest in (...)

...Assisted in (...)

...Always attentive to (...)

...Reliable in/as (...)

...Good fundamental understanding of (...)

...Capable of good work in (...)

...Does decent job as/in (...)

...Adequate work in/as (...)

...Acts responsible in/when (...)

...Uses time wisely to (...)

...Good job of (...)

...Has effective way of (...)

...Has moderate success in/as (...)

...Adaptable to change in (...)

126

...Considerate of (...)

...Versatile in (...)

...Does careful work in/on (...)

...Average ability to (...)

...Attentive to needs of (...)

...Conforms to (...)

...Does effective job in/as (...)

...Always efficient in (...)

...Efficient work in area of (...)

...Good knowledge in/of (...)

...Always prepared to/for (...)

...Gives normal effort in (...)

...Productive effort in (...)

...Promising future as/in (...)

...Respectful work in/as (...)

...Willing to (...)

...Responsible for (...)

...Always compatible with (...)

...Contributes effectively to (...)

...Responsive to needs of (...)

...Suitable for work in/as (...)

...Routinely does (...)

127

Effective Personal Performance (Levels 6-5)

The "daily routine" is work without
a challenge; it breeds complacency.
From the book: **Successful Leadership Today**

"Progress comes from the intelligent
use of experience." ELBERT HUBBARD
From the book: **Successful Leadership Today**

128

CHAPTER 5

ACTIVE - ACTION WORDS

WORD BANK THESAURUS

ACTIVE and **ACTION WORDS**, add P**OWER** to your statement.

ACCOMPLISHES	ACHIEVES	ACTION
ACTIVATION	ACTIVE	ACTIVELY
AGGRESSIVE	AGITATES	AGITATOR
ANALYZES	ANIMATES	ANIMATING
ANTICIPATES	ANXIOUS	APPLIES
ARDENT	AROUSAL	AROUSES
ARTICULATES	ASPIRES	ASPIRING
ASSERTS	ASSIGNS	ASSISTS
ASSURES	AVID	BOLD
BOLSTERS	CAPITALIZES	CATALYST
CHALLENGING	COMPELS	COMPETITIVE
COMPETES	COMPULSIVE	CONCEIVES
CONDUCTS	CONFRONTS	CONTRIBUTES
CONTRIVES	COORDINATES	CREATES
CREATIVE	CULTIVATES	DELEGATES
DEMONSTRATES	DETERS	DEVELOPS
DEVISES	DISPLAYS	DOMINATES
DRIVE	EAGER	ELICITS
EMBODIES	EMERGES	EMULATES
ENCOURAGES	ENDEAVORS	ENERGETIC
ENERGIZES	ENERGY	ENFORCES
ENHANCES	ENLIVENS	ENRICHES
ENTERPRISING	ENTHUSIASTIC	ENTHUSES
ENTICES	ERUPTS	ESCALATES
ESTABLISHES	EXCEEDS	EXCELS
EXCITABLE	EXCITES	EXCITEMENT
EXCITING	EXECUTES	EXECUTION

129

EXPANDS	EXPEDITES	EXPEDITIOUS
EXPLOITS	EXPLORES	EXPLOSIVE
EXUBERANCE	EXUBERANT	EXULTANT
FABRICATES	FACILITATES	FEISTY
FEVERISH	FIERCE	FIERY
FLASHY	FOCUSES	FORCES
FORMULATES	FRANTIC	FRENZY
GENERATES	GRASPS	HASTENS
HECTIC	HIGH-FLYING	HIGH-POWERED
HIGH-PRESSURE	HIGH-SPIRITED	HONES
HURDLES	HURRIES	HYPER
IDENTIFIES	IGNITES	IMPASSIONED
IMPATIENT	IMPELS	IMPETUS
IMPLEMENTS	IMPOSES	IMPROVES
IMPROVISES	IMPULSIVE	INCISIVE
INCITES	INDUCES	INFECTS
INFECTIOUS	INFUSES	INITIATES
INNOVATIVE	INSATIABLE	INSPIRES
INSPIRITS	INSURES	INTENSIVE
INTERFUSES	INVIGORATES	INVIGORATING
JUBILANT	KINDLES	LAUNCHES
LIVELY	MAINTAINS	MANIPULATES
MOTIVATES	ORGANIZES	ORIGINATES
OUTLASTS	OVERCOMES	OVERSEES
OVERWHELMS	PERFORMS	PERPETUATES
PERSEVERING	PERSUADES	PLANS
POSSESSES	POTENCY	POTENT
POWERFUL	POWERHOUSE	PRACTICES
PREPARES	PRODS	PRODUCES
PROJECTS	PROMOTES	PROMPTS
PROPAGATES	PROPELS	PROSPEROUS
PROVOCATIVE	PROVOKES	PROVOKING
PURGES	QUANTIFIES	QUEST

Active - Action Words

QUICKEN	RADIANCE	RADIATES
RALLIES	RECOGNIZES	RECTIFIES
REFINES	REFORMS	REGENERATES
REHABILITATES	REINFORCES	REJUVENATES
RELENTLESS	RENEWS	RENOVATES
REORGANIZES	REQUIRES	RESILIENT
RESOLVES	RESTLESS	RESURGE
RESURGENT	REVIVES	SACRIFICES
SACRIFICING	SCRUTINIZES	SEEKS
SOLVES	SPARKS	SPEARHEADS
SPEEDY	SPIRITED	SPONTANEOUS
SPRY	STIMULATES	STIMULUS
STRENGTHENS	STRINGENT	STRIVES
STOKES	SUPERVISES	SUPPORTS
SURPASSES	SUSTAINS	SWIFT
SWIFTNESS	TENACIOUS	TENACITY
THRIVES	TRANSFORMS	UNBEATABLE
UNSTOPPABLE	UTILIZES	VIGOR
VIGOROUS	VIGILANT	VITALITY
VITALIZATION		

"In all good things,
reason should prevail."
WILLIAM PENN
From the book:
Successful Leadership Today

Active - Action Words

CHAPTER 6

PERSONALITY & WORK RELATIONSHIPS

(LEVELS 10-5)

PERSONAL PERFORMANCE LEVELS

LEVELS 10-9
* Contributes GREATLY to organization mission
* CONTINUALLY seeks additional responsibility
* THOROUGHLY understands all job components
* Works well independent of supervision

LEVELS 8-7
* Contributes HIGH LEVEL to organization mission
* Seeks additional responsibility
* Exhibits drive for self-improvement
* Proposes good solutions to difficult problems

LEVELS 6-5
* Contributes SOME to organization mission
* ACCEPTS additional responsibility
* Requires LIMITED supervision
* Good understanding of major jobs

LEVELS 4-3
* DOES NOT contribute to organization mission
* DOES NOT desire additional responsibility
* Requires ROUTINE supervision
* Satisfied with less than quality work

LEVELS 2-1
* HINDERS organization mission
* AVOIDS added responsibility
* Requires CONSTANT supervision
* DOES NOT or CAN NOT understand job

PERSONALITY & WORK RELATIONSHIPS

WORD BANK

NOTE: The words in this word bank, USED ALONE, describe FAVORABLE TRAITS. When combined with other "qualifying" words, many of these words can be used to describe UNFAVORABLE TRAITS.

EXAMPLE: CHEERFUL (FAVORABLE)
                 NOT CHEERFUL (UNFAVORABLE)

Words listed in other word banks can similarly be used to describe unfavorable traits.

ACHIEVER	ADAPTABLE	ADEPT
ADMIRABLE	ADMIRE	ADROIT
AFFABLE	AFFECTION	AFFECTIONATE
AGGRESSIVE	AGILE	AGILITY
ALERT	ALL-AROUND	ALTRUISTIC
AMIABLE	AMICABLE	AMITY
ANIMATED	ANIMATOR	APPEALING
ARTISTIC	ASSERTIVE	ASSURED
BENEVOLENCE	BENEVOLENT	BIG-HEARTED
BOLD		BRISK
BROAD-MINDED	CALM	CANDID
CAUTIOUS	CHARISMATIC	CHARITABLE
CHARM	CHARMER	CHARMING
CHEERFUL	CHEERY	COMMANDING
COMPASSION	COMPASSIONATE	COMPETITOR
COMPOSED	CONFIDENT	CONGENIAL
CONSIDERATE	CONVINCING	COOPERATIVE
CORDIAL	COURAGE	COURAGEOUS
COURTEOUS	DAUNTLESS	DECISIVE
DEDICATED	DELIBERATE	DETERMINATION
DETERMINED	DEVOTED	DIGNIFIED

133

DIGNIFY	DIPLOMACY	DIPLOMAT
DIPLOMATIC	DIPLOMACY	DISCREET
DISTINGUISHED	DYNAMIC	EAGER
EAGER BEAVER	EAGERNESS	EARNEST
EFFERVESCE	EFFERVESCENT	ELEGANCE
ELEGANT	ELOQUENT	EMPATHIC
EMPATHIZE	EMPATHY	ENCHANT
ENCHANTING	ENERGETIC	ENGAGING
ENGENDER	ENTERPRISING	ENTHUSIASTIC
ENTHUSIASM	ENTHUSIAST	ETHICAL
EQUITABLE	ETIQUETTE	EVEN-TEMPERED
EXCITER	EXPERIENCED	EXTROVERT
EXUBERANT	FAIR	FAIR-MINDED
FAITHFUL	FEARLESS	FESTIVE
FINESSE	FINISHED	FIRM
FLAIR	FORCEFUL	FOREHANDED
FORESIGHTED	FORGIVE	FORGIVENESS
FORGIVING	FORTHRIGHT	FORTITUDE
FORWARD-LOOKING		FRANK
FRIENDLY	FRIENDSHIP	GALLANT
GENEROSITY	GENEROUS	GENIAL
GENIALITY	GENTEEL	GOOD FAITH
GOOD-FELLOWSHIP		GOOD-HEARTED
GOOD-HUMORED	GOOD-NATURED	GOOD-TEMPERED
GOODWILL	GRACIOUS	GRACE
GRACEFUL	GREATHEARTED	GREGARIOUS
GRIT	GUNG HO	HARMONIOUS
HARMONY	HAPPY	HEARTFELT
HELPFUL	HIGH-MINDED	HONEST
HONESTY	HONOR	HONORABLE
HOSPITABLE	HUMANE	HUMANITARIAN
HUMOR	HUMOROUS	IMPASSION
IMPASSIONATE	IMPOSING	IMPRESSIVE

134

INCORRUPTIBLE	INDOMITABLE	INDUSTRIOUS
INDUSTRY	INFLUENTIAL	INITIATIVE
INNOVATIVE	INQUISITIVE	INSPIRE
INSPIRED	INSPIRING	INTEGRITY
INTESTINAL	FORTITUDE	JACOSE
JOCULAR	JOLLY	JOVIAL
JOYFUL	JUDICIOUS	JUST
KIND	KINDHEARTED	KINDLY
KINDLINESS	KINDNESS	LARGE-MINDED
LEVELHEADED	LIGHTHEARTED	LIKABLE
LIMPID	LIVELINESS	LIVELY
LOYAL	LOYALTY	MAGNETIC
MANNERLY	MATURITY	MATURE
MERRY	METHODICAL	METICULOUS
MILD	MORALISTIC	OBSERVANT
OPENHEARTED	OPEN-MINDED	OPENNESS
PATIENT	PATRIOT	PATRIOTISM
PERSEVERING	PERSONABLE	PERSONIFY
PERSUASIVE	PLEASANT	PLEASING
PLEASURABLE	POISE	POLISH
POLISHED	POLITE	PRESTIGIOUS
PRIDE	PROFESSIONAL	PROFESSIONALISM
PROMINENCE	PROMINENT	PROPRIETY
PROMPT	PROUD	PRUDENCE
PRUDENT	QUIET	RADIANT
RECEPTIVE	REFINED	RELIABLE
RELIANT	RENOWN	RENOWNED
REPUTABLE	RESERVED	RESOLUTE
RESPECT	RESPECTABLE	
RESPECTFUL	RESPONSIVE	RESTRAINED
RETIRING	RIGHTEOUS	SCRUPULOUS
SEDATE	SELF-COMPOSED	SELF-CONFIDENCE
SELF-CONTROL		SELF-CONTROLLED

Personality & Work Relationships (Levels 10-5)

SELF-DETERMINATION   SELF-DISCIPLINE
SELF-ESTEEM   SELFLESS   SELF-RELIANCE
SELF-RELIANT   SELF-RESPECT   SELF-RESTRAINT

SELF-SACRIFICE   SELF-SACRIFICING
SELF-STARTER   SELF-WILL   SENSITIVE
SENSITIVITY   SERENE   SERIOUS

SINCERE   SINCERITY   SOBER
SOCIABLE   SOCIAL   SOCIALIZE
SPIRIT   SPIRITED   STABLE

STALWART   STANDARD-BEARER
STATELINESS   STRAIGHT-FORWARD
STUDIOUS   SUAVE   SYMPATHETIC

SYMPATHIZE   SYMPATHY   TACT
TACTFUL   TEAM PLAYER   TEMPERATE
TEMPERANCE   TENACIOUS   TENDER

TENDERHEARTED   TENDERNESS   THANKFUL
THOUGHTFUL   THOUGHTFULNESS
TRANQUIL   TRUSTWORTHY   TRUSTFUL

TRUSTING   UNASSUMING   UNFLAPPABLE
UNIFIER   UNINHIBITED   UNSELFISH
UPRIGHT   VERSED   VERE

VIGOR   VIGOROUS   VIM
VIRTUE   VIRTUOUS   VITALITY
VIVACIOUS   WARM   WARMHEARTED

WELL-BEHAVED   WELL-BRED   WELL-CONDITIONED
WELL-DISPOSED   WELL-GROOMED   WELL-MANNERED
WHOLESOME   ZEAL   ZEALOT

ZEALOUS   ZEST   ZESTFULNESS
ZESTY   ZIP   ZIPPY

"Do your duty and leave the
rest to heaven." PIERRE CORNEILLE
From the book: **Successful Leadership Today**

136

Personality & Work Relationships (Levels 10-5)

BULLET PHRASE STATEMENTS

Select one or two words in COLUMN 1 to go with a word in COLUMN 2.

EXAMPLE: COOPERATIVE ATTITUDE
DIGNIFIED, POLISHED MANNER

COLUMN #1		COLUMN #2
ADAPTABLE	FRIENDLY	
AFFABLE	GOOD-NATURED	ATTITUDE
AGREEABLE	HARMONIOUS	BEHAVIOR
AMICABLE	IMPECCABLE	CHARACTER
APPEALING	KIND	MANNER
CHARISMATIC	LIVELY	PERSONALITY
CHARMING	MAGNETIC	PRESENCE
CHEERFUL	PLEASANT	
COMPASSIONATE	PLEASING	
COMPOSED	POLISHED	
CONGENIAL	REFINED	
COOPERATIVE	SELF-CONFIDENT	
CORDIAL	SENSITIVE	
COURTEOUS	SINCERE	
DIGNIFIED	SOCIABLE	
DISTINGUISHED	THOUGHTFUL	
ELEGANT	WARM	
ENCHANTING	WARMHEARTED	
ENGAGING	WELL-MANNERED	

...Dynamic personality

...Shows compassion

...Highly personable

...Impeccable character

...Dignified presence

...Vigorous personality

...Eager willingness

...Powerful figure

...Mild mannered

...Sound character

...Positive attitude

...Engaging personality

...Exudes optimism

...Pleasant manner

...Friendly personality

...Sincere manner

137

...Emotionally stable

...Unflagging zeal

...Emotionally mature

...Sparks excitement

...Probing personality

...Team player

...Pleasant, even-tempered

...Well mannered

...Even tempered

...Steadying influence

...An inspiration

...Impeccable character

...Pleasing personality

...Refined presence

...Dignified manner

...Inspires self-improvement

...Warm personality

...Friendly disposition

...Amicable person

...Good Samaritan

...Extremely friendly

...Polished manner

...Caring nature

...Highly cooperative

...Congenial person

...Uncommonly likable

...Mental courage

...Energetic personality

...Courteous nature

...Energetic spirit

...Optimistic outlook

...Personal magnetism

...Always enthusiastic

...Equitable treatment

...Encourages understanding

...Instills motivation

...Stimulates harmony

...Equal treatment

...Exemplary character

...Effervescent personality

...Quick witted

...Dignified presence

...Sociable manner

...Easy-going mannerism

138

...Unwavering self-reliance   ...Dignified manner

...Self motivated   ...Enchanting person

...Cheerful readiness   ...Exemplary character

...Refined personality   ...Uncompromising principles

...Nice, polite individual   ...Good, steady disposition

...An energetic personality   ...Easy going nature

...A modest individual   ...Generous, caring individual

...Patient and understanding   ...Considerate of others

...A cheerful individual   ...A likable person

...Humane and compassionate   ...Personal integrity unassailable

...Stable in character   ...High moral principles

...Good personal values   ...Amicable, friendly disposition

...Tremendous personal courage   ...Friendly, radiant personality

...Highest personal integrity   ...Cheerful and good-natured

...Impeccable moral fiber   ...Kind, benign disposition

...Firm, resolute character   ...Stands on principles

...Talented and charismatic   ...High ethical principles

...Ethical, honest personality   ...Great personal courage

...Strong moral character   ...Ethical, honest individual

...Fosters friendly goodwill   ...Never loses temper

...Impeccable moral character   ...Cordial and affable

...Probing, alert personality   ...Friendly and sociable

...Strength of character   ...Competitive, winning spirit

139

Personality & Work Relationships (Levels 10-5)

...Resilient, resolute personality ...Elegant, cultivated manner

...Cleverness and guild ...Good-natured and friendly

...Intrepid, resolute character ...Alert, energetic personality

...Pleasant, pleasing person ...Unselfish and trusting

...Kind, amiable disposition ...Sincere, outgoing personality

...Forthright, confident manner ...Sincere counseling techniques

...Friendly and cooperative ...Infectious positive attitude

...A winning spirit ...Positive, cooperative spirit

...Thoughtful of others ...Compassion for others

...Kind in manner ...Possesses social grace

...Warm, friendly personality ...Fair, open minded

...An unyielding fair-mindedness ...Commanding in presence

...Resilient and energetic ...Composed and calm

...Affable, pleasant personality ...Friendly and cheerful

...Even, steadying temperament ...Amiable and good-natured

...Cheerful and helpful ...Sincere and likable

...Concerned and humane ...Alert, energetic personality

...Polite and elegant ...Humorous and witty

...Graceful in manner ...Sensitive and understanding

...Patient and understanding ...Thoughtful and caring

...Friendly, cooperative spirit ...Honest, respectful reputation

...Sincere, easy-going manner ...Tactful and courteous

140

...Frank and forward   ..Honest and faithful

...Respected by all   ...Presence and poise

...Refreshing, lively personality   ..."Can do" enthusiasm

...Firm, caring attitude   ...High moral principles

...Cheerful and good-natured   ...Good personal values

...Brilliant, lively wit   ...Fair and open-minded

...Infectious positive attitude   ...Cheerful in nature

...Cordial and affable   ...Affable, pleasant personality

...Friendly and sociable   ...Positive, cooperative spirit

...Full of compassion   ...Forthright, confident manner

...Friendly, cooperative attitude   ...Pleasing, sincere personality

...Flexible and cooperative   ...Stands on principles

...Warm, friendly personality   ...High ethical principles

...Friendly, even disposition   ...Courage of conviction

...Fosters friendly goodwill   ...Strong moral character

...Friendly, radiant personality   ...Courteous and good-natured

...Polite and cordial nature   ...Personable and well liked

...Easy to work with   ...Strong will of mind

...Respectful of others   ...Trusting in others

...Model for others   ...Builds on understanding

...Consideration for others   ...Good mannered and polite

...Even temper and disposition

...Courteous, respectful manner

141

Personality & Work Relationships (Levels 10-5)

...Engaging, engrossing personality

...Cooperative, cheerful personality

...Harmonious working relationships

...Agreeable, pleasant personality

...Sincere, outgoing personality

...Personality radiates enthusiasm

...Dynamic, energetic personality

...Open-minded and even-tempered

...Good personal relationships

...Possesses unrestrained enthusiasm

...Engaging, engrossing personality

...Unshakable, unyielding character

...Influential, persuasive personality

...Confident, easy-going manner

...Friendly, enchanting personality

...Unequaled personal demeanor

...Powerful, influential personality

...Impeccable personal moral character

...Possesses great moral strength

...Strong courage of character

...Great personal moral strength

...Personal vision and courage

142

...Possesses infectious positive attitude

...Stays calm and collective

...Keeps composure under pressure

...Flexible and cooperative spirit

...A real morale booster

...Superior rapport with others

...Uncompromising standards of conduct

...Keen sense of humor

...Impartial, just and ethical

...Pleasing and poised personality

...Sense of fair play

...Ingrained respect for others

...Good sense of humor

...Effervescent and enchanting personality

...Patient and understanding nature

...Fantastic sense of humor

...Pleasant manner and personality

...Considerable finesse and diplomacy

...Straightforward and above board

...Magnetic charm and appeal

...Stable and well-adjusted personality

...Dominating presence and personality

...Courteous, mannerly and polite

143

...Always has positive attitude

...Genuine concern for others

...Fair and without prejudice

...Unbeatable character and personality

...Sterling example for others

...Terrific sense of humor

...Noteworthy demeanor and presence

...Amicable personality bolsters morale

...Resilient and cheerful personality

...Radiates energy and enthusiasm

...Genuine concern for others

...Proper and correct manner

...Optimistic outlook and attitude

...Briskly alert and energetic

...Keen sense of humor

...A pillar of strength

...Shrewdly astute and alert

...Strong spirit and character

...Boundless enthusiasm and energy

...Shows courage under pressure

...Engenders trust and confidence

...Believes in fair play

144

...Elegant and cultivated manner

...Booster of high morale

...Dedicated to helping others

...Indestructible sense of humor

...Presence and demeanor noteworthy

...Fair and without prejudice

...Calm and affable manner

...Keen interest in others

...Fosters cooperation and harmony

...Fantastic wit and humor

...Sincere affection for others

...Excellent rapport with others

...Enforces fairness and equality

...Charismatic and outgoing personality

...A real "team player"

...Calm and affable nature

...Ingrained respect for others

...Well liked by others

...Cultivates harmony and understanding

...Impartial, just and ethical

...Pleasing and poised personality

...Polite and polished manner

...Keen sense of humor

145

...Unbeatable character and personality

...Unquestionable personal moral standards

...Stable and well-adjusted personality

...Blessed with social grace

...Calm and controlled personality

...Magnetic charm and appeal

...Self-starter with inspirational personality

...Always polite and courteous

...Quite manner. Commanding presence

...Easy to get along with

...Heedful to needs of others

...Gets along well with others

...Highest standards of moral integrity

...Courage to stand on principles

...Highest personal honor and integrity

...Great moral strength and courage

...Good emotional stability and strength

...Fully developed sense of loyalty

...High sense of personal pride

...High ideals, morals and ethics

...Keen sense of ethical conduct

...Has personal power of persuasion

146

...Fine sense of moral prudence

...Own enthusiasm infiltrates the ranks

...Rare ability to radiate enthusiasm

...Exudes emotional confidence and spirit

...Abundant initiative and personal drive

...Spreads sense of good will

...Personable, well-liked and highly respected

...Inspirational zeal and personal courage

...Dynamic individual with cheerful disposition

...Cheerful, witty personality. An asset

...Enhances morale and team work

...Even temperament and steadying influence

...Warm and helpful personal manner.

...Strong desire to help others

...Displays social poise and tact

...Sincere and uncommonly likable individual

...Honest, sincere with unquestionable integrity

...Polite and elegant in manner

...Cooperative, always willing to help

...Sensitive to needs of others

...Sincere manner and caring nature

...Unbiased in reason and action

...Thoughtful and caring by nature

147

...Strong advocate of equal opportunity

...Well mannered with pleasant personality

...Attentive to needs of others

...Bubbling enthusiasm permeates entire organization

...Concern for welfare of others

...Displays an air of dignity

...Extremely friendly and sociable nature

...Indestructible sense of good humor

...Highest standards of personal behavior

...Always willing to help others

...Strong believer in human equality

...Committed to fair, unbiased principles

...Places high emphasis on cooperation

...Displays social poise and tact

...High moral and ethical principles

...Ready wit and outgoing personality

...Keen sense of fair play

...Thoughtful and caring by nature

...Proper in manner and behavior

...Good-fellowship highlights personal traits

...Completely without bias or prejudice

...Possesses highest standards of integrity

148

...Advocates equal treatment and opportunity

...Courage of conviction without being contentious

...Personal integrity repeatedly earn high praise

...Willing to stand for principles and beliefs

...Pillar of moral strength and courage

...Strength of character to tackle any assignment

...Popular and sociable. A real morale booster

...Genial, cooperative with courage of conviction

...Pleasant personality blends well in any group

...Wit and charm quickly win acceptance in any surrounding

...In harmony and accord with others

...Cheerfulness and enthusiasm cornerstones to success

...Affable personality and willingness to assist others

...Inspired with a sense of purpose

...Cultivates team work and a winning spirit

...Contributes significantly to betterment of morale

...Demonstrates visible concern for welfare of others

...Continuing willingness to lend others a helping hand

...Routinely goes out of way to assist others

...A "team player." Highly cooperative with others

...Instills sense of unity and harmony

...Imparts sense of motivation and pride in others

...Personality spiced with good wit and humor

149

...Sincere and honest in interpersonal actions

...Particularly effective creating harmonious work environment

...Secures complete trust and confidence of others

...Quick to lend a helping hand

...Unswerving devotion to principles of equal opportunity

...Deep concern for well being of others

...Wins trust and confidence of others

...Always proper in manner and behavior

...Good sense of humor and a ready wit

...Good Samaritan, dedicated to helping others

...Genuine concern for welfare of others

...Strong, steady advocate of equal opportunity

...Understands worth and dignity of each individual

...Places high values on human goals

...Enjoys complete trust and confidence of others

...Enhances high morale and team work

...Remarkable ability to get along with others

...Generates spirit of harmony and cooperation

...Special talent for getting along with others

...Compassionate with good sense of humor

...Working with and understanding people is strong asset

...Displays a genuine concern for others

150

...Has cooperative attitude and friendly personality

...Has a good sense of humor and a polished manner

...Moral character is of the highest order

...Deep and abiding personal concern for welfare of others

...Displays a genuine concern for others

...Engenders trust & confidence through genuine interest in ....

CHAPTER 7

PROBLEM SOLVING, MENTAL FACULTY, & JUDGMENT   (LEVELS 10-5)

BULLET PHRASE STATEMENTS

Select a word in COLUMN 1 and use the appropriate ending in COLUMN 2.

EXAMPLE: SUPERIOR INGENUITY

COLUMN #1   **COLUMN #2**

CAPABLE   CURIOSITY
CREDIBLE   IMAGINATION
FINE   INGENUITY
FIRST-RATE   INNOVATOR
OUTSTANDING   JUDGMENT
SUCCESSFUL   KNOWLEDGE
SUPERIOR   WISDOM
ACUTE
ASTUTE
GIFTED
KEEN

OTHERS:
COMMON SENSE   CREATIVE POWER
DEDUCTIVE POWER   INNOVATIVE IDEAS
INTELLECTUAL AWARENESS INTELLECTUAL CAPACITY
LEARNING CAPACITY   LOGICAL THOUGHT
MATURE JUDGMENT   MENTAL KEENNESS

"Energy and persistence
conquer all things."
BENJAMIN FRANKLIN
From the book:
Successful Leadership Today

PROBLEM SOLVING, MENTAL FACULTY, & JUDGMENT

WORD BANK

NOTE: The words in this word bank, USED ALONE, describe FAVORABLE TRAITS. When combined with other "qualifying" words, many of these words can be used to describe UNFAVORABLE TRAITS.

EXAMPLE: CAREFUL (FAVORABLE)
NOT CAREFUL (NOT FAVORABLE)

Words used in other word banks can similarly be used to describe UNFAVORABLE TRAITS.

ABLE	ABSTRACT THOUGHT	
ACCOMPLISHED	ACUITY	ACUMEN
ACUTE	ACUTENESS	AGILE-MINDED
ALERT	ANALYTIC	ANALYTICAL
APT	APTITUDE	APTNESS
ARTFUL	ARTISTIC IMAGINATION	
ASTUTE	AWARE	AWARENESS
BOLD IMAGINATION	BRAINCHILD	BRAIN TRUST
BRIGHT	BRILLIANCE	BRILLIANT
CALCULATING	CAREFUL	CLEAR-HEADED
CLEAR-SIGHTED	CLEAR-WITTED	CLEVER
CLEVERNESS	COGENT	COGITATE
COGITATION	COGNIZANCE	COGNIZANT
COHERENCE	COMMON SENSE	
COMPREHENDABLE	COMPREHENSIBLE	
COMPREHENSION	CONCEIVE	CONCEIVABLE
CONCENTRATE	CONCENTRATING	CONCEPTION
CONCEPTIVE	CONCEPTUAL	
CONCEPTUALIZE	CONSCIOUSNESS	
CONSTRUCTIVE-IMAGINATION		CONTEMPLATE
CRAFTINESS	CRAFTY	CREATE

154

CREATIVE   CREATIVE ABILITY
CREATIVE IMAGINATION   CREATIVENESS
CREATIVE POWER   CREATIVE THOUGHT

CREATIVITY   CULTIVATED   CULTURED
CUNNING   CURIOSITY   CURIOUS
DEDUCTIVE POWER   DEEP-THINKING

DEDUCTION   DELIBERATING   DEXTERITY
DEXTEROUS   DIFFERENTIATE   DISCERN
DISCERNIBLE   DISCERNING   DISCREET

EDUCABLE   EDUCATED   EDUCATOR
ENLIGHTEN   ENLIGHTENED   ENTERTAIN IDEAS
ENLIGHTENMENT   ENVISION   ERUDITE

ERUDITION   EXPERIENCE   EXPERTISE
FABRICATE   FACILITY   FACULTIES
FACULTY   FARSEEING   FARSIGHTED

FECUND   FERTILE   FERTILE MIND
FORSEE   FORESIGHT   FORESIGHTED
FARSIGHTEDNESS   FREE-SPOKEN

FREE THINKER   GIFTED   GENIUS
HEADWORK   HIGHER EDUCATION
HIGHER LEARNING   HINDSIGHT

IDEA   IDEAL   IDEALISTIC
IDEALIZE   IMAGE   IMAGINABLE
IMAGINARY   IMAGINATION   IMAGINE

IMAGINATION   IMAGINATIVE   INCISIVE
INDEPENDENT   INFORMED   INGENIOUS
INNATE   INSIGHT   INSIGHTFUL

INSPIRATION   INSPIRATIONAL
INTEGRATIVE POWER
INTELLECT   INTELLECTION   INTELLECTUAL

INTELLECTUAL FACULTY   INTELLECTUAL GRASP
INTELLECTUAL POWER   INTELLIGENCE
INVENTION   INVENT   INVENTIVE

155

Problem Solving, Mental Faculty, & Judgement (Levels 10-5)

INVENTIVENESS   INVENTOR   IRRADIATE
JUDGMENT   JUDICIAL   JUDICIOUS
KEEN   KEENNESS   KEEN-WITTED

KEEN-WITTEDNESS   KNOW
KNOW-HOW   KNOWING   KNOWLEDGE
KNOWLEDGEABLE   LEARN   LEARNED

LEARNING   LETTERED   LEVELHEADED
LEVELHEADEDNESS   LITERACY   LITERARY
LITERATE   LIVELY IMAGINATION

LOGIC   LOGICAL   LOGICAL THOUGHT
MASTERY   MATURE   MEDIATE
MENTAL   MENTAL ALERTNESS

MENTAL CAPACITY   MENTAL FACULTY   MENTALITY
MENTAL PROCESS   MENTOR   METHODICAL
MINDFUL   NIMBLE   OMNISCIENT

ORIGINATE   ORIGINALITY   OUTLOOK
OUTTHINK   OUTWIT   PENETRATE
PENETRATING   PENETRATION   PERCEIVE

PERCEPTION   PERCEPTIVE   PERSPICACIOUS
PICTURED   POLITIC   PONDER
PONDERABLE   POSTULATE   POSTULATOR

POWERFUL   POWER OF MIND
POWER OF REASON   POWER OF THOUGHT
PRACTICAL   PRACTICAL WISDOM

PRAGMATIC   PRESENCE OF MIND
PRODUCTIVE   PRODUCTIVE IMAGINATION
PROFICIENCY   PROFICIENT   PROFOUND

PROFOUND KNOWLEDGE
PRUDENCE   PRUDENT   PUNGENT
QUICK   QUICKNESS   QUICK THINKER

QUICK-THINKING   QUICK WIT   QUICK-WITTED
RATIONAL   RATIONALE   RATIONAL FACULTY
RATIONALISM   RATIONALITY   RATIONALIZE

Problem Solving, Mental Faculty, & Judgement (Levels 10-5)

READY WIT	REASON	REASONABLE
REASONING	REASONING FACILITY	
RECALL	RECEPTIVE	RE-EXAMINE

REMARKABLE	RESOLUTION	RESOLVE
RETENTIVE	RETENTIVITY	RETHINK
REVALUATE	RICH IMAGINATION	SAGACIOUS

SAGACITY	SAGE	SANE
SAPIENT	SAVVY	SCHOLAR
SCHOLARLY	SCHOLASTIC	

SEASONED UNDERSTANDING		SELF-TAUGHT
SENSIBLE	SENSIBILITY	SHARP
SHARPNESS	SHARP-WITTED	

SHARP-WITTEDNESS		SHREWD
SHREWDNESS	SKILLFUL	SLY
SMART	SMARTNESS	SOUNDNESS

SOUND UNDERSTANDING		SPECULATE
SPECULATION		SPECULATIVE
STRAIGHT THINKING		STUDIOUS

TALENT	TALENTED	TEACH
TECHNIQUE	THINK	THINKABLE
THINKER	THINK-UP	THOUGHT

UNDERSTAND	UNDERSTANDING	UNDERSTUDY
VISION	VISUALIZATION	VISUALIZE
VIVID	VIVID IMAGINATION	VOCABULARY

WELL-GROUNDED	WELL-INFORMED	WELL-READ
WELL-VERSED	WIDELY-READ	WISDOM
WISE	WISENESS	WIT

| WITS | WITTED | WITTICISM |
| WITTY | WORLDLY-WISE | |

Leadership is something you do
WITH people, not TO people.
From the book: **Successful Leadership Today**

157

Problem Solving, Mental Faculty, & Judgement (Levels 10-5)

BULLET PHRASE STATEMENTS

...Inspiring imagination

...Forward-thinking

...Intellectually gifted

...Keenly analytical

...Sound judgment

...Advanced knowledge

...Matchless ingenuity

...Analytical mind

...Creative intelligence

...Superior knowledge

...Insatiable curiosity

...Intellectually active

...Unusually resourceful

...Highly innovative

...Mentally quick

...Mental sharpness

...A rational person

...An inquisitive individual

...Correct mental approach

...Practical, prudent wisdom

...Quick in mind

...Ingenious nature

...Skilled innovator

...Creatively inclined

...Retentive mind

...Mentally alert

...Discriminating mind

...Extensive knowledge

...Intellectual courage

...Advanced knowledge

...Original thinker

...Inquisitive mind

...Mentally skillful

...Irrepressible curiosity

...Great inter-discipline

...Stimulating imagination

...Boundless analytical ability

...Comprehends direction well

...Positive mental attitude

...Exercises good judgment

...Acute, thorough thinker

...Dares to dream

158

...Knowledgeable and mature

...A disciplined mind

...Explores new ideas

...Unlimited learning capacity

...Quick, penetrating mind

...Well calculated actions

...Unending intellectual capacity

...Grasps essentials quickly

...Great mental grasp

...Thirst for knowledge

...Bold, forward thinker

...Clear in thought

...Sharp mental keenness

...Sound in thought

...Vast intellectual capacity

...Keen intellectual perception

...Great intellectual awareness

...Enjoys mental challenge

...Sorts out pertinent facts

...Mentally artful and skillful

...Has vision and foresight

...Superior mental qualifications

...Possesses intellectual courage

...Fresh, new ideas

...Develops logical priorities

...Innovative and imaginative

...Creative, positive outlook

...Sound, prudent judgment

...Keen rational powers

...Exercises sound judgment

...Perceptive and alert

...A quick thinker

...Quick to learn

...Broad, varied intellect

...Well organized mentally

...Highly perceptive intellect

...Good in judgment

...Clear, analytical mind

...Sound, sensible judgment

...Productive innovative ideas

...Great intellectual capacity

...Vision for the future

...Thinks and plans ahead

...Ability to think logically

159

Problem Solving, Mental Faculty, & Judgement (Levels 10-5)

...Unquenchable thirst for knowledge

...Contributes innovative ideas

...Possesses stimulating imagination

...Well-rounded, knowledgeable individual

...Analytical decision-making ability

...Offers sound, innovative suggestions

...Mentally alert and foresighted

...Creativity is virtually inexhaustible

...Quick and innovative mind

...Endless constructive mental energy

...Imaginative and inventive mind

...Mentally quick and active

...Capable of complex reasoning

...Demonstrates sound, mature judgment

...Can originate new ideas

...Good judgment and foresight

...Unmatched capacity for learning

...Exercises sound, logical judgment

...Good analytical thought process

...Rational, logical and responsive

...Inquisitive mind. Exacting nature

...Adept, well adjusted mentally

...Logical and coherent mind

...Exercises orderly, rational reasoning

...Can comprehend new information

...Seeks to expand knowledge

...Good capacity for learning

...Grasps pertinent details rapidly

...Sound of mind and judgment

...Quick to perceive and act

...Ideas and suggestions well organized

...Continuing source of innovative ideas

...Ideas quick to win acceptance

...Ideas and actions spur results

...Excellent foresight and planning ability

...Discriminates between important and unimportant

...Well developed sense of judgment

...Plans ahead with great success

...Has vision for the future

...Good mental faculty and attitude

...Positive mental attitude and outlook

...Imaginative skill and mental dexterity

...Clear and logical in thought

...Logical in decision making process

...Originates well thought out ideas

161

...Finds solutions to problem areas

...Discriminates between fact and fiction

...Innate ability to think logically

...Always comes to realistic conclusions

...Unlimited capacity for problem solving

...Unequaled academic abilities and accomplishments

...Rational and logical in thought

...Learning and growth potential unlimited

...Continually improves on old ideas

...Capable of resolving complex problems

...Not restrained by conventional thought

...Explores new situations and possibilities

...Responds resourcefully with valid ideas

...Good mental agility and skill

...Unending intellectual energy and capacity

...Always thinks through problem areas

...Logical and analytical thought process

...Blessed with great independent judgment

...Independent, perceptive and penetrating thinker

...Ingenuity in solving complex problems

...Widely read with retentive memory

...Logical and direct in approach

Problem Solving, Mental Faculty, & Judgement (Levels 10-5)

...Plans ahead. Has great foresight

...Learns quickly. Retains that learned

...Mature mind. Thinks and acts rationally

...Intelligent and creative. Never at loss to find solutions

...Knowledgeable individual. Well prepared for any contingency

...Demonstrates creative thinking and innovative problem
solving abilities

...Exercises high degree of ingenuity in problem solving

...Able to strike out mentally in new directions

...Keen ability to develop correct and logical conclusions

...Possesses decision-making faculty that focuses on important
issues

...Has good judgment, common sense and a sense of reality

...Uses sound judgment to solve difficult problems

...Able to rapidly acquire in-depth knowledge on any subject
matter

...Makes decisions after weighing pertinent facts

...Mature sense of judgment and responsibility

...Quick thinker who makes positive, correct decisions

...Disciplined mind. Grasps and retains pertinent detail

...Blessed with mental dexterity and intellectual capacity

...Resourceful in mentally complicated or unusual situations

...Ability to accommodate and correlate large amount of details

...Exercises high degree of imagination and ingenuity

163

...Ability to coordinate myriad of mental details simultaneously

...Mental dexterity and good judgment to tackle any assignment

...Excellent blend of common sense and logic

...Thrives on difficult and complex problems

...A cornerstone of technical knowledge and skill

...Judgment and ability to obtain quality results

...Innovative and creative mind and manner

...Capable of independent decision and action

...Creative thinking and innovative problem solving abilities

...Mind is quick, innovative and decisive

...Constant source of innovative, workable ideas

...Mentally stable with an orderly mind

...Selects logical and correct courses of action

...Good spontaneous judgment and decision making

...Good practical knowledge and the skill to use it

...Properly weighs and evaluates complex matters

...Ability to see through and solve problems

...Finds fruitful solutions to old problems

...Ability to grasp and understand perplexing matters

...Uses common sense to tackle problems

...Presence of mind to act independently

...Actions marked by efficiency and practical logic

...Analytical mind, adaptable to changing situations

164

Problem Solving, Mental Faculty, & Judgement (Levels 10-5)

...Quick to pick up on things

...Good ability to learn and understand quickly

...Continually alert for ways and means to improve

...Aggressive in seeking out answers to developing problems

...Clear mental picture of what is ahead

...Judicious and sound decision making facilities

...Continuing source of innovative, workable ideas

...Uses good intellect to get things going in right direction

...Mental aptitude and competence to tackle most demanding tasks

...Independent decisions have merit and substance

...Special talent for areas requiring intellectual challenge

...Exercises sound judgment in practical matters

...Impressive breadth of experience and knowledge

...Great ability to perform in an academic setting

...Uses penetrating and objective analysis in arriving at decisions

...Analytical in thought, reasoned in mind

Focus on RESULTS not ACTIVITY.
From the book:
Successful Leadership Today

"A man who is always ready to
believe what is told him will
never do well." GAIUS PETRONIUS
From the book: **Successful Leadership Today**

165

Problem Solving, Mental Faculty, & Judgement (Levels 10-5)

CHAPTER 8

LEADERSHIP, SUPERVISION, & MANAGEMENT
(LEVELS 10-5)

LEADERSHIP

LEVELS 10-9
* Delegates responsibility successfully
* Promotes individual involvement and development
* Inspires self-improvement and high morale
* Inspires complete respect and confidence
* Maintains SUPERIOR rapport with others

LEVELS 8-7
* Delegates responsibility effectively
* Sincere concern for others
* Enjoys respect and confidence of others
* Maintains GOOD morale and rapport with others

LEVELS 6-5
* Influences others to work consistently and accurately
* USUALLY delegates responsibility effectively
* Maintains SATISFACTORY rapport with others

LEVELS 4-3
* DOES NOT delegate responsibility effectively
* Dictates activities to others
* Cannot maintain good morale
* Shows little concern for welfare of others

LEVELS 2-1
* RESTRICTS self-improvement of others
* FAILS to delegate responsibility properly
  AVOIDS others

166

LEADERSHIP, SUPERVISION AND MANAGEMENT

WORD BANK

ADMINISTER   AUTHORITY   COMMAND
CONDUCT   CONTROL   CONTROLLER
DICTATE   DIRECT   DIRECTION
GOVERN   GUIDANCE   HEAD
IN CHARGE   LEAD   LEADER
MANAGE   MANAGEMENT   OVERLOOK
OVERSEE   PRESIDE   RULE
SUPERVISE   SUPERVISION

BULLET PHRASES

Select a word in COLUMN 1 to go with COLUMN 2 and
COLUMN 3 and add the appropriate ending with a word from
COLUMN 4

COLUMN #1	COLUMN #2 (NAME OF ORGANIZATION)	COLUMN #3 IN or WITH	COLUMN #4
			ARTICULATE MANNER
			BOLD IMAGINATION
ADMINISTERS			COMPASSION
CONTROLS			COMPETITIVE SPIRIT
DIRECTS			DIPLOMATIC MANNER
GOVERNS			EXCELLENT FASHION
HEADS			FIRM CONTROL
MANAGES			FIRM RESOLVE
OVERSEAS			FIRST RATE RESULTS
SUPERVISES			GREAT DETERMINATION
			GREAT INDUSTRY
			INFECTIOUS ENTHUSIASM
			INSPIRED LEADERSHIP
			POISE, POLISH
			POSITIVE MANNER
			RELENTLESS DRIVE
			UNBLEMISHED RECORD
			UNENDING ENERGY

167

Select one or more words in COLUMN 1 and end with a word in COLUMN 2.

EXAMPLE: ENERGETIC, ASTUTE MANAGER

COLUMN #1		COLUMN #2
ACCOMPLISHED	EXPEDITIOUS	
ACTIVE	EXTRAORDINARY	
ADROIT	FAULTLESS	LEADER
AGGRESSIVE	GREAT	PLANNER
ARDENT	IMPRESSIVE	ADMINISTRATOR
ARTICULATE	INNOVATIVE	DIRECTOR
ASPIRING	INTENSE	MANAGER
ASTUTE	METICULOUS	ORGANIZER
BOLD	OUTSTANDING	SUPERVISOR
CHALLENGING	PASSIONATE	
COMPETITIVE	PERSEVERING	
DOMINANT	POTENT	
EMINENT	POWERFUL	
ENERGETIC	RESILIENT	
ENERGIZING	PROMPT	
ENTERPRISING	STRICT	
ENTHUSIASTIC	STRONG	
EXACTING	SUPERIOR	
EXCELLENT	UNBEATABLE	
EXEMPLARY	UNRIVALED	
EXPEDIENT	VIGILANT	

...Inspires others

...Infectious enthusiasm

...Composed leader

...Radiates confidence

...Great organizer

...No-nonsense leader

...Generates enthusiasm

...Good disciplinarian

...Constructive counseling

...Great motivator

...Life-giving leadership

...Motivates others

...Impartial treatment

...Delegates responsibility

...Nurtures subordinates

...Acts decisively

168

Leadership, Supervision, & Management (Levels 10-5)

...Impressive leader

...Commanding presence

...Unifying presence

...Exciting leader

...Generates self-confidence

...Inspires performance

...productive supervisor

...Positive motivator

...Unites others

...Accomplished leader

...Instills pride

...Fosters self-dignity

...Develops initiative

...Takes charge

...Take-charge individual

...Ignites action

...Mature leader

...Promotes harmony

...Imposing presence

...Generates goodwill

...Positive influence

...Decisive character

...Team leader

...Authoritative presence

...Engenders self-development

...Morale builder

...Gets results

...Creates excitement

...Cultivates juniors

...Uncommon leadership

...Inspires greatness

...Fosters competition

...Maintains discipline

...Wins loyalty

...Stimulates teamwork

...Encourages self-development

...Respects others

...Master counselor

...Charismatic leader

...Facilitates cooperation

...A real motivator

...Inspires and encourages

...Stirs the imagination

...Well-rounded leadership skills

...Firm, resolute leader

...Recognizes top performers

169

Leadership, Supervision, & Management (Levels 10-5)

...Patient and understanding ...Considerate of others

...Humane and compassionate ...Tailors leadership needs

...Stirs up enthusiasm ...Gets impressive results

...A charismatic leader ...Concern for others

...Interested in others ...Makes things happen

...Clear, consistent guidelines ...Always an inspiration

...Attains superior performance ...Natural team leader

...Engenders mutual respect ...Real morale booster

...Tactful and diplomatic ...Respected by others

...Leads by example ...Concerned, caring leader

...Applies strict discipline ...Offers demanding challenges

...Promotes team work ...Strong, dedicated leadership

...Earns everyone's trust ...Decisive leadership style

...Exemplifies ideal leader ...Promotes sound leadership

...Develops new personnel ...Vigorous leadership style

...A motivating force ...Radiates team spirit

...Leads by example ...Promotes team harmony

...Equitable, fair treatment ...Firm, sympathetic leader

...Engenders winning attitude ...Inspires quality work

...Polished, mature leader ...Generates positive spirit

...Strict, firm disciplinarian ...Wins genuine respect

...Strong, decisive leader ...Skillful, direct leadership

170

Leadership, Supervision, & Management (Levels 10-5)

...Fosters winning attitude

...Firm but fair

...Tactfully leads others

...Fair, impartial treatment

...Interested in others

...Astute, experienced leader

...Leads with style

...A dynamic leader

...Firm, yet fair leader

...Exerts necessary influence

...Sparks real enthusiasm

...Secures others' loyalty

...Cares about people

...Taxes others' abilities

...Intense, compassionate personality

...Sound management practices

...Invigorating, successful leader

...Creative management initiatives

...Prompt, diligent administrator

...Watchful, discerning manager

...Achieves maximum productivity

...Sound leadership fundamentals

...Enforces professional development

...Spirited, determined leader

...Inspires great trust

...Can motivate anyone

...Active, involved leader

...Potent, productive leader

...Stimulates professional growth

...Tactful and diplomatic

..Considerate of others

...Morally just and fair

...Elicits maximum effort

...Innate managerial skills

...Respectful of others

...Astute money manager

171

Leadership, Supervision, & Management (Levels 10-5)

...Uncommon leadership perceptiveness

...Encourages professional pride

...Spreads infectious enthusiasm

...Impressive leadership record

...An accomplished counselor

...Demands best performance

...Runs cohesive organization

...Exuberant, enthusiastic leader

...Promotes harmonious atmosphere

...Constructive counseling abilities

...Fosters unparalleled productivity

...Excellent counseling techniques

...Aggressive management acumen

...Experienced, knowledgeable manager

...Exceptionally fine administrator

...Innovative management techniques

...Regularly meets commitments

...Top administrative acumen

...Enforces established policy

...Sound administrative skills

...Sound leadership fundamentals

...Meticulous administrative skills

...Supports self-dignity and worth

...Arouses and excites interest

...Molds character and courage

...Motivates and leads others

...Instills pride and purpose

...Has personal leadership magic

...Has "follow me" confidence

...Propagates goodwill and trust

...Engenders trust and confidence

...Instills loyalty and pride

...Tactful leader and motivator

...Exercises sound leadership principles

...Inspires zeal and obedience

...Energetic personality, Stimulating leader

...Encourages excellence among others

...Equitable and impartial leadership

...Epitome of tactful leadership

...Able leader. Adept counselor

...Strict, yet fair disciplinarian

...Encourages open, two-way communications

...Positive influence on others

...Persuasive and tactful leader

...A "take charge" individual

173

...Tailors leadership to needs

...Extracts most from others

...Positive, strong leadership attributes

...Ability to inspire others

...Acts decisively under pressure

...Generates positive work environment

...Leadership respected by others

...Inspires enthusiasm and confidence

...Recognizes self-worth and dignity

...Makes positive things happen

...Radiates confidence and trust

...Positive influence on others

...Molded efficient, smooth-running organization

...Improves potential of others

...Fair and unbiased leadership

...Artful management of resources

...Exercises superior leadership principles

...Forceful without being overbearing

...Economically sound management practices

...Strict without generating resentment

...Uses tact and diplomacy

...Instills pride in accomplishment

174

...Skillful manager of time

...Poised and mature leader

...Skillfully directs others' activities

...Uses goal-oriented management techniques

...Fosters a competitive spirit

...A well informed leader

...Impressively managed equipment assets

...Inspires others to success

...Superior ability to inspire

...Offers sound management advise

...Knows how to lead

...Helps others grow professionally

...Masterful use of available resources

...Demands, receives positive results

...A charismatic, caring leader

...Runs a smooth operation

...Arouses others to action

...Leads stressing team work

...Promotes harmony, team work

...Radiates confidence to others

...Well balanced leadership traits

...Fully taxes others' capabilities

...Demonstrates sound, fundamental leadership

175

Leadership, Supervision, & Management (Levels 10-5)

...Positive & constructive leadership

...Knows how to motivate

...Demands best of others

...Maintains unusually high morale

...Doesn't accept mediocre performance

...Inspires teamwork and unity

...Fosters pride and dignity

...A real morale builder

...Always rewards superior performance

...Truly cares about people

...Secures loyalty of others

...Excites a competitive spirit

...Stimulates drive in others

...Applies corrective counseling techniques

...Provides unifying, cohesive direction

...Influences others to success

...Always receives cooperative effort

...Earns trust of others

...Creates excitement and enthusiasm

...Excellent use of tact

...Engenders spirit of trust

...Respects rights of others

176

...Understands individual dignity, worth

...Nurtures subordinate professional development

...Catalyst of high morale

...Gains support of others

...Accepts only quality performance

...Maintains excellent rapport with others

...Takes charge. A real leader

...Motivates and charges up others

...Inspires others to higher performance

...Excites competitive spirit in others

...Knows success is team effort

...Sensitive to needs of others

...Acts decisively in trying situations

...Fosters high level of unity

...Earns genuine respect of others

...Frank, honest and direct leader

...Fully taxes abilities of others

...Well defined plans and goals

...Instills loyalty, harmony and teamwork

...Decisive in decision and action

...Inspires and ignites the imagination

...Capacity to successfully lead others

...Creates excitement in doing job

177

Leadership, Supervision, & Management (Levels 10-5)

...Able to win others' loyalty

...An exceptional leader and organizer

...Skillful employment of personnel resources

...Deep ingrained respect for others

...Charismatic leader who gets results

...Invigorating supervisor and direct leader

...The epitome of tactful leadership

...Own confidence radiated to others

...A mature, poised, confident leader

...Gives loyalty and provides leadership

...Artfully leads and controls others

...A confident and determined leader

...Always makes positive things happen

...Provides vigorous and work-aggressive leadership

...Highly respected for tactful manner

...Affords others a demanding challenge

...Earns others' trust and confidence

...Bold and imaginative leadership techniques

...The organization's leadership standard bearer

...Delegates responsibility wisely and successfully

...Prudent, economical use of resources

...Proponent of leadership by example

...Skillful employment of personnel resources

...Real motivator in team action

...Unified and coherent management philosophy

...Demands best efforts of others

...Thoroughly proficient and efficient manager

...Makes others want to work

...Attuned to overall management priorities

...Sincere, concerned and honest leader

...Uses consistently successful management techniques

...Maximizes the strengths of others

...Fosters prudent business management principles

...Especially adept dealing with others

...Extremely well organized and mission-oriented

...Believes in fair, equitable treatment

...Designs clear-cut goals and objectives

...Propagates goodwill and an unmistakable drive and desire for excellence

...Own radiant energy and zeal quickly picked up by others

...Provides balanced blend of strong leadership and personal compassion

...Ensures each individual's capabilities are fully taxed

...Highly effective in training others to assume more challenging and demanding positions of authority and responsibility

...Successfully faced challenges of leadership rarely afforded others

179

...Enlightened leadership technique arouses interest and participation

...Well organized. Plans for the future

...Makes good use of available resources

...Balances workload according to required priorities

...Exudes spirit of well being, confidence and determination in others

...Innovative and decisive style of leadership provided impetus

 in maintaining professional work environment

...Employs open and direct manner in supervising personnel and is highly successful in obtaining maximum results regardless of situation or circumstances

...Exercises sound leadership fundamentals with care and concern for others

...Concerned and caring leader, keenly aware of personal side of leadership

...Provides the electricity, the spark of action that drives others in a positive, constructive direction

...A unifying presence to any organization

...Leadership instilled new sense of pride and purpose in others

...A real motivator. Knows how to stir the imagination and work effort of others

...Dedicated supervisor. Standards of integrity and bearing are of highest caliber

...Personalized style of leadership highly respected and effective.

...Leads others to desired level of performance.

180

...A real leader: Gives 100%, demands the best from others, and looks out for their interests and needs

...Contributes significantly to betterment of morale and team work

...Exceptionally well organized and perceptive to the problems and needs of others

...Careful, exact planner who gets positive results

...Establishes and enforces firm, sound management practices

...Alert, perceptive, prompt-to-act manager

...Extremely accurate and careful about administrative detail

...Has a special flair for expert management of assets

...Sets positive, realistic expectations and standards

...Breathed new life into a declining organization

...Demonstrates strong aptitude for administrative work

...Has firm grip on organizational management procedures

...Meticulous record keeping and timely submission

...Consistently the leading element in planning and implementing new operational and management procedures

...Keen managerial abilities evident in exceptional manner in which tasking is always based on available resources

...Can quickly identify problem, formulate solution, direct action, and take corrective follow-up action without outside assistance

...Uses sound management logic to arrive at valid conclusions

...Has ability to organize work groups effectively

...Successful at correlating various fractions of a job into one overall concept

181

...Ability to make correct, spontaneous management decisions

...Possesses ability to foresee and prepare for future management needs

...Analytical mind, adaptable to changing organizational situations

...Calm and affable manner are prime assets in daily management of details

...A dynamic individual whose cheerful attitude and strong loyalty ensures complete zeal, obedience and support of others

...Knows key to quality performance is a positive leadership style

...Instills loyalty, drive and desire to excel in others

...Recognizes and rewards top performers. People work to earn a personal "well done"

...Fully and successfully exploits capabilities of others

...Authoritative in action with commanding presence. Gets results

...Leadership, determination and experience leads peer group

...Effective leadership qualities executed in exemplary manner

...The personification of the model leader: Self-motivated, enthusiastic, & has willing support & cooperation of others

...Impressive leader. Receptive to suggestions and solicits comments from others

...Personal leadership style motivates others to a higher level of individual performance

...Understands leadership means giving a common vision and purpose to others

...Knows that for successful leadership, you lead people by example

182

...Gained the respect and admiration of others by using frank and fair leadership

...Truly a person who represents the highest caliber of talent and leadership available

...A master of positive leadership. Truly cares about people

...A leader of dynamic character and stamina, and an unlimited capacity for challenge

...Created and maintained excellent work environment

...Cultivates team work and a winning professional attitude

...Established new highs in team harmony and unity

...Secures the energy and spirit of subordinates through innovative and imaginative leadership

...Makes things happen and is not content with anything less than maximum effort

...Arouses interest and excites competitive spirit of others

...Highly capable leader. Always receives willing and spontaneous support of others

...Radiant personality and confident manner quickly wins willing support of others

...Sparks a spirit of job excitement and self-sacrifice in others

...Successfully researches projects and staff work

...Accomplished manager, attains all desired ends

...Alert, astute manager, can turn negative situations into profitable advantage

...Ideally suited for top management positions

...Skillful manager with proven ability to get things done

Leadership, Supervision, & Management (Levels 10-5)

...A good sense of organization and a reputation for dependable results

...Establishes and pursues precise, clear-cut management goals

...Performed multitude of administrative tasks with enviable punctuality and error free productivity

...Exceptionally adept at fine-tuning administrative matters

...Displayed aggressive and imaginative management acumen

...Management contributions have been a welcomed shot in the arm

...Superb management resulted in unequaled performance throughout organization

...Management expertise and organizational insight are personal trademarks

...Poised and mature manager with reputation for getting the job done

...Attains positive management results regardless of difficulty

...Detailed planning and intensive coordination assure positive results

...Demonstrates superior knowledge of operations and administrative matters

...Great faculty for exercising strong management control

...Possesses innate managerial skills and ingrained aggressive pursuit of excellence

...Quick to grasp management principles and concepts involved in correct function of any operation

...Displays quality management skills and unstinting commitment to proficiency

...Instituted rigid accountability procedures in all areas

184

...Compiled impressive record over a broad range of management and administrative matters

...Astute and close scrutiny of assets ensured most effective use of scarce personnel and equipment resources

...Competent and capable leader, leads by doing and showing

...Discipline enforced on fair and consistent basis

...Guidance to others is clear and comprehensive

...Commands superior performance and takes prompt corrective action of substandard performance

...Understands and effectively uses principle of delegation

...Skillful leader with proven ability to attain superior results

...Establishes challenging yet attainable goals for others

...Quiet in demeanor, tactful and thorough in positive handling of others

...Ability to quickly gain respect and loyalty of others

...Leads by doing and showing--a pace setter

...Intelligent, dynamic leader. Thrives on new challenges

...Day-to-day performance elicits positive and productive response from others

...Earned both abiding loyalty and deepest respect of others

...Professional attitude radiates to others, causing them to respond with full effort

...Establishes dialogue process with others that enhances understanding and mutual respect

...Directs efforts of others without dulling initiative

...Concerned with well-being of others while maintaining positive control

185

Leadership, Supervision, & Management (Levels 10-5)

..."Follow me" style of leadership elicits maximum effort

...Displays excellent combination of tact and direct supervision

...Ability to apply corrective counseling and have it accepted in positive manner

...Ability to elicit the best effort of others

...Engenders spirit in others to perform to absolute best

...Personable, well-liked and highly respected leader

...Ability to create and maintain individual and team confidence

...Clearly demonstrated capacity for effectively and efficiently directing activities of others

...Gets others involved in change and new ideas. Leads them where they should be going

...Understands worth and dignity of each individual

...Handles others firmly and positively, but with such dexterity and tact as to inspire a feeling of respect and devotion

...Superior leader, can distinguish between motivating and non motivating factors

...Doesn't get entangled in day-to-day individual problems. Sets and achieves multiple long-range goals and objectives

...Great ability to plan and direct group operations and activities of any scope or size

...Makes optimum use of assigned personnel

...Management style has measurably improved overall organization

...Displayed unique ability to grasp not only broad scope of responsibilities, but also to manage the incredible number of details associated with job

Leadership, Supervision, & Management (Levels 10-5)

...Maintains characteristic courage and coolness during management crisis situations

...Excellent ability to coordinate group efforts

...Management skills led to unparalleled high level of performance

...Unwavering support in achieving management objectives

...Provides valuable resolutions to wide range of problems through successful use of available resources

...Persistent management efforts led to steadily improving organization quality and efficiency

...Early identification of deficiencies and shortcomings in organization led to incalculable savings in manpower & money

...Well known for impressive management ability

...Unencumbered by superfluous detail. Gets to the heart of any management problem area and provides good fix

...The many documents called upon to originate are properly staffed and researched

...All paperwork submitted in a correct, concise and timely manner

...An expert at drafting smooth official correspondence and directives

...Thorough in management and staff work, leaves nothing to chance

...Met or exceeded all tasking with unique managerial skills and ability to foresee and plan for problem areas before they fully develop

...Applied managerial skills to good advantage and purpose

...Can apply management knowledge and skill to any situation without waiting for specific guidance or approval

187

Leadership, Supervision, & Management (Levels 10-5)

...Daily planning and long-range strategy based on sound management principles

...Successfully faces difficult management challenges

...Continually searches for ways to improve procedures and raise efficiency

...Many management suggestions incorporated into organization philosophy

...Built a corps of supervisors who take pride in "taking charge" and working together in cohesive, productive manner

...Instills constructive loyalty and pride in others

...Characteristic courage and coolness under pressure provide steadying influence to others

...Knows how to lead people, and more importantly, knows where to take them

...A quality leader. A person who inspires others to join in on a common effort and team goal

...A natural supervisor with exceptional ability to make even the most difficult principles easily understandable

...Unique ability to coordinate group efforts toward attainment of common goals

...Led organization to an unparalleled high level of performance

...Responsible to needs of others. A popular leader

...Takes personal interest in welfare and well-being of others

...Reliable, friendly leadership creates favorable attitude and work environment

...Instills motivation in others by own willingness to listen and learn

...Has positive and distinctive leadership qualities that help mold any organization into cohesive, productive unit

...Establishes and enforces clear-cut goals. Demands positive results

...When in charge, successful conclusion never in doubt

...A take-charge individual. Displays strong initiative and infectious enthusiasm

...Strength of character and natural team leader traits are the mainstay of a well rounded leadership style

...Leads unified, enduring and proud team of professionals

...Has the leadership spirit and faith to lead people into action

...Organizational leadership contributes immeasurably to morale

...Enriches team spirit and pride in accomplishment

...Repeatedly demonstrated exceptional leadership and initiative that served as forerunner in organization and led to unsurpassed excellence

...Bearing, professional expertise and personal involvement are cornerstones of individual leadership success

...Gives others a helping hand or a pat on the back when most needed

...Diligent efforts and resourcefulness inspired others and greatly contributed to total work effort

...Careful, exact planner who gets positive results

...Has strong leadership attributes and driving desire to excel

...Displays genuine sincerity and concern for others while achieving maximum results

...Has ability to inspire others to act decisively under stressful situations

189

...Generates positive attitude and spirit throughout organization

...Varied background and experience, and ability to make correct decisions in even the most stressful situations

...Genuinely and warmly respected by others for leadership qualities and dedication to job

...Has inspiring enthusiasm and unending leadership spirit

...Individual vitality and "can do" spirit has permeated entire organization, from top to bottom

...A "leader by example" who obtains superior results

...Helps individuals recognize self-dignity and worth through strong and effective personal counseling and leadership

...Displays uncommon leadership, enthusiasm and initiative

...Extremely perceptive and hard working, takes charge and makes positive things happen

...Charismatic leader, wins support and maximum effort of others

...Molded an efficient and smooth-running organization

...Dedicated to betterment of others. They know it and always contribute maximum effort and energy

...Excites and arouses others to action

...Leadership style elicits productive vigor and fosters complete harmony and team work

...Promotes harmony and team work and achieves maximum results

...Fits each individual with challenging assignments, encourages self-esteem

...Possesses professional competence to know what to do, the fortitude to decide how to do it, and the dynamic leadership to inspire others to accomplish it

190

...An informed leader who genuinely cares about the development and well-being of others

...Delegates authority effectively, does not run a one-person show. Delegation based on trust and mutual understanding

...Morale never higher, yet demands and receives full day's work from each individual

...Careful preparation and planning led to achieving outstanding level of performance in a broad operating spectrum

...Exemplary management acumen and personal performance consistently enhanced organizational reputation

...A unifying presence to any organization

...Possessed of sound judgment and management acumen

...Supplies effective application of sound management practices

...Exceptionally well versed at solving management problems

...Undertook exacting managerial duties with keen sense of direction and well-defined goals

...Repeatedly demonstrated impressive management qualifications

...Organization functions like a well oiled machine

...Maintains highly accurate and easily understood methods of tracking and monitoring organizational work and accomplishment

...Can quickly and efficiently diagnose problems

...Identifies problems and supplies effective remedies without delay

...A professional manager. Understands principle of delegation

...Mentally alert with a gift for devising organizational instructions and administrative procedure

191

Leadership, Supervision, & Management (Levels 10-5)

...Delegates authority effectively, does not run a one-person operation

...Alert, with creative mind, able to develop effective and efficient procedural methods

...Prepares excellent written instructions that are easily understood

...Highly flexible, adjusts management techniques to meet requirements

...Does not act before all facts have been properly evaluated

...Executes excellent management practices by blending concern for individuals with the job at hand

...Thinks clearly and logically, able to accommodate and correlate large number of details in efficient and effective use of available manpower and material

...Has a firm grasp of effective management principles

...Manages and controls with unusual definition and precision

...Has capacity to make spontaneous and intuitive management judgments of considerable value

...Exceptional manager and organizer, ensures upward mobility of others

...Draws on abilities and strengths of others

...A student of human nature with superior ability to inspire cooperation among others

...Provides meaningful work assignments with which others can identify and become personally involved

...Has spiritual force and moral fiber necessary to be a leader

...Possesses the spark of leadership, creative ability, and self-confidence to excel in any assignment

...Possessed of the vision, courage of conviction, moral integrity and the capacity to inspire others to strive for excellence

...Displays firm grasp and use of effective leadership principles

...Ability to recognize potential of others and provide the leadership to realize that potential

...Possesses those special qualities it takes to be a leader.

Communicates easily, instills pride, and commends people for effort and dedication to job

...Exerts personal influence over others while allowing sufficient latitude for growth and creativity

...Comes across to others with force and confidence. A real leader with a special knack for getting the job done

...Discusses strong and weak points with individuals and takes sincere interest in improving their performance

...Strengthens morale by cultivating sense of well being and pride in belonging

...Directs others without dulling their initiative or deadening their interest or enthusiasm

...Pleasant personality blends well in any work group, yet never loses sight of responsibilities as leader and supervisor

...Consistently demands and receives only best from others

...Uses past experience, common sense, and excellent direct supervision to elicit most from each individual

...A loyal, energetic and conscientious leader

...Demonstrates visible concern for the welfare and well being of others

...Personal achievements and ability to lead, in any capacity, contributed immeasurably to sustained superior performance

...Persuasive and tactful in conveying ideas

193

...Gives others responsibility. Lets them grow, and creates team spirit and unity

...A person of great common sense. A leader of uncommon perceptiveness

...Helps others grow and develop skills through timely advise, guidance and counseling

...Organization functions smoothly, effectively and reliably

...Balances schedule and workload according to priorities and produces quality results

...Masterful use of available assets demonstrated on daily basis

...Efficient organizer with sense of duty and desire to succeed

...Maintains awareness of changing situations, provides preventive rather than remedial management

...Grasps essentials of problem quickly, follows through with rapid logic

...Manages the job at hand, not distracted by inconsequential

...Extremely quick to adapt to changing situations and never at a loss to find correct solutions

...Every goal and objective met timely and correctly the first time

...Anticipates future tasking and through prior planning is never placed in a position of pushing a deadline

...Exceptionally well qualified to examine existing organization and procedure to determine economy and efficiency

...Ability to adjust to day-to-day workload variations

...Possesses constructive imagination necessary for problem solving

...Highly competent manager and administrator with knack for passing own knowledge and experience

194

...A knowledgeable individual of great foresight. Well prepared for any contingency

...Proficiently exercises broad directive control over various tasks and projects simultaneously

...Quick to take the lead in coordinating activities

...Integrates organization requirements and individual capabilities

...Works well within developed and defined long-range management objectives

...Initiated programs designed to achieve maximum economy of funds and optimum use of materials

...Demonstrates creative thinking and innovative problem solving techniques

...An excellent administrator, will handle any job in highly creditable manner

...Ability to cut through confusion and get to crux of any problem

...Solicits others for their thoughts and ideas. Knows how to lead

...Has special talent for bringing out the very best effort in each individual

...Eager and capable of doing superior leadership job across broad range of responsibilities

...Recognizes that success is a team effort. Gets others involved so that they can learn and grow professionally

...Action oriented. Not content with anything less than maximum effort of others

...Solid leader. Steers straight and direct course for others

...Down-to-earth leader. Others find it easy to converse on personal matters

195

...Encourages personal development at every opportunity

...Personal time management concepts and leadership ability have significantly contributed to increased efficiency

...Repeatedly demonstrated impressive ability to motivate others in any work environment

...Optimistic outlook and "can do" enthusiasm radiates in all directions and inspires others to put forth their own best effort

...Projects positive leadership by own exacting and vibrant enthusiasm for any and all challenges

...Knows how to reach an objective and uses good leadership to achieve the desired ends

...Tactful leader. Considerate of others and uses restraint while obtaining desired results

...Establishes and maintains atmosphere of pride and involvement and accomplishment

...Poised and mature leader with an authoritative manner

...Provides positive guidance that improves skill level of others

...Gives energizing, stimulating leadership and tact to lead

...An assertive and considerate leader who gets positive results

...A proponent of strong, solid leadership

...Provides skillful direction through tactful leadership
...Impressive ability to motivate others

...Ignites the human spirit and provides assertive, positive leadership

...Concerned, caring leader. Allows others to grow in new directions

...Leads with intensity, compassion and energy

...High morale and exceptional enthusiasm demonstrated by others on a daily basis attest to leadership skills

...Has management ability to succeed in multiple and diverse responsibilities with uncommon success

...A master at achieving maximum use of limited resources
...Innate ability to anticipate management problems early

...Managerial skills are of highest caliber

...Tenacity of purpose drives daily management principles

...Always gives superb performance under stressful situations

...Knows how to plan an ambitious, achievable workload

...Organization consistently maintained in high state of readiness

...Maintains good work organization discipline

...Capacity to analyze facts correctly and supply correct fix

...Maintains excellent blend between short- and long-term objectives

...Paramount interest is efficiency of organization

...Great foresight, prepared for any eventuality

...Established new, effective managerial control system

...Exercises high degree of imagination in problem solving

...Excellent planner and organizer, does not wait for instructions

...Invariably submits timely and perceptive solutions to staff problems

...Exercises initiative, responds well to unusual situations

...Displays superior administrative ability and managerial skill

...Fostered development from an embryonic state to a highly effective and responsive organization

197

...Excellent manager and organizer who is willing to accept any assignment

...As a manager and an organizer, radiates confidence, composure and competence

...Ability to organize own time and that of others effectively

...Mental ability to develop correct and logical conclusions

...Operates organization in climate that permits swift resolution of unforeseen circumstances

...Professional, accomplished administrator and manager who understands and effectively uses principle of delegation

...Skillful manager with proven ability to attain high standards

...Displays quality leadership and unstinting commitment to job accomplishment and excellence

...A highly motivated leader whose commitment to job accomplishment consistently results in productive output of highest quality

...Made visible impact on intangible areas of pride, morale and positive attitude

...Knows and understands worth and dignity of subordinates and successfully integrates this human element in daily leadership

...Stimulates the creative effort and work of others

...Provides timely recognition for superior performance

...Rewards superior performance. Corrects substandard performance

...Develops skills of new personnel at a rapid pace

...A personal and professional inspiration to each member of the organization

...Firmly and fairly enforces rules and standards

198

...Equitable treatment of others optimizes their performance

...Personal leadership has measurably improved overall performance

...An individual who commands the fullest respect and support

...Fosters high morale and a total winning attitude and spirit

...Definitely leader-type, clearly demonstrated capacity to lead others

...Positive attitude and personal application of leadership without equal

...Consistently inspires higher achievement in others

...Fair and exacting. Leads by example

...Astute on-scene leadership always produces quality results

...A dynamic individual who leads the way in job accomplishment

...Leadership skills are of the highest quality

...Can unite and rally the collective efforts of others

...A rare leader who possesses maturity, intelligence and technical know-how

...Cheerful and cooperative. Fair and unbiased in exercising authority over others

...Exerts personal influence with tact and force

...Intelligent, industrious manner inspires trust and confidence

...Personal commitment to good leadership principles

...Tactful, decisive leadership promotes esprit de corps

...Uses authority correctly in accomplishing all tasks

...Transfers goals and objectives into concrete, workable plans

...Anticipates upcoming requirements and stays well ahead of rapidly unfolding situations

...Ability to assimilate information and data and apply it to the task at hand

...Anticipates future requirements and takes necessary steps to assure proper action

...An invaluable manager and source of knowledge in every area of responsibility

...Always prepared for emergency procedures, ready for action

...Possesses decision-making facility that focuses on high issues

...Management effectiveness has set new standards

...Manages work assignment with uncommon expertise

...Instituted wide range of management-related initiatives

...Efficient organizer with desire and ability to do good job

...Management decisions always based on best available information

...Possesses commendable faculty for getting projects started

...Balances schedule and workload according to required priorities

...Assumptions logically derived from facts at hand

...Clearly demonstrated capacity for managing activities that lead to high quality results

...Good judgment, quick and decisive in action

...Continually searches for ways to improve procedures

...Outstanding manager, performs without prompting

200

...Quickly grasps essential elements of management problem solving

...Uses initiative and keen logic in seeking management solutions

...Possesses ability to devise operational procedures that get the job done properly and economically

...Thinks out new ways and means to improve effectiveness

...Accepts management responsibility and challenge in stride

...Demonstrates versatility and exceptional managerial skills

...Carefully evaluates all options before making final decision

...Highly talented with a good sense of organization

...Ability to devise operational procedures and follow-on administrative details

...Intelligently drafts instructions that are easily understood

...Recognizes potential of others and provides necessary guidance to reach that potential

...Consistently successful in obtaining cooperation of others

...Innate ability to get to crux of personal problems and provide cure

...Leads others with vision and sense of purpose

...Takes personal interest in supporting and developing professional skills of others

...Leadership style instills self-confidence and motivation

...Leadership methods promote harmony and foster high morale

...Reinforces good work and corrects faulty workmanship

...Leads a very effective and productive organization

201

...Especially adept at fitting people to jobs and training them quickly

...Method of personal leadership designed to improve efficiency

...Not naive or abrupt, uses tact and diplomacy

...Strengthens morale by cultivating sense of belonging

...Leadership merits special praise and gratitude

...Provides inner drive to others that moves them to positive action

...A catalyst of team work and high morale

...Earns the admiration and respect of others

...Embodies finest qualities of leadership

...Rare ability to create and maintain confidence and respect

...Consistently demands and receives only the best performance

...Gives others strong sense of direction without dulling their initiative

...Possesses unending ability to generate enthusiasm

...Quick to offer positive advice to others on ways to increase their personal and professional worth

...A forceful figure, others actively fall in behind the able and capable leadership and guidance provided

...Admirable blend of tact and direct leadership

...Potent and productive supervisor. Overcomes difficulties

...A demanding leader who gets impressive results

...Possesses well developed, positive counseling techniques

...Personal contribution to morale and team work have been a welcomed shot in the arm

202

Leadership, Supervision, & Management (Levels 10-5)

...Calm and stable leader in crisis situations

...Arouses interest and maximum effort in team work

...Demonstrates superb leadership and unbridled enthusiasm

...A confident leader. Radiates trust and enthusiasm

...Contributed immeasurably to high morale and performance by unique combination of direct leadership and compassion

...Superb leadership resulted in unequaled performance of others

...A guiding and steadying influence on others

...Provided commendable results in many stressful leadership situations

...Instituted rigorous training program that proved tremendously successful

...Enviable ability to generate enthusiasm in others

...Instills in others desire to do top notch work

...Enjoys complete trust and confidence of others

...Practices and enforces strict adherence to established policy

...Maintains high standard for own performance and instills, with success, this trait in others

...Understands needs and knows capabilities of others

...Accepts leadership responsibility and challenge in stride

...Unique ability to solicit and receive full effort of others

...Assertive yet considerate. Sets the leadership example

...Secures the complete loyalty and obedience of others

...Informed leader with genuine concern for each individual

203

Leadership, Supervision, & Management (Levels 10-5)

...Highly talented with a good sense of organization and a spontaneous propensity to leadership

...Tactful and considerate of others. Inspires mutual respect and confidence

...Designs clear-cut goals and moves toward them with willing and able support of others

...Places high values on leadership that stresses team work and individual effort

...Uses authority to assign and accomplish tasks in fair manner

...Strong leadership. Instills in others burning desire to excel

...Personable, highly respected, exhibits outstanding qualities as a leader

...Sets high goals for self and expects no less of others

...Leadership practices stimulate sense of personal identification, belonging and esprit de corps

...Introduces new ideas and encourages development of individuals

...Encourages others to put forth best effort

...Straight forward but empathic approach to others quickly resolves many problems

...Fair, impartial leader. Respects rights of others

...Inspires fullest cooperation and support of others

...Stands up for others and they respond in kind

...Tactful, positive manner quickly gains respect and loyalty

...Motivates others instead of driving them

...Individual of remarkable leadership talent and directional one-on-one motivation

204

...A master at providing direction and leadership to new personnel

...Rare ability to apply corrective counseling and have it accepted in positive manner

...Directs others with firm but fair hand

...Provides unified purpose and sense of direction

...Directs and guides others with understanding and tact

...Leads others by giving them vision and a purpose

...Unique ability to create team enthusiasm

...Sympathetic and understanding leadership, yet gets the job done

...A dynamic leader. Aggressive in job accomplishment

...Sells ideas and influences others with great success

...Has personal and professional interest in each individual

...Rare ability to facilitate cooperative effort of others

...Quick to take the lead in providing guidance and direction

...Establishes climate that makes people receptive to leadership

...Integrates job requirements with individual needs and capabilities

...Clarifies and enforces unified action. Challenges others

...Infectious enthusiasm enlists willing support and cooperation

...Applies a strict application of discipline and control

...A natural flair for bringing out the best in others

...The personification of a dynamic and caring leader

205

...Positive attitude generates enthusiasm at all levels

...Provides corrective counseling in positive, fruitful manner

...Achieves unusually high standards of performance from others

...Industrious manner and ability to get a job done correctly inspires great trust and confidence in others

...Can reach a troubled person and provide sound counseling

...Strong professional attitude radiates to others

...Calm, sincere and constructive counseling techniques

...Informed leader who genuinely cares about the well-being of others

...Sets stringent, achievable performance standards for others

...Extremely versatile leader. Adapts leadership style to changing personnel and situations

...Good leader, creates excitement and enthusiasm

...Fair, impartial and honest treatment of others

...Considerate of the feelings of others

...Skillful direction and counseling ensure few problems

...Concerned for the welfare and feelings of others

...Serious minded. Keeps organization on an even keel

...Skillful in leading others to desired goals

...Possesses that creative spark of leadership

...A dynamic leader who thrives on challenge

...Fosters high morale and a total winning attitude

...Easily gains the cooperation and support of others

206

Leadership, Supervision, & Management (Levels 10-5)

...Uses excellent blend of tact and direct supervision

...Displays an understanding and an informed sense of judgment when dealing with people

...A real leader. Knows how to motivate others

...Directs activities of others with a firm but fair hand

...Unequaled ability to obtain maximum support of others

...Leads tactfully to achieve desired level of performance

...Highly capable of making sound, independent judgments and decisions

...Commands the fullest respect and support of others

...Personally encourages others to set highest personal standards

...Inspires teamwork, unity of purpose, and high productivity

...Never too busy to listen to the problems of another person

...Animating leader, arouses enthusiasm and interest of people
...Active leader. Others come together in common action

...Establishes an exciting and professional work environment

...Supervises others with goal of improving each individual's skills

...Instills pride and dignity in others

...Provides calm, patient leadership to new personnel

...Met every diverse demand and challenge through exceptional ability to motivate others

...A personal morale builder to every member of the organization

...Sets an example anyone would do well to follow

...Vigorous leadership contributed directly to organization

...Capitalized on individual strengths and provided training and counseling in weak areas

```
Leadership also means
to stay out of the way.
From the book:
Successful Leadership Today
```

```
"Anyone who stops learning is old,
whether at twenty or eighty.
Anyone who keeps learning
stays young." HENRY FORD
From the book: Successful Leadership Today
```

CHAPTER 9

SELF EXPRESSION & COMMUNICATION SKILLS

(LEVELS 10-5)

LEVELS 10-9
* Commands large vocabulary
* Submits flawless written products
* Projects ideas in most straightforward, comprehensive manner

LEVELS 8-7
* Good command of English language
* ABLE to translate thoughts into clear, understandable sentences
* Submits written work in timely manner

LEVELS 6-5
* Average command of English language
* Neat, accurate correspondence
* Gets point across
* Able to prepare routine reports

LEVELS 4-3
* Limited vocabulary
* CANNOT get meaning across in concise, organized means on paper

LEVELS 2-1
* POOR USE of English grammar and composition
* VERY LIMITED vocabulary

SELF-EXPRESSION & COMMUNICATION SKILLS

DEFINITIONS

ACCENTUATE	To highlight or emphasize something.
ARTICULATE	Express oneself effectively.
CLARITY	Being clear.
CLEAR	Easily understood.
COHERENT	Logically consistent.
COMMUNICATE	Convey something to another.
CONCISE	Brief and to the point.
CONVERSATIONALIST	One who excels in conversation.
CONVERSE	Exchange thoughts through speech.
CONVEY	To communicate to another.
DICTION	Verbally express in clear, correct manner.
EDIT	Adhere to written acceptance or standard.
ELOQUENT	Fluent expression.
ENUNCIATE	Speak articulate words.
EXPOUND	Cover something in detail.
EXPRESS	To make something known in words.
FLUENT	Speak or write with ease.
GRAPHIC	Clear and lively description.
IMPART	Communicate to another.
LINGUAL	Articulated speech.
LINGUIST	One who speaks more than one language.
LINGUISTIC	Language.
ORATOR	A skilled public speaker.
PRONOUNCE	To articulate words.
SUCCINCT	Express without useless words.
SELF-EXPRESSION	Express oneself.
TERSE	Brief, smooth and elegant expression.
VERBAL	Speech or talk.
VIVID	Sharp, clear impression.
VOCABULARY	Total words used or known.

Having a voice in the decision
stimulates the action.
From the book: **Successful Leadership Today**

210

BULLET PHRASE STATEMENTS

Select one or more words in COLUMN 1 and match with the appropriate word in
COLUMN 2.

EXAMPLE: EXCELLENT SPEAKER
　　　　　　EXCELLENT, CONVINCING SPEAKER

COLUMN #1		COLUMN #2
ACCOMPLISHED	INFLUENTIAL	
ANIMATING	INNOVATIVE	
ARTICULATE	INTERESTING	
ASPIRING	INVIGORATING	COMMUNICATOR
CLEAR	OUTSTANDING	CONVERSATION-ALIST
COMPELLING	PASSIONATE	ORATOR
CONVINCING	PERSUASIVE	PUBLIC SPEAKER
CREATIVE	POLISHED	SPEAKER
DIVERSE	POTENT	TALKER
ELOQUENT	POWERFUL	VOCABULARY
EMINENT	PRECISE	WORDSMITH
ENERGETIC	REFINED	WRITER
ENGROSSING	SHREWD	
ENTERPRISING	SKILLED	
ENTHUSIASTIC	EXACTING	
EXCELLENT	EXCEPTIONAL	
EXCITING	EXEMPLARY	
STIMULATING	EXPEDIENT	
SUPERB	EXTRAORDINARY	
SUPERIOR	EXUBERANT	
UNBEATABLE	FAULTLESS	
UNRIVALED	FORCEFUL	
GREAT	HIGH-POWERED	
IMPASSIONED	IMPRESSIVE	
INFECTIOUS		

> "Be just and fear not."
> WILLIAM SHAKESPEARE
> From the book:
> **Successful Leadership Today**

211

...Clear, orderly self-expression

...Drafts correspondence correctly

...Commands large vocabulary

...Makes points clearly

...Voice reflects confidence

...Reports easy to understand

...Easily understood by others

...Reports convey desired meaning

...Correct grammar and enunciation

...Reports prompt, thorough and accurate

...Correspondence always precise and descriptive

...Conveys thoughts and concepts succinctly

...Articulate use of English language

...Correct and coherent in speech

...Speaks in clear, concise terms

...Special talent for communicating effectively

...Written reports concise and coherent

...Logical and factual in discussion

...Written work requires minimum editing

...Gives vivid and descriptive presentations

...Presents ideas clearly and effectively

...Speaking inspires confidence of others

...Compositions are orderly and coherent

212

Self Expression & Communication Skills (Levels 10-5)

...Prepares skillful and punctual reports

...Communications not shallow in content

...Enunciates well with excellent diction

...Brief and concise written communications

...Innate ability to communicate clearly

...Good orator, thinks on feet

...Excellent ability to communicate clearly

...Effective in relating point of view

...Discusses wide variety of subjects with confidence and conviction

...Skillful and effective in oral and written communications

...Reports, letters and memos well constructed and comprehensive

...Authoritative manner of speaking commands complete attention

...Meticulous and methodical in staff work

...Communicates ideas in vivid, descriptive terms

...Staff work on time and complete

...Presents ideas in clear, easily understood manner

...Written material always to the point

...Written reports always well researched and ready for signature

...Presents sound, clear views in written or oral presentation

...Speaks and writes with great clarity

...Use of English language articulate and easily understood

213

...Ability to express views clearly and concisely

...Uses correct grammar. Spells and punctuates correctly

...Exceptionally valuable in presenting conference or group speeches

...Direct speaking manner without being blunt

...Oral and written directives concise, firm and clear

...Completes large volume of staff work correctly

...Excellent understanding and use of English language

...Verbal expressions reflect self assurance and poise

...Good and varied command of English language

...Written work has substance and content

...Particularly good expressing ideas and thoughts in writing

...Good versatility in use of English language

...Clear, terse method of speaking and writing

...Presents ideas in easily understood manner

...Written material requires virtually no editing

...Submits highly accurate and professionally written reports

...Reports are succinct, exact and graphic

...Excellent ability to put thoughts into words

...Conveys views and feelings with clarity and conviction

...Speaks easily and straight-forward. Easily understood

...Speaks with good tone and inflection ...Noteworthy talent for drafting smooth correspondence

214

...Vivid and descriptive in oral and written communications

...Well read, has good working knowledge of English language

...Oral presentations command complete attention of listening audience

...Ability to communicate effectively with others at all levels

...Superb ability to write clearly and precisely

...Ideas presented with power and persuasion

...Effective in relating point of view and winning an unbiased listener

...Presents succinctly and eloquently prepared briefs

...Thoughts are well organized and orally expressed

...Articulate and precise in speech and the written word

...Written products are clear and cogent

...Excellent ability to enunciate new ideas verbally

...Especially skilled at painting vivid word picture

...Spoken and written word punctuated by correctness and exactness

> "So much of what we call management consists of making it difficult for people to work."
> PETER DRUCKER
> From the book:
> **Successful Leadership Today**

CHAPTER 10

FAVORABLE THESAURUS

(LEVELS 10-5)

FAVORABLE THESAURUS

A

ABET	ABILITY	ABSOLUTE
ABSTRACT THOUGHT		ABUNDANT
ACCLAIM	ACCOMMODATING	ACCOMPLISHED
ACCURATE	ACE	ACHIEVE
ACHIEVEMENT	ACHIEVER	ACME
ACTIVATION	ACTIVE	ACUITY
ACUMEN	ACUTE	ACUTENESS
ADAPTABLE	ADEPT	ADHERE
ADHERENCE	ADMIRABLE	ADMIRE
ADROIT	ADVANCED	ADVOCATE
AFFABLE	AFFECTION	AGREEABLE
AGGRESSIVE	AGILE	AGILE-MINDED
AGILITY	AGOG	ALACRITY
ALERT	ALIVE	ALL-AROUND
ALL-IMPORTANT	ALL-STAR	ALTRUISTIC
AMBITIOUS	AMENITY	AMIABLE
AMICABLE	AMITY	ANALYST
ANALYZE	ANALYTIC	ANALYTICAL
ANIMATE	ANIMATED	ANIMATOR
ANTICIPATE	ANXIOUS	ANXIOUSNESS
AI (A-One)	APEX	APPEALING
APPLAUD	APT	APTITUDE
APTNESS	ARDENT	AROUSE
ARTFUL	ARTICULATE	ARTISTIC

216

ARTISTIC IMAGINATION

ASPIRATION ASPIRE AROUSAL
ASSERT ASSERTIVE ASPIRING
ASSET

ASSIDUOUS ASSURED ASTUTE
ATTENTIVE ATTRACTIVE ATTRIBUTE
AUSPICIOUS AVID AWARE
AWARENESS

B

BANNER BENEFICIAL BENEVOLENCE
BENEVOLENT BEHAVE BENIGN
BEST BIG-HEARTED BLITHE

BOLD BOLD IMAGINATION
BOLSTER BOUNDLESS BRAINCHILD
BRAINSTORM BRAIN TRUST BRIGHT

BRILLIANCE BRILLIANT BRISK
BROAD-MINDED

C

CALCULATING CALM CAMARADERIE
CANDID CANDOR CANNY
CAPITALIZE CAREFUL CATALYST

CAUTIOUS CERTAIN CERTAINTY
CHALLENGING CHAMPION CHARISMA
CHARISMATIC CHARITABLE CHARM

CHARMER CHARMING CHEERFUL
CLAIRVOYANCE CLAIRVOYANT CLARITY
CLEAR-CUT CLEAR-HEADED CLEAR-SIGHTED

CLEAR-WITTED CLEVER CLEVERNESS
COGENT COGITATE COGITATION
COHERENCE COHERENT COHESION

217

COHESIVE	COLOSSAL	COMFORT
COMMANDING	COMMEND	COMMENDABLE
COMMENDATION	COMMITMENT	COMPASSION
COMPASSIONATE	COMPEL	COMPELLING
COMPETITIVE	COMPETITOR	COMPLEXITY
COMPLEX	COMPLICATE	COMPLICATED
COMPLIMENT	COMPOSED	COMPOSURE
COMPREHEND	COMPREHENDABLE	
COMPREHENSIBLE	COMPREHENSION	
COMPREHENSIVE	CONCEIVABLE	CONCEIVE
CONCENTRATE	CONCENTRATING	CONCEPTION
CONCEPTIVE	CONCEPTUAL	CONCEPTUALIZE
CONCERNED	CONCISE	CONDOLE
CONDOLENCE	CONFIDENCE	CONFIDENT
CONGENIAL	CONGRUENT	CONGRUITY
CONGRUOUS	CONSCIOUS	CONSCIOUSNESS
CONSCIENTIOUS	CONSIDERATE	CONSIDERATION
CONSONANCE	CONSONANT	
CONSTRUCTIVE-IMAGINATION		CONTAGIOUS
CONTEMPLATE	CONTRIBUTE	CONTRIBUTION
CONTRIVE	CONVERSANT	CONVINCING
COOPERATION	COOPERATIVE	CORDIAL
CORRECT	CORRIGIBLE	COURAGE
COURAGEOUS	COURTEOUS	COURTESY
CREATE	CREATIVE	CREATIVE ABILITY
CREATIVE IMAGINATION		CREATIVENESS
CREATIVE POWER		CREATIVE THOUGHT
CREATIVITY	CREDENTIAL	CREDIBILITY
CREDIBLE	CRISP	CRITICAL
CULTIVATE	CULTIVATED	CULTURED
CUNNING	CURIOUS	CURIOSITY

> "When you betray someone else,
> you also betray yourself." ISAAC BASHEVIS SINGER
> From the book: **Successful Leadership Today**

218

D

DAPPER	DECISIVE	DECORUM
DEDICATED	DEDUCTION	DEDUCTIVE POWER
DEEP-THINKING	DEFT	DELIBERATE
DELIBERATION	DELVE	DEPEND
DEPENDABLE	DESIRABLE	DETER
DETERMINATION	DETERMINED	DEVOTED
DEXTERITY	DEXTEROUS	DEXTEROUS
DEVISE	DICTION	DIFFERENTIATE
DIFFICULT	DIGNIFIED	DIGNIFY
DIGNITY	DILIGENT	DIPLOMACY
DIPLOMAT	DIPLOMATIC	DISCERN
DISCERNIBLE	DISCERNING	DISCIPLINE
DISCREET	DISCRIMINATING	DISTINGUISHED
DIVERSE	DOMINANT	DOMINATE
DOMINEERING	DRAMATIC	DRASTIC
DRIVE	DYNAMIC	

E

EAGER	EAGER BEAVER	EAGERNESS
EARNEST	EDUCABLE	EDUCATE
EDUCATED	EDUCATOR	EFFECTUAL
EFFERVESCE	EFFERVESCENT	EFFICIENCY
EFFICIENT	EFFORT	ELABORATE
ELATED	ELEGANCE	ELEGANT
ELEVATED	ELICIT	ELOQUENCE
ELOQUENT	ELUCIDATE	EMBODIMENT
EMERGE	EMBODY	EMINENT
EMOTIONAL	EMPATHIC	EMPATHIZE
EMPATHY	EMPHASIZE	EMPHATIC
EMPLOY	EMULATE	EMULATION

219

ENABLE	ENCHANT	ENCHANTING
ENCHANTMENT	ENCOURAGE	ENCOURAGEMENT
ENCOURAGING	ENDEAVOR	ENDURABLE
ENDURANCE	ENDURE	ENERGETIC
ENERGIZE	ENERGY	ENFORCE
ENGAGING	ENGENDER	ENGROSSING
ENHANCE	ENJOY	ENJOYMENT
ENLIGHTEN	ENLIGHTENED	ENLIGHTENMENT
ENLIVEN	ENRICH	ENTERPRISE
ENTERPRISING	ENTERTAIN IDEAS	ENTHUSE
ENTHUSIASM	ENTHUSIAST	ENTHUSIASTIC
ENTICE	ENTRUST	ENUNCIATE
ENVIABLE	ENVIOUS	ENVISION
EPITOME	EPITOMIZE	ERUDITE
ERUDITION	ERUPT	ESCALATE
ESPRIT DE CORPS	ESSENTIAL	ESTABLISH
ESTEEM	ETHICAL	ETIQUETTE
EUPHORIA	EVEN-TEMPERED	EXACT
EXACTING	EXALT	EXCEED
EXCEEDING	EXCEL	EXCELLENCE
EXCELLENT	EXCEPTIONAL	EXCITE
EXCITEMENT	EXCITER	EXCITING
EXEMPLARY	EXEMPLIFY	EXHORT
EXPAND	EXPECTATION	EXPEDIENCE
EXPEDIENCY	EXPEDIENT	EXPEDITE
EXPEDITIOUS	EXPERIENCE	EXPERIENCED
EXPERT	EXPERTISE	EXPLICIT
EXPLOIT	EXPLORE	EXPLOSIVE
EXPOSTULATE	EXPOUND	EXTENSIVE
EXTRA	EXTRAORDINARY	EXTROVERT
EXUBERANCE	EXUBERANT	EXULTANT

Cheerful people spread cheerfulness.
Unhappy people spread unhappiness.
From the book: **Successful Leadership Today**

Favorable Thesaurus (Levels 10-5)

FABULOUS	FACILITATE	FACTUAL
FACULTIES	FACULTY	FAIR
FAIR-MINDED	FAIRNESS	FAIR PLAY
FAIR-SPOKEN	FAITH	FAITHFUL
FANTASTIC	FAR-REACHING	FARSEEING
FARSIGHTED	FASCINATING	FASCINATION
FAULTLESS	FAVORABLE	FEARLESS
FEAT	FECUND	FEISTY
FELICITOUS	FELICITY	FELLOWSHIP
FERTILE	FERTILE MIND	FERVENT
FERVOR	FESTIVE	FEVERISH
FIDELITY	FIDUCIARY	FIERCE
FIERY	FINE	FINELY
FINESSE	FINE-TUNE	FINISHED
FIRM	FIRST	FIRST CLASS
FIRST-RATE	FIRST-STRING	FIVE-STAR
FLAIR	FLEXIBLE	FLOURISH
FLEXIBILITY	FLUENT	FLUID
FOCUS	FOOLPROOF	FORCE
FORCIBLE	FOREHANDED	FOREMOST
FORGIVE	FORGIVENESS	FORGIVING
FORESEE	FORESIGHTED	FORESIGHTEDNESS
FORMATIVE	FORMIDABLE	FORMULATE
FORTE	FORTHRIGHT	FORTIFY
FORTITUDE	FORWARD-LOOKING	FOUR-STAR
FRANK	FREETHINKER	FREEWHEELING
FRESH	FRIENDLY	FRUITFUL
FULL-FLEDGED	FULL-SCALE	

Most people can learn more,
if they are exposed to more.
From the book: **Successful Leadership Today**

Favorable Thesaurus (Levels 10-5)

G

GALLANT GENERATE GENEROUS
GENIAL GENIALITY GENIUS
GENTEEL GENTILE GENUINE

GIFT GIFTED GLAD
GLORIOUS GLORY GOOD
GOOD DEAL GOOD FAITH

GOOD-FELLOWSHIP GOOD-HEARTED
GOOD-HUMORED GOOD-NATURED
GOOD-TEMPERED GOODWILL GRACE

GRACIOUS GRATIFY GRATIFYING
GRAVITY GREAT GREATHEARTED
GREGARIOUS GRIT GRUELING

GUILE GUMPTION GUNG HO
GUSTO

H

HANDS-ON HARMONIOUS HARMONY
HASTEN HASTY HEADLONG
HEADWAY HEADWORK HEARTFELT

HEARTY HEAVYHEARTED HEED
HEEDFUL HELPFUL HERO
HIGHER EDUCATION HIGHER LEARNING HIGH-GRADE

HIGH-MINDED HIGH-POWERED HIGH-PRESSURE
HIGH-SPIRITED HONE HONEST
HONESTY HONOR HONORABLE

HOPE HOPEFUL HOSPITABLE
HUMANE HUMANITARIAN HUMOR
HUMOROUS HURDLE

Favorable Thesaurus (Levels 10-5)

I

IDEA	IDEAL	IGNITE
ILLUSTRATE	ILLUSTRIOUS	IMAGINE
IMAGINABLE	IMAGINATION	IMMACULATE
IMMERGE	IMMERSE	IMPARTIAL
IMPASSION	IMPASSIONED	IMPECCABLE
IMPETUS	IMPLICIT	IMPONDERABLE
IMPORTANCE	IMPORTANT	IMPOSE
IMPOSING	IMPRESSIVE	IMPROMPTU
IMPROVE	IMPROVEMENT	IMPROVISATION
IMPROVISE	IMPUGN	INBORN
INBRED	INCENTIVE	INCISIVE
INCITE	INCITEMENT	INCONTESTABLE
INCONTROVERTIBLE		INCORRUPT
INCORRUPTIBLE	INCREDIBLE	INDEFECTIBLE
INDEPENDENT	IN-DEPTH	INDESTRUCTIBLE
INDIVIDUALITY	INDOCTRINATE	INDOMITABLE
INDUCT	INDUCEMENT	INDUSTRIOUS
INDUSTRY	INERRANT	INEXHAUSTIBLE
INEXTINGUISHABLE	INFINITE	INFALLIBLE
INFECT	INFECTIOUS	INFLUENCE
INFLUENTIAL	INFORM	INFORMED
INFUSE	INGENIOUS	INGENUITY
INGRAIN	INGRAINED	INITIATE
INITIATIVE	INNATE	INNOVATE
INNOVATION	INNOVATIVE	INQUISITIVE
INSATIABLE	INSATIABILITY	INSIGHT
INSIGHTFUL	INSPIRATION	INSPIRATIONAL
INSPIRE	INSPIRED	INSPIRING
INSPIRIT	INSTANTANEOUS	INSTIGATE
INSTILL	INSTINCTIVE	INSTRUMENTAL
INTEGRAL	INTEGRATE	

Favorable Thesaurus (Levels 10-5)

INTEGRATIVE POWER INTEGRITY
INTELLECT INTELLECTION INTELLECTUAL
INTELLECTUAL FACULTY INTELLECTUAL GRASP

INTELLECTUAL POWER INTELLIGENCE
INTELLIGENT INTENSE INTENSITY
INTERESTED INTERFUSE

INTESTINAL FORTITUDE INTREPID
INTRICATE INTRIGUE INTRINSIC
INTUITIVE INUNDATE INVENT

INVENTION INVENTIVE INVENTIVENESS
INVENTOR INVIGORATE INVINCIBLE
IRRADIATE IRREFUTABLE

J

JACK-OF-ALL-TRADES JACOSE
JOCULAR JOLLY JOURNEYMAN
JOVIAL JOY JOYFUL

JOYOUS JUBILANT JUDICIAL
JUDICIOUS JUGGLE

K

KEEN KEENNESS KEEN-WITTED
KEEN-WITTEDNESS KEYNOTE KIND
KINDLE KINDLY KINDNESS

KINGPIN KINDNESS KNACK
KNOW KNOW-HOW KNOWING
KNOWLEDGE KNOWLEDGEABLE
KNUCKLE DOWN KUDO

> All problems become smaller if you don't dodge
> them but confront them." ADMIRAL WILLIAM F. HALSEY
> From the book: **Successful Leadership Today**

L

LABOR	LABORIOUS	LABOR-SAVING
LANDMARK	LARGE-HEARTED	LARGE-MINDED
LASTING	LATITUDE	LAUDABLE
LAUDATORY	LAUNCH	LAUREL
LEADING	LEARN	LEARNED
LEARNING	LEGACY	LEGIBLE
LEGITIMACY	LEGITIMATE	LETTERED
LETTER-PERFECT	LEVELHEADED	
LEVELHEADEDNESS	LIFE BLOOD	LIGHTHEARTED
LIKEABLE	LIMELIGHT	LIMITLESS
LIMPID	LITERACY	LITERAL
LITERALLY	LITERARY	LITERATE
LIVELINESS	LIVELY	LIVELY IMAGINATION
LOGIC		
LOGICAL	LOGICAL THOUGHT	LONG-LIVED
LONG-RANGE	LOYAL	LOYALTY
LUCID	LUCIDITY	LUSTROUS

M

MAGNETIC	MANAGE	MANAGEMENT
MANAGER	MANAGERIAL	MANIPULATE
MANIPULATION	MANNERLY	MARVELOUS
MASTERFUL	MASTERLY	MASTERMIND
MASTERY	MATURE	MATURITY
MAXIMIZE	MAXIMUM	MEDITATION
MEDIATE	MENTAL ALERTNESS	
MENTAL PROCESS	MENTOR	MERCIFUL
MERCY	MERIT	MERITORIOUS

225

MERRY	METHODICAL	METICULOUS
MIGHT	MILD	MINDFUL
MODEST	MODESTY	MONUMENTAL

MORALE	MORALISTIC	MORALITY
MORALIZE	MOTIVATE	MOTIVATION
MOTIVE	MYRIAD	MYSTIQUE

N

NEAT	NICE	NICETY
NIMBLE	NOBEL	NO-NONSENSE
NOTABLE	NOURISH	NURTURE

O

OBEDIENT	OBEY	OBSERVANT
OBSESSION	OMNISCIENT	OPENHANDED
OPENHEARTED	OPEN-MINDED	OPENNESS

OPTIMUM	ORATOR	ORCHESTRATE
ORDERLY	ORGANIZE	ORIENTATED
ORIGINAL	ORIGINALITY	ORIGINATE

OUTCLASS	OUTDO	OUTGOING
OUTLAST	OUTMATCH	OUTSHINE
OUTSTANDING	OUTTHINK	OVERCOME

OVERSEE	OVERSHADOW	OVERWHELM
OPEN-EYED		

STRESS: What people place on
themselves to make something
seem more difficult.
From the book: **Successful Leadership Today**

P

PACIFIC	PAINSTAKING	PARAGON
PARAMOUNT	PASSION	PASSIONATE
PATHFINDER	PATRIOT	PATRIOTISM
PEERLESS	PENETRATE	PENETRATING
PENETRATION	PEP	PERCEIVE
PERCEPTION	PERCEPTIVE	PERFECT
PERFECTIBLE	PERFECTION	PERFECTIONISM
PERFORM	PERFORMANCE	PERPETUAL
PERPETUATE	PERSEVERANCE	PERSEVERE
PERSEVERING	PERSIST	PERSISTENCE
PERSISTENT	PERSONABLE	PERSONIFICATION
PERSONIFY	PERSPICACIOUS	PERSPICUOUS
PERSUADE	PERSUASION	PERSUASIVE
PERVADE	PILLAR	PINNACLE
PLAUDIT	PLEASANT	PLEASANTRY
PLEASING	PLEASURABLE	PLEASURE
PLIABLE	POIGNANT	POISE
POISED	POLISH	POLISHED
POLITE	POLITIC	POLYGLOT
PONDER	PONDERABLE	POPULAR
POSITIVE	POTENCY	POTENT
POTENTIAL	POWER	POWERHOUSE
POWERFUL	POWER OF MIND	
POWER OF REASON		
POWER OF THOUGHT		PRACTICAL
PRACTICAL KNOWLEDGE		PRACTICAL WISDOM
PRAGMATIC	PRAISE	PRECISE
PRECISION	PREDOMINANT	PREDOMINATE
PREEMINENT	PREMIUM	PREPARE
PREPAREDNESS	PREPONDERANT	PREPONDERATE

227

PREPOTENCY	PRESENCE OF MIND	
PRESTIGE	PRESTIGIOUS	PREVAIL
PREVAILING	PREVALENT	PRIDE

PRIME	PRIVILEGE	PRIVILEGED
PROD	PRODIGY	PRODUCE
PRODUCTIVE IMAGINATION		PROFESSIONALISM

PROFICIENCY	PROFICIENT	PROFOUND
PROFOUND KNOWLEDGE		PROGRESS
PROGRESSIVE	PROLIFERATE	PROLIFIC

PROMINENCE	PROMINENT	PROMOTE
PROMOTER	PROMPT	PROMPTITUDE
PROPAGATE	PROPEL	PROPENSITY

PROPER	PROPITIOUS	PROPONE
PROPONENT	PROPOSAL	PROPRIETY
PROSPER	PROSPERITY	PROSPEROUS

PROTEGE	PROTOTYPE	PROD
PROVIDENT	PROWESS	PRUDENCE
PRUDENT	PRUDENTIAL	PUNCTUAL

PUNGENT	PURE	PURGE
PURPORT	PURPOSE	PURPOSEFUL

Q

QUALIFIED	QUALITY	QUANTIFY
QUERY	QUEST	QUICK
QUICKEN	QUICKNESS	QUICK-THINKER

QUICK-THINKING	QUICK WIT	QUICK-WITTED

"The best test of a
man is authority." PROVERB
From the book:
Successful Leadership Today

R

RADIANCE   RADIANT   RALLY
RAPID   RARE   RARITY
RATIONAL   RATIONALE   RATIONALISM

RATIONALITY   RATIONALIZE   RATIONAL FACULTY
READY   READY WIT   REALISM
REALIST   REALISTIC   REALITY

REASON   REASONABLE   REASONING
REASONING FACILITY   RECALL
RECEPTIVE   RECTIFY   REDRESS

RE-EXAMINE   REEVALUATE   REFINE
REFINED   REFORM   REFRESHING
REGENERATE   REHABILITATE   REJUVENATE

RELENTLESS   RELIABLE   RELIANCE
RELIANT   REMARKABLE   REMEDIAL
REMEDY   REMORSE   REMORSEFUL

RENASCENT   RENEW   RENOWN
RENOWNED   REORGANIZE   REPUTABLE
RESERVED   RESILIENCE   RESILIENT

RESOLUTE   RESOLUTION   RESOLVE
RESOUNDING   RESOURCE   RESOURCEFUL
RESPECT   RESPECTABLE   RESPECTED

RESPECTFUL   RESPONSIBILITY RESPONSIBLE
RESPONSIVE   RESTRAINED   RESURGE
RESURGENT   RETENTIVE   RETENTIVITY

RETHINK   REVIVE   RICH IMAGINATION
RIGHTEOUS   RIGOR   RIGOROUS
ROBUST   ROSY

"There are no bad soldiers,
only bad officers." NAPOLEON
From the book: **Successful Leadership Today**

229

S

SAGACIOUS SAGACITY SAGE
SALIENT SAMARITAN SANE
SANITY SAPID SAPIENT

SAVIOR-FAIRE SAVVY SCHEME
SCHOLAR SCHOLARLY SCHOLASTIC
SCRUPULOUS SCRUTINIZE SCRUTINY

SEASONED UNDERSTANDING SELF-ASSERTION
SELF-ASSURANCE SELF-COMPOSED
SELF-CONFIDENCE SELF-CONTROL

SELF-CONTROLLED SELF-DETERMINATION
SELF-DISCIPLINE SELF-ESTEEM
SELF-EXAMINATION SELF-IMPROVEMENT

SELFLESS SELF-MADE SELF-RELIANCE
SELF-RELIANT SELF-RESPECT SELF-RESTRAINT
SELF-SACRIFICING SELF-STARTER

SELF-SUFFICIENT SELF-TAUGHT
SELF-WILL SENSIBILITY SENSIBLE
SENSITIVE SENSITIVITY SERIOUS

SHARP SHARPNESS SHARP-WITTED
SHARP WITTEDNESS SHIPSHAPE
SHREWD SHREWDNESS SIGNIFICANCE

SIGNIFICANT SILVER-TONGUED
SINCERE SINCERITY SINGLE-HANDED
SKILL SKILLED SKILLFUL

SMART SMARTNESS SMOOTH-SPOKEN
SMOOTH-TONGUED SNAPPY SOBER
SOCIABLE SOCIAL SOCIALIZE

SOLACE SOLID SOLIDIFY
SOPHISTICATED SOUNDNESS

230

SOUND UNDERSTANDING
SPARKLE   SPARTAN   SPARK
SPECIALIST   SPECIALIZE   SPEARHEAD
                                       SPECIALTY

SPECTACLE   SPEEDY   SPIRIT
SPIRITED   SPLENDID   SPONTANEOUS
SPOTLESS   SPRUCE   SPURT

STABILITY   STABILIZE   STABLE
STAGGERING   STALWART   STAMINA
STANDARD-BEARER   STANDOUT

STAR   STATELINESS   STAUNCH
STEADFAST   STERLING   STIMULANT
STIMULATE   STIMULATOR   STIMULUS

STOKE   STRAIGHT-FORWARD
STRENGTH   STRENGTHEN   STRENUOUS
STRONG   STRONG-MINDED   STRONG-WILLED

STUDIOUS   STUPENDOUS   SUAVE
SUBSTANTIAL   SUCCEED   SUCCESS
SUCCESSFUL   SUCCINCT   SUPERB

SUPERFINE   SUPERIOR   SUPERLATIVE
SUPPORTER   SUPPORTIVE   SUPREMACY
SUPREME   SURE   SURPASS

SURPASSING   SURVIVOR   SWIFT
SWIFTNESS   SYMBOLIZE   SYMPATHETIC
SYMPATHIZE   SYMPATHY   SYSTEMATIC

T

TACT   TACTFUL   TACTICIAN
TALENT   TALENTED   TEACH
TEMPERANCE   TEMPERATE   TENACIOUS

TENACITY   TENDER   TENDERHEARTED
TERRIFIC   TERSE   THANKFUL
THINKER   THINKING   THINK-UP

Favorable Thesaurus (Levels 10-5)

THOUGHTFUL	THRIFT	THRIFTY
THRIVE	TIDY	TIME-SERVING
TIRELESS	THOROUGH	TOP-LEVEL
TOUGH	TOUGH-MINDED	THOUGHTFUL
THOUGHTFULNESS	TRAILBLAZER	TRANSFORM
TRENCHANT	TROUBLE-SHOOTER	
TRUSTFUL	TRUSTING	TRUSTWORTHY
TRUTHFUL		

U

UNBEATABLE	UNBIASED	UNBOUNDED
UNCANNY	UNDAUNTED	UNEQUIVOCAL
UNERRING	UNFAILING	UNFLAPPABLE
UNIFIER	UNINHIBITED	UNLIMITED
UNMISTAKABLE	UNPARALLELED	UNPREJUDICED
UNQUESTIONABLE	UNRELENTING	UNRIVALED
UNRUFFLED	UNSELFISH	UNSTOPPABLE
UNTIRING	UP-AND-COMING	UPRIGHT

V

VALIANT	VALOR	VALUABLE
VERACIOUS	VERACITY	VERBALIST
VERSATILE	VERSED	VERE
VIGILANT	VIGOR	VIGOROUS
VIM	VIRTUE	VIRTUOUS
VISION	VISUALIZATION	VISUALIZE
VITALITY	VITALIZATION	VIVACIOUS
VIVID	VIVID IMAGINATION	

> Loyalty is a two-way street.
> From the book: **Successful Leadership Today**

Favorable Thesaurus (Levels 10-5)

W

WARM	WARMHEARTED	WATCHFUL
WEARINESS	WEIGHTY	WELL-ADVISED
WELL-BEHAVED	WELL-BRED	WELL-CONDITIONED
WELL-DEFINED	WELL-DISPOSED	WELL-DONE
WELL-FOUNDED	WELL-GROOMED	WELL-GROUNDED
WELL-HANDED	WELL-INFORMED	WELL-KNOWN
WELL-MANNERED	WELL-OFF	WELL-READ
WELL-ROUNDED	WELL-SPOKEN	WELL-TAKEN
WELL-TIMED	WELL-VERSED	WHIZ
WHOLEHEARTED	WHOLESOME	WIDE-RANGING
WIDELY-READ	WILY	WINNER
WISDOM	WISE	WISENESS
WIT	WITS	WITHSTAND
WITTED	WITTICISM	WITTY
WONDERWORK	WONDROUS	WORDPLAY
WORDSMITH	WORKAHOLIC	WORKHORSE
WORKMANSHIP	WORLDLY-WISE	WORTHFUL
WORTHWHILE	WORTHY	

Z

ZEAL	ZEALOT	ZEALOTORY
ZEALOUS	ZENITH	ZEST
ZESTFULNESS	ZIP	ZIPPY

233

CHAPTER 11

BELOW AVERAGE PERSONAL PERFORMANCE

(LEVELS 4-3)

PERSONAL PERFORMANCE LEVELS

LEVELS 10-9
* Contributes GREATLY to organization mission
* CONTINUALLY seeks additional responsibility
 * THOROUGHLY understands all job components
* Works well independent of supervision

LEVELS 8-7
* Contributes HIGH LEVEL to organization mission
* Seeks additional responsibility
* Exhibits drive for self-improvement
* Proposes good solutions to difficult problems

LEVELS 6-5
* Contributes SOME to organization mission
* ACCEPTS additional responsibility
* Requires LIMITED supervision
* Good understanding of major jobs

LEVELS 4-3
* DOES NOT contribute to organization mission
* DOES NOT desire additional responsibility
* Requires ROUTINE supervision
* Satisfied with less than quality work

LEVELS 2-1
* HINDERS organization mission
* AVOIDS added responsibility
* Requires CONSTANT supervision
* DOES NOT or CAN NOT understand job

BELOW AVERAGE

WORD BANK

NOTE: The words in this word bank, USED ALONE, describe BELOW AVERAGE PERFORMANCE. When combined with other "qualifying" words, many of these words can be used to describe higher or lower performance.

EXAMPLE: DEFICIENT (BELOW AVERAGE)
ALWAYS DEFICIENT (UNSATISFACTORY)
* NEVER DEFICIENT (ABOVE AVERAGE)

* When writing on SUPERIOR PERFORMANCE, try not to use a negative word in conjunction with a positive "qualifying" word ("NEVER"). An appropriate SUPERIOR PERFORMANCE bullet to the above could be "ALWAYS CORRECT."

Words listed in other word banks can similarly be used to describe higher or lower performance.

ABNORMAL	ALMOST	AMBIGUITY
AMBIGUOUS	AMBIVALENT	AMISS
ARBITRARY	ARTIFICIAL	ASTRAY
AVERSION	AWKWARD	AWRY
BARELY	BELOW-PAR	BLAND
BLEMISH	BREAKDOWN	CAPRICIOUS
COMPLACENCY	COMPLACENT	CONFUSE(D)
CONFUSION	CRUDE	CUMBERSOME
DABBLER	DAMAGE	DEFECT
DEFECTIVE	DEFICIENCY	DEFICIENT
DEVIATES	DIFFICULT(Y)	DILUTE
DIMINISH	DISAGREE(ING)	DIFFICULT(Y)
DILUTE	DIMINISH	DISAGREE
DISAPPOINT	DISAPPOINTING	DISAPPOINTMENT
DISINCLINED	DISREGARD	DISRUPT(IVE)
DISSATISFIED	DOCILE	DODGE
DRAB	DRAWBACK	DUBIOUS
EBB	ERODE	ERRATIC

235

ERRONEOUS	FADE	FADING
FALLACY	FALLIBLE	FALTER
FICKLE	FIGUREHEAD	FINICKY
FLAPPABLE	FLAW(ED)	FLEDGLING
FLIMSY	FLIP-FLOP	FLOUNDER
FLUCTUATE	FLUTTER	FOOT-DRAGGING
FORGET(FUL)	FORMLESS	FOUL-UP
FRAGMENT	FRAGMENTARY	FRAIL
FRIVOLOUS	FRUITLESS	FRUSTRATE
FRUSTRATION	FUZZY	GLITCH
GRUDGING	HALF-BAKED	HALF-COCKED
HALF-HEARTED	HAMPER	HAPHAZARD
HAPLESS	HERKY-JERKY	HINDER
HINDRANCE	HIT-OR-MISS	HUMDRUM
IDLE	IGNORE	IMITATE
IMITATION	IMPAIR	IMPARITY
IMPEDE	IMPERFECT	IMPERFECTION
IMPOTENT	IMPROPER	INACCURACY
INACCURATE	INADEQUACY	INADEQUATE
INADVERTENT	INADVISABLE	INAPPROPRIATE
INATTENTION	INATTENTIVE	INAUSPICIOUS
INCOMPLETE	INCONCLUSIVE	INCONSEQUENTIAL
INCONSISTENCY	INCONSISTENT	INDIFFERENCE
INDIFFERENT	INEFFECTIVE	INEFFECTUAL
INEFFICIENCY	INEFFICIENT	INESSENTIAL
INEXACT	INEXPERIENCE(D)	INEXPERT
INEQUITABLE	INFERIOR	INFRACTION
INFRINGE	INOPPORTUNE	INORDINATE
INTERFERE	INTERRUPT	IRREGULAR
IRRESPONSIVE	IRRELEVANT	LACK
LACKADAISICAL	LACKING	LACKLUSTER
LAG	LAPSE	LAX
LAXITY	LESS	LESSEN

236

LETHARGIC	LETHARGY	LIMITED
LIMP	LOW	LOW-GRADE
LOWER	LOW-LEVEL	MALFUNCTION
MALINGER	MAR	MARGINAL
MEANDER	MEDIOCRE	MEDIOCRITY
MEEK	MENIAL	MERE
MERELY	MINOR	MISAPPLY
MISBEHAVE	MISCHIEVOUS	MISGUIDED
MISHANDLE	MISHAP	MISUSE
MIX-UP	MUNDANE	NOMINAL
NONCHALANT	NONESSENTIAL	NUISANCE
OBSCURE	OSCILLATES	OVERDUE
OVERLOOK	OVERSIGHT	PALTRY
PARTIAL	PARTIALITY	PAUCITY
PERFUNCTORY	PERMISSIVE	PETTY
PITFALL	PLOD	PLODDER
POINTLESS	PROBLEM	PROCRASTINATE
PROCRASTINATING	QUESTIONABLE	QUIBBLE
READY-MADE	REDUNDANT	REGRESS
REGRESSION	RELAPSE	RELUCTANCE
RELUCTANT	REMISS	RHETORICAL
ROUGH	RUDIMENTAL	RUDIMENTARY
RUSTY	SCANT(Y)	SECOND-RATE
SEMI-SKILLED	SEMI-PRODUCTIVE	SHABBY
SHAKY	SHALLOW	SHALLOWNESS
SHIRK	SHODDY	SHORTCOMING
SHORTFALL	SHORTSIGHTED	SLACKER
SLOW(LY)	SLUMP	SMALL
SMALL-SCALE	SMALL-TIME	SLUGGISH
SPARSE	SPORADIC	SPOTTY
SQUANDER	STYMIE(D)	SUBNORMAL
SUBSTANDARD	SUPERFICIAL	SUPERFLUOUS
TEMPERAMENTAL	THWART	UNCERTAIN(TY)

Below Average Personal Performance (Levels 4-3)

UNCOMPLETED	UNCONCERNED	UNCOOPERATIVE
UNDERACHIEVER	UNFAMILIAR	UNFAVORABLE
UNFINISHED	UNIMPORTANT	UNIMPRESSIVE
UNMINDFUL	UNOBSERVANT	UNORGANIZED
UNPOLISHED	UNPREDICTABLE	UNREFINED
UNRESOURCEFUL	UNRESPONSIVE	UNRULY
UNSOUND	UNTIDY	UNSEASONED
WANE	WANING	WEAK
WEAKEN	WEAKLY	WEAKNESS
WEARIFUL	WEARISOME	WEARY
WISHY-WASHY	WOULD-BE	

Good treatment leads to good morale.
From the book: **Successful Leadership Today**

"There is nothing so powerful as truth--and
often nothing so strange." DANIEL WEBSTER
From the book: **Successful Leadership Today**

238

BULLET PHRASE STATEMENTS

Select a word in COLUMN #1 to go with a word in COLUMN #2.

EXAMPLE: COMPLACENT WORKER

COLUMN #1

CARELESS
COMPLACENT
CONFUSED
INDIFFERENT
INEXPERIENCED
LACKADAISICAL
LAX
LETHARGIC
MARGINAL
MEDIOCRE
RELUCTANT
SUPERFICIAL
TEMPERAMENTAL

COLUMN #2

INDIVIDUAL
OFFICER
MANAGER
PERSON
SUPERVISOR
TECHNICIAN
TYPIST
WORKER
(or, use
Professional
title)

...Mediocre performer

...Easily distracted

...Minimum contribution

...Erratic performance

...Inconsistent worker

...Little progress

...Lacks persistence

...Requires supervision

...Overly perfectionist

...Inconsistent results

...Somewhat reliable results

...Carefree attitude

..Nonchalance attitude

...Limited potential

...Meager productiveness

...Sometimes complaisant

...Mediocre abilities

...Marginal performer

...Unimpressive work

...Reluctant performer

...Barely acceptable effort

...Work is tolerable

239

...Moderate job performance

...Becomes easily distracted

...Exerts minimum effort

...Becomes easily frustrated

...Slow and methodical

...Requires regular guidance

...Work not timely

...Unimpressive work habits

...Has limited success

...Very limited potential

...Cannot stay motivated

...Limited growth potential

...Sometimes positive attitude

...Work mostly commonplace

...Slow to act

...An unambiguous individual

...Usually average worker

...Work has flaws

...Not very efficient

...Results mostly insignificant

...Achieves minor success

...Inattention to detail

...Tolerant of mediocre effort

...Gives some effort

...Slow, plodding performance

...Requires regular reminders

...Irregular work habits

...Shows little effort

...Accepts direction reluctantly

...Not always punctual

...Limited growth potential

...Not very efficient

...Exerts minimum effort

...Work is inconsistent

...Lacks steadfast dedication

...Commits minor infractions

...Prone to forgetfulness

...Difficulty completing tasks

...Can be forgetful

...Inexact in detail

...Does amateur work

...Partially completes work

...Paltry work output

...Not very efficient

...Almost gets things right

...Limited success in some jobs

240

Below Average Personal Performance (Levels 4-3)

...Puts forth minimum effort

...Not careful about work

...Fails to meet expectations

...Does some jobs well

...Makes errors in judgment

...Does make some mistakes

...Does most simple jobs well

...Tires of work on occasion

...Does not seek additional work

...Not overly serious about job

...Slow worker at best

...Abilities better than performance

...Tries hard, accomplishes little

...Routinely displays indifference

...Sometimes premature in judgment

...Achieves minimal work requirements

...Gives steady, semi-productive effort

...Misunderstands some directions

...Usually passable performance

...Sometimes sloppy workmanship

...Consistent marginal performance

...Sometimes unsatisfactory performance

...Tires of work easily

...Doesn't use time wisely

...Lacks aggressive work habits

...Has lapses of memory

...Has tendency to forget

...Some work is passable

...Gives good effort on occasion

...Shows little interest in work

...Tires hard but achieves little

...Tends to be troublesome

...All deadlines not met

241

Below Average Personal Performance (Levels 4-3)

...Routinely second-rate performance

...Somewhat lacking in cooperativeness

...Shirks responsibility if possible

...Loses self-confidence too easily

...Unpredictable attention to detail

...Enjoys being a nonconformist

...Some jobs completed inaccurately

...Completes only simple jobs effectively

...Apprehensive about accepting new jobs

...Sometimes performs to full expectations

...Slow and deliberate work pace

...Performance is not always satisfactory

...Lax in carrying out duties

...Of little worth to organization

...Lax in performance and behavior

...Cosmetic results, no real substance

...Passable work in unimportant matters

...Too many instances of oversight

...Plagued by irregular work habits

...Not a potent, productive worker

...Too many instances of misjudgment

...Work suffers from inferior quality

...Can become confused about job

242

Below Average Personal Performance (Levels 4-3)

...Good work on small-time jobs

...Suffers from errors in judgment

...Finds too much idle time

...There are too many misunderstandings

...Work is so-so at best

...Work is of common variety

...Mostly ineffective, inefficient work habits

...Finds too much idle time

...Some work of inferior quality

...Is not a hard charger

...Has difficulty overcoming minor obstacles

...Unable to meet diverse challenges

...Does not stay productively employed

...Unable to tackle difficult tasks

...Unable to get properly organized

...Lack of confidence in abilities

...High ambitions but low performance

...Not overly excited about job

...Job not always first priority

...Does only what is essential

...Does minimum amount of work

...Not totally dedicated to job

243

Below Average Personal Performance (Levels 4-3)

...Completes some jobs on time

...Desire to excel sometimes wanes

...Enjoys too much idle time

...Lacks persistence in trying situations

...Works hard when the mood strikes

...Does only the simple jobs well

...Does just enough to get by

...Has only rudimentary knowledge of job

...Routinely gets caught up in petty details

...Somewhat lacking in persistence to attack jobs

...Remains uncertain on how to perform job

...Becomes confused and frustrated too easily

...Does not always perform to expected standards

...Work suffers from plainness and simplicity

...Good judgment sometimes impaired by short temper

...Inclined to slack off work when possible

...Walks on thin edge between right and wrong

...Prone to becoming bogged down in petty details

...Exerts only minimum initiative needed to complete job

...Performance migrates between acceptable and unacceptable

...Has only waning interest in work

...Shows little desire or interest in improving performance

...Unable to deal with complex problems

244

Below Average Personal Performance (Levels 4-3)

...Neglectful and forgetful if not watched

...Can be counted on to make some mistakes

...Work deteriorates as day goes on

...Uses illogical approach to some jobs

...Quality of work not a prime concern

...Must be watched on a regular basis

...Unable to cope with difficult jobs

...Does not work well without direct supervision

...Doesn't always do the best job possible

...Normally content with watching others do the work

...Work isn't always completed on time

...Doesn't always measure up to full potential

...Spirit of cooperation not always up to par

...Puts forth maximum effort if in the mood

...Personal interests sometimes come before job

...Finds ways to make idle time

...Becomes inactive if left alone too long

...Prone to occasions of lackluster work

...Can become preoccupied with personal matters

...Does not have a competitive spirit

...Unable to become motivated about job

...Mostly unimpressive record of accomplishment

...Does not always stay on schedule

245

Below Average Personal Performance (Levels 4-3)

COMPLETE THE PHRASE

...Limited in ability to(...)

...Ordinary ability to(...)

...Good effort adversely affected by(...)

...Tires to improve, but needs to(...)

...Interest in work oscillates between (...) and (...)

...Only moderately interested in (...)

...Can attain favorable results, however (...)

...Strives to do good job, unfortunately (...)

...Attempts to complete jobs, but (...)

...Endeavors to work correctly, however (...)

...Can do skillful work, but (...)

...Capable of putting forth good effort, but on occasion (...)

...In general achieves good results, but (...)

...Attempts to be careful and accurate, however (...)

...Sometimes has trouble in/with (...)

...Normally does a good job, however at times (...)

...Otherwise adequate performance sometimes hindered by (...)

...At times has difficulty (...)

...Despite good effort, has problems (...)

...Although an average worker, (...)

...Modest attempts at job hampered by (...)

...Does decent job except for (...)

246

Below Average Personal Performance (Levels 4-3)

...Ordinarily performs well, except for (...)

...Otherwise good performance hindered by inability to (...)

...Tries hard, but has difficulty (...)

...Performs well except when (...)

...Capable worker, but (...)

...Responsibilities are sometimes too much to overcome when (...)

...Tries hard. Good ability, but (...)

...Good work except when (...)

...Work occasionally marred by (...)

...Occasionally lax in (...)

...Gives efficient effort, but lacks ability to (...)

...Gives good effort unless (...)

...Completes respectable work, however (...)

...Otherwise satisfactory work marred by (...)

...Occasional mediocre performance in (...)

...Tries to do good job, but (...)

...Strives for excellent results, unfortunately (...)

...Attempts to (...), but (...)

...Not very good at (...)

...Of limited value because (...)

...Tries to get it together, but (...)

...Of little benefit or use because (...)

247

Below Average Personal Performance (Levels 4-3)

...Sometimes has trouble (...)

...Gives good effort, however (...)

...Sometimes unsuccessful in/when (...)

...Does many things well, but (...)

...Sometimes gives meaningless performance as/in (...)

...Unable to focus properly on (...)

...Has flaws in (...)

...Positive attitude fails when (...)

...Wasted motions sometimes leads to (...)

...Eagerness to work fails when (...)

...Job not always to satisfaction of (...)

...Becomes confused if/when (...)

...Work sometimes marred by (...)

...Slow to respond to (...)

...Gets caught unprepared when (...)

...Lacks necessary persistence to (...)

...Gives up too easily when (...)

...Not a very professional (...)

...Sometimes not careful about (...)

...Makes some mistakes when (...)

...Work can become ineffective when/if (...)

...Deficient in area of (...)

248

Below Average Personal Performance (Levels 4-3)

...Inadequate in (...)

...Work marred by (...)

...Ineffective in area of (...)

...Oversight in judgment when/if (...)

...Disregards rules when/if (...)

...Unmindful of job when/if (...)

...Inadequate attempt at/to (...)

...Unconcerned about (...)

...Offers second-rate (...)

...Erratic performance in area of (...)

...Displays some negligence when/if (...)

...Imperfect work habits cause (...)

...Futile effort to (...)

...Inadequate skill in (...)

...May not meet expectations when/if (...)

...Has a mild problem of (...)

...Not overly serious about (...)

...Gets into awkward situations when/if (...)

...Gives below-par work when/if (...)

...Sometimes careless when it comes to (...)

...Will become overly complaisant when/if (...)

...Gets confused when/if (...)

...A disappointment when it comes to (...)

249

Below Average Personal Performance (Levels 4-3)

...On occasion displays disregard for(...)

...Doesn't always measure up to abilities when (...)

...Prone to error when/if (...)

...Loses confidence when/if (...)

...Only a slight improvement in (...)

...Has a flaw in (...)

...Inability to work on/in (...)

...Preoccupied with (...)

...Inadvertently failed to (...)

...Careless when it comes to (...)

...Unconcerned about (...)

...Falters when it comes to (...)

...Work becomes flawed when/if (...)

...Offers flimsy excuses for (...)

...Can do haphazard work when/if (...)

...On occasion demonstrates inability to (...)

...Accuracy of work in question when/if (...)

...Can become indifferent about job when/if (...)

...Work flounders when/if (...)

...If not careful, will forget (...)

...Does best work when closely watched, otherwise (...)

...Convenient lapse of memory can occur when/if (...)

250

Below Average Personal Performance (Levels 4-3)

...Sporadic work when (...)

...Can become uncertain when/if (...)

...Gives inferior work when/if (...)

...Weak in area(s) of (...)

...Will complain when/if (...)

...Needs routine reminders when/if (...)

...Has little initiative when/if (...)

...Lacks vitality needed to (...)

...Inadequately prepared despite (...)

...Has deficiency in (...)

...Below normal in ability to (...)

...Becomes unpredictable when/if (...)

...Not suited for work on/in (...)

...Continues to be unorganized in (...)

...Deficient in area of (...)

...Inefficient work on/in (...)

...Indifferent to (...)

...Overlooks opportunities to (...)

... Overly complacent when/in (...)

...Insufficient progress in/to (...)

...Rudimentary knowledge of/in (...)

...Inefficient when it comes to (...)

...Work or little value when/if (...)

251

Below Average Personal Performance (Levels 4-3)

...Sometimes loses sight of (...)

...Although well trained, sometimes has trouble (...)

...Occasionally wastes time by (...)

...Not always responsive to (...)

...Loses confidence when (...)

...Doesn't always take pride in (...)

...Lacks skill in (...)

...Has only superficial knowledge in/of (...)

...Unsuccessful in attempts to (...)

...Deficient in (...)

...Major shortcoming is (...)

...Insufficient interest for/in (...)

...Occasionally uncertain about (...)

...Sporadic work output when/if (...)

...Undependable when it comes to (...)

...Unready to take on (...)

...Has incomplete knowledge in/on (...)

...Can be worthless in area of (...)

...Sometimes hampers (...)

...Unable to get interested in (...)

...Reliability fails when/if (...)

...Otherwise good performance marred by (...)

252

Below Average Personal Performance (Levels 4-3)

...Not always dependable and reliable because (...)

...Gives good effort only when (...)

...Sometimes not responsive to (...)

...Achieves success only when (...)

...Not a great amount of skill in/doing (...)

...Delivers accurate work only when (...)

...Barely satisfactory effort when/in (...)

...Fruitless attempts to (...)

...Has misconception about/of (...)

...Occasionally forgets to (...)

...Has difficulty understanding (...)

...Is indifferent to (...)

...Does not always do successful work because (...)

...Rarely seeks opportunity to (...)

...Avoids work when (...)

...Work sometimes suffers because of (...)

...Not dependable when (...)

...Sometimes loses sight of (...)

...Indecision sets in when (...)

...May fall behind in work when/if (...)

...Performs well when/if (...)

...Will complete work if (...)

...Not overly concerned about (...)

253

Below Average Personal Performance (Levels 4-3)

...Good work habits break down when/if (...)

...Not qualified to/for (...)

...Work inadequate when/if (...)

...Unprepared in area of (...)

...If not closely watched will (...)

...Unproductive in (...)

...Suffers loss of confidence when/in (...)

...Indifferent in attempts to (...)

...Unskilled in ability to (...)

...Has shortcoming in (...)

...Crude in attempts to (...)

...Unequipped to deal with (...)

...Sometimes loses sight of (...)

...Personal talent limited to (...)

...Work up to par only when (...)

...Inclined to slack off when/if (...)

...Concern for daily work effort lacking when/if (...)

...Misses opportunities to (...)

...Inattentive to job when/if (...)

...Does not complete (...)

...Occasionally careless in (...)

...Deficient in (...)

...Major shortcoming is (...)

Below Average Personal Performance (Levels 4-3)

...Insufficient interest for/in (...)

...Occasionally careless in (...)

...Will do a good job if (...)

...Not overly concerned about (...)

...Work effort fails when (...)

...Gives menial effort when/if (...)

...Achieved limited success when (...)

...Personal initiative affected by (...)

...Has a problem when/if (...)

...Fails to fully pursue (...)

...Work effort affected by (...)

...Loses confidence when/if (...)

...Good ability hindered by (...)

...Is unable to (...)

...Subject to failure when/if (...)

...Occasional faulty work when/if (...)

...Major drawback is (...)

...Unable to (...)

...Doesn't balance workload when (...)

...High level of performance fails when (...)

> The louder you talk,
> the angrier you become.
> From the book:
> **Successful Leadership Today**

255

Below Average Personal Performance (Levels 4-3)

CHAPTER 12

UNSATISFACTORY PERSONAL PERFORMANCE

(LEVELS 2-1)

PERSONAL PERFORMANCE LEVELS

LEVELS 10-9
* Contributes GREATLY to organization mission
* CONTINUALLY seeks additional responsibility
* THOROUGHLY understands all job components
* Works well independent of supervision

LEVELS 8-7
* Contributes HIGH LEVEL to organization mission
* Seeks additional responsibility
* Exhibits drive for self-improvement
* Proposes good solutions to difficult problems

LEVELS 6-5
* Contributes SOME to organization mission
* ACCEPTS additional responsibility
* Requires LIMITED supervision
* Good understanding of major jobs

LEVELS 4-3
* DOES NOT contribute to organization mission
* DOES NOT desire additional responsibility
* Requires ROUTINE supervision
* Satisfied with less than quality work

LEVELS 2-1
* HINDERS organization mission
* AVOIDS added responsibility
* Requires CONSTANT supervision
* DOES NOT or CAN NOT understand job

UNSATISFACTORY PERSONAL PERFORMANCE

WORD BANK

NOTE: The words in this word bank, USED ALONE, describe UNSATISFACTORY PERFORMANCE. When combined with other "qualifying" words, many of these words can be used to describe higher performance.

EXAMPLE: WRONG (UNSATISFACTORY)
SOMETIMES WRONG (BELOW AVERAGE)
* NEVER WRONG (ABOVE AVERAGE)

* When writing on SUPERIOR PERFORMANCE, try not to use a negative word in conjunction with a positive "qualifying" word ("NEVER"). An appropriate SUPERIOR PERFORMANCE bullet to the above could be "ALWAYS RIGHT."

Words listed in other word banks can similarly be used to describe higher or lower performance.

ABUSIVE	BACKWARD	BLUNDER
BOTCH(ES)	BUNGLE(S)	BUNGLING
CARELESS	CATASTROPHE	CHAOTIC
COLLAPSE	COVER-UP	DECEIT
DECEIVE	DECEPTION	DEFRAUD
DEPLORABLE	DEPLORE	DERELICT
DERELICTION	DEROGATORY	DESTRUCT
DESTRUCTION	DESTRUCTIVE	DETRIMENTAL
DISASTROUS	DISASTER	DISGRACE(FUL)
DISHONEST	DISLOYAL(TY)	DISOBEDIENCE
DISOBEDIENT	DISOBEY	DISORDER(LY)
DOWNFALL	EMPTY	ERR
ERRANT	ERROR	FAIL(ED)
FAILURE	FAKE	FALSE
FALSEHOOD	FALSITY	FAULT(Y)
FIASCO	FLAGRANT	FLUNK
FRAUD	FRAUDULENT	FUMBLE
FUTILE	FUTILITY	HARASS

257

HARM(FUL)	HARSH	HAZARDOUS
HELPLESS	HORRENDOUS	ILL-ADVISED
ILLEGAL	ILL-FATED	ILL-FOUNDED
ILLICIT	IMPIOUS	IMPOTENCE
IMPOTENT	IMPROPRIETY	INABILITY
INACTION	INACTIVE	INAPT
INAPTITUDE	INEPTNESS	INAUSPICIOUS
INCAPABLE	INCAPACITY	INCOMPETENCE
INCOMPETENT	INCONGRUOUS	INCONSIDERATE
INCORRECT	INDOLENT	INEPT
INEPTITUDE	INJURE	INJURY
INSUBORDINATE	INTIMIDATE	INTOLERABLE
INVALID	IRRESPONSIBLE	IRRESPONSIVE
LEAST	LAZY	LIFELESS
LOSER	LOSS	LOST
LOWEST	MEANINGLESS	MENACE
MINIMAL	MINUSCULE	MINUTE
MISAPPROPRIATE	MISCONDUCT	MISFIT
MISFORTUNE	MISTAKE	NEGATE
NEGATIVE	NEGLECT(FUL)	NEGLIGENCE
NEGLIGENT	NONPRODUCTIVE	OBSOLETE
OBSTRUCT(ION)	OUTLANDISH	OUT-OF-DATE
PATHETIC	PETULANT	PITIFUL
POOR	PURPOSELESS	QUIT
QUITTER	REBELLIOUS	REFUSAL
REFUSE	REJECT	REPREHENSIBLE
RETARD	RUIN	RUN-DOWN
SELF-DEFEATING	SHAM	SHAMEFUL
SHIFTLESS	SHIFTY	SLIPSHOD
SLOPPY	SLOPWORK	SORROWFUL
STAGNANT	STAGNATE	SUCCUMB
THOUGHTLESS	THRIFTLESS	TROUBLE(D)
UNABLE	UNACCOMPLISHED	UNAPT

258

Unsatisfactory Personal Performance (Levels 2-1)

UNDEPENDABLE	UNDERHANDED	UNDESIRABLE
UNDISCERNING	UNDISTINGUISHED	UNFAIR
UNFIT	UNLAWFUL	UNPROFESSIONAL
UNRESPONSIBLE	UNRELIABLE	UNSATISFACTORY
UNSKILLED	UNSKILLFUL	UNSUCCESSFUL
UNSUITABLE	UNTRUSTWORTHY	UNWILLING
UNWORTHY	USELESS	USURP
VALUELESS	VICTIMIZE	VIOLATE
VIOLATION	VITIATE	WASHED-UP
WASTE(D)	WASTEFUL	WORSE
WORSEN	WORST	WORTHLESS
WRECK	WRONG	WRONGDOER
WRONGDOING	WRONGFUL	

Good leadership comes from the heart.'
From the book: **Successful Leadership Today**

Ignorance is usually
a self-inflicted wound.
From the book:
Successful Leadership Today

Unsatisfactory Personal Performance (Levels 2-1)

BULLET PHRASES

Select a word from COLUMN 1 to go with a word in COLUMN 2.

EXAMPLE: REPEATEDLY FAILS

COLUMN #1	COLUMN #2
FREQUENTLY	BLUNDERS
CARELESS	
HABITUALLY	COMPLACENT
	CONFUSED
OFTEN	FAILS
	FRUITLESS
REPEATED	INACCURATE
	INATTENTIVE
REPEATEDLY	INCORRECT
	INEFFECTIVE
ROUTINELY	INEPT
	INEXACT
	NEGLIGENT
	UNAPT
	UNDEPENDABLE
	UNOBSERVANT
	UNPREDICTABLE
	UNRELIABLE
	UNSUCCESSFUL
	WRONG

BULLET PHRASE STATEMENTS

...Lacks confidence

...Incomplete work

...Not manageable

...Professionally stagnant

...Overly complacent

...Pathetic performance

...Misuses position

...Avoids responsibility

...An underachiever

...Inferior workmanship

...Impotent work

...Unambitious individual

...Inappropriate actions

...Substandard performer

260

...Loses control

...Totally unconcerned

...Impedes progress

...Shirks responsibility

...Inhibits work

...Blatant negligence

...Undermines morale

...Not job-aggressive

...Constantly complains

...Creates problems

...Sloppy workmanship

...Usually careless

...Continuous poor attitude

...Below average performer

...Efforts routinely futile

...Deplorable work ethics

...Shows little forethought

...Erodes good order

...Needs continued reminders

...Violates the rules

...Inferior quality work

...Neglectful and incompetent

...Inconsiderate of others

...Lacks imagination

...Completely helpless

...Ignores reality

...Wasted opportunities

...Shuns work

...Disruptive influence

...Ignores direction

...Flouts authority

...Not trustworthy

...Lacks self-discipline

...Not reliable

...Defeatist attitude

...Habitually flouts authority

...Provides useless assistance

...Unsatisfactory work results

...Not a self-starter

...A complete disappointment

...No future potential

...Interprets rules loosely

...Abnormal work behavior

...Frequent misconduct problems

...Routinely obstructs progress

...Routinely faulty work

261

...Incompetent at job

...Plagued by indecision

...Intentionally avoids work

...Indecisive under pressure

...Lack of initiative

...Acts on impulse

...Prone to indecisiveness

...Incapable and inept

...Throws weight around

...Seriously endangers morale

...Deviates from standards

...Erratic work habits

...A non-productive worker

...Fault-finding to excess

...Questionable work ethics

...Lacks mental coordination

...Not an orderly thinker

...Unable to master job

...Exhibits lack of desire

...Subject to daily failure

...Unpredictable work habits

...Unwilling to conform

...Interferes with progress

...Discourages team unity

...Lags behind others

...Reluctant, unwilling worker

...Lack of desire

...Plots and schemes

...Misrepresents the facts

...Impervious to counseling

...Of little value

...No physical vigor

...Careless work habits

...Failed to improve

...Jumps to conclusions

...Asks undue questions

...Operates in a vacuum

...Fails to observe rules

...Difficult to reason with

...Idealistic to a fault

...Conveniently misunderstands directions

...Illogical performance and actions

Unsatisfactory Personal Performance (Levels 2-1)

...Consistently poor performance

...Deliberately refuses direction

...Makes frequent misjudgments

...Disobedient and disrespectful

...Insignificant work accomplishment

...Requires constant supervision

...Adversely affects operations

...Unimpressive job performance

...Faulty, defective workmanship

...Produces inaccurate, faulty work

...Flagrant violation of directions

...A generally unorganized person

...Common errors in judgment

...Doesn't give passable effort

...Mostly insignificant work accomplishment

...Burdensome to this organization

...Frequently deviates from standards

...Uncertain, indecisive in action

...Frequently makes false statements

...Intentionally makes minor mistakes

...Efforts frequently prove fruitless

...Blames shortcomings on others

...Ignores direction and guidance

263

Unsatisfactory Personal Performance (Levels 2-1)

...Has excessive minor infractions

...Gross deviation from procedure

...Avoids work and responsibility

...Lacks proper mental discipline

...Not dependable or reliable

...Complete disregard for authority

...Less than moderate success

...Unwilling to obey direction

...Makes careless, avoidable mistakes

...Prejudicial to good order

...Substandard performance routinely displayed

...Intractable unwillingness to conform

...Immaturity and bad judgment

...Detrimental to team spirit

...Less than marginal performer

...Openly disagrees with superiors

...Obvious lack of motivation

...Fails to accomplish tasks

...Negative outlook and disposition

...Not receptive to counseling

...Careless attention to detail

...Fails to achieve consistency

Unsatisfactory Personal Performance (Levels 2-1)

...Remains helpless without supervision

...A burden on others

...Spreads discontent and resentment

...Reluctant to accept direction

...Too many petty mistakes

...Incompetent on most jobs

...Always subject to failure

...Will botch any job

...Completely without useful skill

...Indulges in own self-interests

...Unsuccessful and fruitless work

...Interrupts work of others

...Hinders and impedes work

...Detriment to good order

...Totally inadequate work habits

...Imperfect to say least

...Work riddled with defects

...Jobs routinely remain uncompleted

...Only partially completes work

...Lack of personal conviction

...Not steadfast in commitment

...Has difficulty understanding directions

...Routinely leaves work place

265

Unsatisfactory Personal Performance (Levels 2-1)

...Requires almost constant supervision

...Engenders disrespect among peers

...Seriously lacking in initiative

...Total lack of motivation

...Ineptness in job accomplishment

...Inappropriate behavior and performance

...Stubbornly opposes corrective counseling

...Routinely gives unacceptable performance

...Steady, prolonged decline in performance

...Unable to take constructive criticism

...Causes extra work for others

...Displays obvious lack of motivation

...Performance degenerated to unacceptable level

...Shows open discontent toward superiors

...Routinely questions motive of others

...Weakens or breaks under pressure

...Performance of work is unsatisfactory

...A liability to the organization

...Shows no desire for improvement

...Ignores explicit direction of superiors

...Unsuited for this type work

...Unproductive most of the time

...Usually empty promises to improve

...Suffers convenient lapses of memory

...Makes one mistake after another

...Evasive when confronted with shortcomings

...Wears down spirit of others

...Inattentive to routine work procedures

...Blames others for own shortcomings

...Not receptive to constructive counseling

...Routinely doubts and questions superiors

...Overly concerned with own self-image

...Opposes improvement efforts of others

...Frequent infraction of the rules

...Unmindful of job at hand

...Incomplete work highlights daily effort

...Poorness of quality in work

...Does insufficient amount of work

...Frequently deviates from set procedures

...Relies too heavily on others

...Intentional disregard for following direction

...Habitually reports to work late

...Devoid of hope for improvement

...Neglectful and forgetful work habits

...Frequently in discord with others

Unsatisfactory Personal Performance (Levels 2-1)

...Deficient in skill and knowledge

...Unable to overcome minor problems

...Incapable of sustained satisfactory performance

...Incompetent without direct, constant supervision

...Unable to perform routine jobs

...Fails to respond to direction

...Causes extra work for others

...Reluctant to abide by rules

...Has innate aversion to work

...Shows little or no effort

...Erodes morale and team spirit

...Careless in manner and action

...Acts on impulse, not plan

...Unable to deal with reality

...Somewhat of a perfectionist with inclination toward stubbornness

...Reluctant to accept responsibility unless specifically assigned

...Has little interest outside specialty area

...Avoids, to maximum extent possible, new responsibilities

...Some assignments stay incomplete for too long

...Unable to stay abreast of job

...Not correct and precise in detail

...Failed to live up to expectations

268

Unsatisfactory Personal Performance (Levels 2-1)

...Uncertain and doubtful in making decisions

...When forced to undertake duties outside normal specialized area, produces only mediocre results

...Sincere and thorough, though somewhat unimaginative and stodgy

...Takes more time than expected to complete jobs due to any number of personal reasons

...Inclined to stray from the truth

...Seldom prepared for the task at hand

...Does not demonstrate a sense of responsibility

...Unwilling to listen to reason or fact

...Evades and shirks job when possible

...Careless. Makes mistakes through lack of attention

...Fails to act according to expected standards

...Frequently breaks rules and fails to follow direction

...Considers all jobs below personal dignity to accomplish

...Does not abide by rules in an orderly fashion

...Will violate any rule not to personal liking

...Professional development lags far behind others

...Alters facts to suit own self-interest

...Unable to stay mentally involved in job

...Frequently becomes preoccupied with personal matters

...Has more than a mild dislike for work

...Unable to choose correct courses of action

Unsatisfactory Personal Performance (Levels 2-1)

...Lax and careless in performing job

...Not responsive to guidance or direction

...Performance highlighted by neglect and negligence

...Acts without giving due consideration or thought

...Will not work unless prompted or prodded

...Too many excuses, not enough work

...Works hard only when personally convenient

...Turns simple tasks into complex problems

...Superficial work doesn't hold up to close examination

...Cannot cope successfully with trying situations

...Inability to adapt to changing conditions

...Unable to stay abreast of events in fast-paced environment

...Does not get things done in timely manner

...Dodges work and responsibility at almost every opportunity

...Not job-aggressive, waits for something to happen before
   acting

...Not overly serious or concerned in doing tasks correctly

...Functions well below level of capabilities

...Manipulates people to meet own ends

...Gives in to pressure during crisis situations

...Does not always get all the facts before acting

...Has strong tendency to stray from normal behavior

...Interprets rules loosely and usually to personal benefit

270

Unsatisfactory Personal Performance (Levels 2-1)

...Becomes withdrawn and distraught when confronted with shortcomings

...Prefers to forsake any personal help or assistance

...Will stray or deviate from work standards if not closely watched

...Abnormally high reluctance to accept direction or guidance

...Not capable of continued good performance

...Even best efforts frequently prove fruitless

...Believes job should be subordinate to personal interests

...Gives undue consideration and attention to personal likes

...Cannot be relied upon to take timely, correct action

...Gets into verbal confrontation with others

...Refuses to yield or relent to change

...A slacker, shirks job when possible

...Exhibits only short periods of success

...Unable to distinguish between right and wrong

...Expects success using guesswork and conjecture

...Work falls short of expectations and abilities

...Failed to live up to expectations

...Twists recollection of events to own ends

...Actual performance falls well short of abilities

...Very difficult for others to work with

...Hesitant and confused in unfamiliar surroundings

Unsatisfactory Personal Performance (Levels 2-1)

...Proved to be a major disappointment

...Asks for an undue amount of justification on any assignment

...Exhibits neither desire nor ability to perform satisfactorily

...Counseling routinely required for sloppy workmanship

...Does not pay attention to detail or instruction

...Performance marked by inconsistency and flaw

...Sporadic in understanding and carrying out directives

...Inability to adjust to expected standards

...Half-truths highlight attitude and behavior problems

...Demonstrates little initiative, or desire for improvement

...Has lack of motivation and a negative attitude

...Late for work on numerous occasions

...Improvement counseling lasts only a short time

...Does not take pride in work or job accomplishment

...Performance, across the board, is unsatisfactory

...Performance is all valleys and no peaks

...Impulsive, subject to actions without due thought

...Negative attitude reflected in continued marginal performance

...Shows total lack of ability to work in structured environment

...Performance well below that expected of peer group

...Frequently voices displeasure at job assignments

...Continually commits minor efforts as if testing superiors
...Unresponsive to normal and special counseling

272

Unsatisfactory Personal Performance (Levels 2-1)

...Exhibits unsatisfactory performance in technical specialty

...Has negative outlook and disposition regardless of subject matter

...Complains openly when not assigned jobs to personal liking

...Unwilling to comply with simplest direction

...Lacks requisite skill despite extensive training

...Works without supervision when the mood strikes

...Unwilling to do personal share of work

...Counseling results in only short-term improvement

...Immature and undisciplined with no potential

...Consistently failed to take corrective action on deficiencies

...Insufficient motivation to overcome even small obstacles

...Will not acknowledge mistakes or failures

...Always blames others for own failures

...Work must remain under constant supervision

...Attempts to correct deficiencies have been in vain

Unsatisfactory Personal Performance (Levels 2-1)

COMPLETE THE PHRASE

Select a word in COLUMN 1 to go with a word in COLUMN 2 and use a word in COLUMN 3 and provide the appropriate ending in COLUMN 4.

COLUMN #1	COLUMN #2	COLUMN #3 AS/TO/IN	COLUMN #4 (COMPLETE)
CARELESS			
DEPLORABLE			
DISAPPOINTING			
DISGRACEFUL	ABILITY		
DUBIOUS			
FAILED			
FLIMSY	APTITUDE		
FUTILE			
HALF-HEARTED			
IMPOTENT			
INADEQUATE	CAPABILITY		
INEFFECTIVE			
INFERIOR			
INSIGNIFICANT			
INSUFFICIENT	PERFORMER		
LIMITED			
LOW-LEVEL			
PATHETIC	PERFORMANCE		
SHABBY			
SHAMEFUL			
SHODDY	RECORD		
SUBSTANDARD			
UNDISTINGUISHED	TALENT		
UNSUCCESSFUL			
USELESS	WORKER		
WEAK			
WORTHLESS			

> "Good words are worth much,
> and cost little." GEORGE HERBERT
> From the book: **Successful Leadership Today**

Unsatisfactory Personal Performance (Levels 2-1)

Select a word in COLUMN 1, COLUMN 2 and COLUMN 3 and add an appropriate ending.

EXAMPLE:

OFTEN (#1)	INCAPABLE (#2)	OF DOING (#3)	SATISFACTORY WORK (ENDING)

COLUMN #1	COLUMN #2	COLUMN #3	ENDING
	CARELESS		
	FORGETS		
	HELPLESS		
FREQUENTLY			
	INADEQUATE		
	INATTENTIVE		
HABITUALLY		FOR	
	INCAPABLE		
	INCOMPETENT		
OFTEN		IF	
	INDIFFERENT		
	INEFFECTIVE		
REPEATED		OF	
	MEANINGLESS		
	NEGLIGENT		
REPEATEDLY		TO	
	OBLIVIOUS		
	OFFENSIVE		
ROUTINELY		WHEN	
	UNABLE		
	UNEQUIPPED		
	UNFIT		
	UNMINDFUL		
	UNSUITED		
	USELESS		
	WRONG		

Successful people see
opportunities, not problems.
From the book:
Successful Leadership Today

275

...Habitually gets into trouble by (...)

...Becomes hostile when approached about (...)

...Failed to achieve consistency in (...)

...Involved in unethical practice of (...)

...Shows apathy and indifference toward (...)

...Disenchanted with present job because (...)

...Will not maintain commitment to (...)

...Lacks vigor or force to (...)

...Has not adjusted well to (...)

...A misfit, not suited for/to (...)

...Becomes agitated and upset when (...)

...Becomes confused and puzzled when (...)

...Hinders and impedes progress by (...)

...Interferes with normal functioning of (...)

...Has made insignificant progress in (...)

...Unable to grasp meaning of (...)

...Open distrust of others causes (...)

...Lacks knowledge or comprehension to (...)

...Lacks the emotional stability to (...)

...Lax in complying and enforcing (...)

...Refused to accept assistance in/to (...)

...Shows marked unwillingness to (...)

...Deliberate lack of consideration for (...)

276

Unsatisfactory Personal Performance (Levels 2-1)

...Excitable temper frequently cause of (...)

...Not an accomplished or skilled (...)

...Impedes work by inability to (...)

...Does not totally comply with (...)

...Usually falls behind others when (...)

...Fails to grasp essentials of (...)

...Not satisfactory in ability to (...)

...Failed to achieve consistency in (...)

...Suspended from regular duties for/because (...)

...Suffered loss of confidence in/by (...)

...Has a noticeable imperfection in (...)

...Despite noble intentions, unable   to (...)

...Has not kept pace with (...)

...Lacks necessary ability to (...)

...Not qualified to be (...)

...Shows only artificial interest in (...)

...Lacking in ability to (...)

...Of little value in/when (...)

...Behavior not conducive to (...)

...Openly defies and challenges (...)

...Lacks mental aptitude to (...)

...Not mature enough to (...)

277

Unsatisfactory Personal Performance (Levels 2-1)

...Lacks the capacity to (...)

...Unable to refrain from (...)

...Upsets normal operations by (...)

...Has open contempt for (...)

...Unsuitable and unfit for (...)

...Made crude attempt to (...)

...Lags behind others in (...)

...Lacks mental restraint to (...)

...Made false statements concerning (...)

...Incompetent in area(s) of (...)

...Lacks inner discipline to (...)

...Careless and negligent in (...)

...Critically undermines morale by (...)

...Requires routine reminders to (...)

...Has bad habit of (...)

...Stirs up trouble by (...)

...Helpless when confronted with (...)

...Has great difficulty in/with (...)

...Has chronic weakness in/of (...)

...Not mentally equipped to (...)

...Becomes easily distressed when/over (...)

...Compounds existing problems by (...)

...Inexperienced in matters of (...)

Unsatisfactory Personal Performance (Levels 2-1)

...Displays marked indifference in (...)

...Has distorted view of (...)

...Showed minimal improvement despite (...)

...Ignores reality. Unable to (...)

...Unwilling to put forth necessary effort to (...)

...Does not give required importance to (...)

...Does not have the ability to (...)

...Below normal level of skill in (...)

...Conduct not fit or becoming of a/an (...)

...Unable to maintain a stable balance of (...)

...Overall performance declined because of (...)

...Is of little or no use in/when (...)

...Lacks mental courage and conviction to (...)

...Did not exercise sound judgment in/when (...)

...Enjoys a low reputation due to (...)

...Rude and impolite, does not show respect to/for (...)

...Slow to learn and develop as a/an (...)

...Performance has deteriorated to point of (...)

...Does not satisfy minimum requirements for/of (...)

...Does not possess the mental vigor or vitality to (...)

...Behavior has declined to point of (...)

...Has a strong moral weakness in (...)

Unsatisfactory Personal Performance (Levels 2-1)

...Suffers frequent minor setbacks because of (...)

...Failure to pay attention to detail caused (...)

...Unable to take full advantage of (...)

...A major cause of disappointment because (...)

...Acts in haste without due regard of/for (...)

...Suffered total loss of integrity because (...)

...Lacks necessary wisdom and judgment to (...)

...Does not possess sufficient knowledge to (...)

...Failed to act with promptness and dispatch in/when (...)

...Sometimes uses ethically dubious means to (...)

...Does not possess the necessary self-confidence to (...)

...Work characterized by complete absence of (...)

...Chronic personal and financial problems have led to (...)

...Despite ample opportunity, failed to improve (...)

...Inconsistent and unimpressive performance led to (...)

...Attitude and performance not in tune with (...)

...Has exaggerated ego problem which frequently results in (...)

...Prone to substandard work because of (...)

...Becomes intensely excited and aroused by/when (...)

...Inconsistent work and irregular work habits caused by (...)

...Occasionally regresses to old habits of (...)

...Personal doubt and indecision hinders performance in/as (...)

Unsatisfactory Personal Performance (Levels 2-1)

...Acts on spontaneous impulse, without due consideration of/for (...)

...Does not have the will or ability to (...)

...Deeply emotional, cannot control urge to (...)

...Sometimes uses excessive force or pressure in/to (...)

...Actions and deeds in sharp contrast with/to (...)

...Carelessness and inattention has led to/caused (...)

...Belabors on nonessential matters to detriment of (...)

...A constant threat to morale by/because (...)

...Finds it most difficult to fit in with (...)

...Personal desires frequently at contrast with (...)

...Generally learned, but totally inexperienced in (...)

...Unable to fall in line with (...)

...Suppresses growth potential of others by/when (...)

...Tries to do a good job, but is hindered by (...)

...Utterly helpless when it comes to (...)

...Has no idea of how to (...)

...Tends to create bad relationships with co-workers because (...)

...Lacks vigor and persistence required to (...)

...Not reliable to work independently, needs help to (...)

...Becomes easily detached from job by (...)

...Unwillingness and inability to act decisively caused (...)

...Has difficulty dealing with others because (...)

281

Unsatisfactory Personal Performance (Levels 2-1)

...Exercised bad judgment and discretion in/by (...)

...Does not support organization policies and directives by/when (...)

...Of little use or value in/when (...)

...Time after time proved a burden to (...)

...Positive aspects of performance outweighed by ....,

...Unable to deal with reality of (...)

...Spends an inordinate amount of time in/on (...)

...Ruined effort to (...)

...Unable to restrain (...)

...Lacking in ability to (...)

...Usually negligent when/in (...)

...Worthless as a (...)

...Without value working in/on (...)

...Does not stay in strict compliance with (...)

...Abuses (...)

...Flagrant violations of (...)

...Has major shortcomings in (...)

...Deficient performance as/in (...)

...Crude method of (...)

...Complete inability to (...)

...Incapable of doing (...)

...Incompetent in area of (...)

282

...Unable to complete (...)

...Incapable of sustained (...)

...Inept when it comes to (...)

...Unqualified for (...)

...Total disregard for (...)

...Indifferent to (...)

...Inadequate for (...)

...Lacks requisite knowledge to (...)

...Displayed improper judgment by/when (...)

...Experienced some incidences of (...)

...Unsuitable for (...)

...Apathetic towards (...)

...Demonstrates lack of interest in (...)

...Not reasonable and rational in thought, unable to (...)

...Struggles to maintain correct balance of (...)

...Personal desires in discord with (...)

...Despite adequate time, failed to (...)

...Becomes rattled when (...)

...Slow to grasp (...)

...Makes mistakes when/while (...)

...Becomes unraveled when (...)

...Just can't seem to (...)

...Has difficulty doing (...)

283

Unsatisfactory Personal Performance (Levels 2-1)

...Impairs morale by (...)

...Not worthy of (...)

...Blatant disregard for (...)

...Loses composure when (...)

...Bad habits include (...)

...Contemptuous disregard for (...)

...Strongly opposed to (...)

...Not serious about (...)

...Misguided efforts cause(d) (...)

...Has difficulty with (...)

...Planned badly for (...)

...Unforgiving nature causes (...)

...Gets easily discouraged when (...)

...Ineffective in (...)

...Despite repeated attempts, can't (...)

...Has trouble (...)

...General poor quality (...)

...Spends too much time (...)

...Fails to take advantage of (...)

...For the most part unimpressive (...)

...A detriment to (...)

...Can't do (...) correctly

Unsatisfactory Personal Performance (Levels 2-1)

...Requires close supervision when working with/in (...)

...At times irritates others by (...)

> "The farther back you can look,
> the farther forward you are
> likely to see." WINSTON CHURCHILL
> From the book: **Successful Leadership Today**

> Turn ideas into action.
> Turn action into reality.
> From the book:
> **Successful Leadership Today**

Unsatisfactory Personal Performance (Levels 2-1)

CHAPTER 13

UNFAVORABLE

PERSONALITY & WORK RELATIONSHIPS

(LEVELS 4-1)

UNFAVORABLE PERSONALITY

AND WORK RELATIONSHIPS

WORD BANK

NOTE: The words in this word bank, USED ALONE, describe UNFAVORABLE TRAITS. When combined with other "qualifying" words, many of these words can be used to describe FAVORABLE PERFORMANCE.

EXAMPLE: ABRUPT (UNFAVORABLE)
                 NEVER ABRUPT (FAVORABLE)

Words listed in other word banks can similarly be used to describe FAVORABLE TRAITS.

ABASE	ABERRANT	ABHORRENT
ABRASIVE	ABRUPT	ABUSIVE
ACCOST	ALOOF	AMBIVALENT
ANTAGONIST	ANTAGONISTIC	ANTAGONIZE
ANTISOCIAL	APPALL	APPALLING
ARGUMENTATIVE	ARROGANCE	ARROGANT
AUDACITY	BASHFUL	BELLIGERENCE
BELLIGERENT	BERATE	BERSERK
BIASED	BLAND	BLUNDER
BLUNT	BOISTEROUS	BRAGGER
BRASH	BRASSY	BUNGLING
CALLOUS	CAUSTIC	CHEAT
CHEATER	CHEERLESS	COCKSURE
COCKY	COLD	COLORLESS
COMPLACENT	CONCEITED	CONDESCENDENCE
CONDESCENDING	CONFUSE	CONSPIRE
CONTEMPT	CONTEMPTIBLE	CORRUPT
CORRUPTIBLE	CRANKY	CRASS
CRUDE	CRUEL	CRUELTY
CRUSTY	CUNNING	CURT
CYNICAL	DECEIT	DECEITFUL

287

DECEIVE(D)	DECEIVER	DECEPTION
DEFEATIST	DEFIANCE	DEFIANT
DEMEAN	DEMORALIZE	DEPERSONALIZE
DEPRESSED	DEPRESSING	DESPISE
DESPITE	DESPITEFUL	DEVIANT
DEVIOUS	DISAGREEABLE	DISCONTENT
DISCORD	DISCOURTEOUS	DISDAIN
DISDAINFUL	DISFAVOR	DISGRACE
DISGRACEFUL	DISGRUNTLE	DISHONEST(Y)
DISHONOR	DISREPUTE	DISRESPECT
DISRESPECTFUL	DISSENSION	DISSENT
DISSENTER	DISTASTEFUL	DRAB
DURESS	ECCENTRIC	EGOCENTRIC
EGOISM	EGOTISM	EGOTISTIC
EMBITTER	ENERVATE	ENRAGE
EVASIVE	FACETIOUS	FAITHLES
FALSE	FALSEHOOD	FALSITY
FASTIDIOUS	FAULTFINDING	FICKLE
FINICKY	FLUSTER	FLUSTERED
FOOLHARDY	FOOLISHNESS	FOPPISH
FORGETFUL	FRAUD	FRAUDULENT
FRUSTRATE	FRUSTRATED	FRUSTRATION
FURIOUS	FUROR	FURY
FUSSY	GALL	GALLING
GARRULOUS	GAUCHE	GRIPE
GROUSE	GUILELESS	HALF-BAKED
HALF-COCKED	HALF-TRUTH	HARDHEADED
HARD-HEARTED	HARD-NOSED	HARD-SET
HARSH	HATRED	HEARTLESS
HECKLE	HIGH HANDED	HIGH-STRUNG
HIGH-TONED	HOSTILE	HOSTILITY
HOT-TEMPERED	HUMILIATE	HUMORLESS
HURTFUL	HYPERCRITICAL	ILL-BEHAVED

Unfavorable Personality & Work Relationships (Levels 4-1)

ILL-HUMORED	ILL-MANNERED	ILL-NATURED
IMMATURE	IMMORAL	IMPATIENCE
IMPATIENT	IMPERSONAL	IMPERSONALIZE
IMPERTINENCE	IMPERTINENT	IMPETUOUS
IMPOLITE	IMPUDENCE	IMPUDENT
INATTENTIVE	INCERTITUDE	INCOGNIZANT
INCOHERENT	INCOMPATIBLE	INCONCEIVABLE
INCONSIDERATE	INDECISION	INDECISIVE
INDIGNANT	INDIGNATION	INDIGNITY
INDISCREET	INEPT	INEPTITUDE
INFURIATE	INGRATITUDE	INHARMONIOUS
INHARMONY	INHOSPITABLE	INHUMANE
INIMICAL	INJUDICIOUS	INSENSIBLE
INSENSITIVE	INSINCERE	INSIPID
INSOLENCE	INSOLENT	INSUBORDINATE
INSULT	INSIDIOUS	IRATE
IRE	IRK	IRKSOME
IRRATIONAL	IRRESOLUTE	IRRITABLE
JEALOUS	JEALOUSY	JOYLESS
KINDLESS	KNOW-IT-ALL	KNUCKLE UNDER
LAZY	LETHARGIC	LIFELESS
LIGHT-HEADED	LOATH	LOATHE
LOATHING	LOATHSOME	LOW-MINDED
LOW-SPIRITED	MALADJUSTED	MALADROIT
MALEVOLENCE	MALEVOLENT	MALFEASANCE
MANNERLESS	MEDDLESOME	MERCILESS
MINDLESS	MISBEHAVE	MISBEHAVIOR
MISGUIDED	MOODY	MOROSE
MUDDLE	NAIVE	NERVELESS
NONCONFORMIST	OBNOXIOUS	OBSESSION
OBSTINATE	OFFENSIVE	OPPRESSIVE
OUTBURST	OUTSPOKEN	OUTRAGE
OVERBEARING	OVERCONFIDENT	OVERREACT

289

Unfavorable Personality & Work Relationships (Levels 4-1)

OVERSIMPLIFY	PANIC	PARANOID
PATRONIZE	PEEVISH	PERT
PERTINACIOUS	PERTINACITY	PESSIMISM
PESSIMISTIC	POMPOSITY	POMPOUS
PORTENTOUS	PREJUDICE	PREJUDICIAL
PROCRASTINATE	PRUDE	PRUDISH
PRY	PRYING	PUGNACIOUS
QUARRELSOME	QUITTER	RAGE
RAMPAGE	REASONLESS	REMORSE
REMORSEFUL	REMORSELESS	REPREHEND
REPREHENSIBLE	REPRESS	REPRESSION
REPRIMAND	REPUGNANCE	REPUGNANT
REPULSE	REPULSION	REPULSIVE
RESENT	RESENTFUL	RESENTMENT
RHETORIC	RHETORICAL	RHETORICIAN
RIDICULE	RIVALRY	RUDE
RUTHLESS	SARCASM	SARCASTIC
SAUCY	SCOFF	SELF-CENTERED
SELF-CONCEIT	SELF-CONSCIOUS	SELF-DOUBT
SELF-IMPORTANT	SELF-INDULGENCE	
SELF-INDULGENT	SELF-INTEREST(ED)	SELFISH
SELF-OPINIONATED	SELF-RIGHTEOUS	
SELF-SEEKING	SELF-SERVING	SHIFTLESS
SHORTSIGHTED	SHORT-TEMPERED	
SHY	SMIRK	SMUG
SNIDE	SNUFFY	SOFT-HEADED
SPIRITLESS	SPITE	SPITEFUL
SPURN	SULLEN	SUPERCILIOUS
SURLY	TACTLESS	TEMPER
TEMPERAMENTAL	TEPID	THOUGHTLESS
TIMID	TIMOROUS	TRICKY
TROUBLEMAKER	TROUBLESOME	TURBULENT
TURMOIL	UNAMBITIOUS	INARTISTIC

Unfavorable Personality & Work Relationships (Levels 4-1)

UNSPARING	UNASSERTIVE	UNCIVIL
UNCONCERNED	UNCONTROLLABLE	
UNCOOPERATIVE	UNCOURTEOUS	UNDECIDED
UNDERMINE	UNDEPENDABLE	UNDISCIPLINED
UNDIGNIFIED	UNDISTINGUISHED	
UNFEELING	UNFRIENDLY	UNGRACIOUS
UNGRACEFUL	UNHAPPY	UNINSPIRED
UNKIND	UNKINDLY	UNMANNERLY
UNMERCIFUL	UNMINDFUL	UNPLEASANT
UNPOLISHED	UNPOPULAR	UNPREDICTABLE
UNPRINCIPLED	UNREALISTIC	UNREASON
UNREASONABLE	UNSCRUPULOUS	UNSOCIAL
UNSTABLE	UNTRUTH	UNTRUTHFUL
VAIN	VINDICTIVE	VIOLENT
WANGLE	WANTON	WEAKHEARTED
WEAK-MINDED	WILE	WILL-LESS
WROTH	WRY	

"You may pardon much of others,
nothing to yourself." AUSONIUS
From the book: **Successful Leadership Today**

Successful people make their own opportunities.
From the book: **Successful Leadership Today**

291

BULLET PHRASE STATEMENTS

Select one or two words from COLUMN 1 to go with a word in COLUMN 2.

EXAMPLE: ARROGANT PERSONALITY
           RUDE, IMMATURE MANNER

COLUMN #1   **COLUMN #2**

ABUSIVE	REPULSIVE	
ARROGANT	RESENTFUL	
BLAND	RUDE	ATTITUDE
BLUNT	SARCASTIC	BEHAVIOR
BOISTEROUS	SELF-CENTERED	CONDUCT
BRASH	SELF-SERVING	DISPOSITION
CHEERLESS	TACTLESS	MANNER
CRASS	TEMPERAMENTAL	NATURE
CRUDE	THOUGHTLESS	PERSONALITY
CYNICAL	UNCOOPERATIVE	
DRAB	UNCOURTEOUS	
FUSSY	UNDIGNIFIED	
HUMORLESS	UNFRIENDLY	
IMMATURE	UNGRACIOUS	
IMPERSONAL	UNPLEASANT	
LIFELESS	UNPOLISHED	
MEDDLESOME	UNSCRUPULOUS	
OVERBEARING	UNSOCIABLE	
OVERCONFIDENT	VIOLENT	
QUARRELSOME		

Good deeds must be
supported by good rewards.
From the book: **Successful Leadership Today**

Unfavorable Personality & Work Relationships (Levels 4-1)

...Emotionally unstable

...Dull personality

...Unenergetic spirit

...Slow wit

...Lacks self-motivation

...Unfriendly disposition

...No tact .

...Not compassionate

...Distasteful attitude

...Attracts trouble

...Disagreeable personality

...Emotionally immature

...Deviant behavior

...Unfriendly disposition

...Disorderly conduct

...Maladjusted personality

...Provokes arguments

...Unpredictable manner

...Low self-esteem

...Emotionally immature

...Carefree attitude

...Incites arguments

...Easily angered

...Uncaring nature

...Cheerless attitude

...Pessimistic outlook

...Unpolished manner

...Negative attitude

...Unrealistic manner

..Without enthusiasm

...Inexcusable behavior

...Lacks charisma

...Unstable personality

...Aberrant behavior

...Antisocial attitude

...Unprincipled manners

...Ill-humored personality

...Temperamental behavior

...Undignified manner

...Without compassion

...Adolescent behavior

...Lacks confidence

...A complainer

...Abrasive personality

...Short temper

...Negative attitude

293

Unfavorable Personality & Work Relationships (Levels 4-1)

...Openly discontent

...Frequent complainer

...Abrupt manner

...Emotional difficulty

...Overly emotional

...Indiscreet personal affairs

...Irrational, erratic behavior

...Disobedient and belligerent

...Argues to excess

...Undesirable personality traits

...Contemptible and arrogant

...Becomes emotionally violent

...Stirs up trouble

...Arrogant and overbearing

...Distant and impersonal

...Disrespectful to others

...Corrupt, immoral character

...Indifferent towards others

...Brash and immature

...Obstinate and impudent

...Undisciplined and unruly

...Drab, dull personality

...Unacceptable behavior

...Weak personality

...Hot tempered

...Unpleasant personality

...Agitates others

...Prone to argument

...Verbally abuses others

...Overbearing and intolerant

...Dull, trite personality

...Corruptive, dishonest nature

...Unjustly exploits others

...Becomes easily excited

...Breaks down morale

...Quarrelsome, touchy nature

...Impolite, insulting manner

...Cold, indifferent attitude

...Argumentative toward others

...Fabricates the truth

...Loses emotional control

...A problem person

...Crude, tactless manner

...Stubborn and obstinate

Unfavorable Personality & Work Relationships (Levels 4-1)

...Inconsiderate and uncaring

...Has defeatist attitude

...Abrupt, blunt manner

...Without personal courage

...Detriment to morale

...Little interest in others

...Causes disorder and unrest

...Irritates and annoys others

...Unable to control emotions

...Overly bold and brash

...Lack of personal conviction

...Without mercy and compassion

...Evasive and indirect manner

...Creates depression and gloom

...Indiscreet and thoughtless actions

...Overbearing and oppressive

...Vain, self-centered personality

...Arrogant, overbearing manner

...Short-tempered and arrogant

...Hostile, aggressive temperament

...Insolent, overbearing personality

...Lackluster, lackadaisical attitude

...Unpleasant, objectionable personality

...Indolent, sluggish personality

...Crude, coarse personality

...Distorts the truth

...Weak moral character

...Not thoughtful of others

...Displays bias and prejudice

...Overly bold and assertive

...Meek and overly humble

...Without sorrow or remorse

295

Unfavorable Personality & Work Relationships (Levels 4-1)

...Aggressive, challenging attitude

...Prankish, childish mannerism

...Overly aggressive personality

...Ingrained disrespectful nature

...Violate, explosive disposition

...Impolite and unmannerly actions

...Creates resentment and disharmony

...Devious and cunning personality

...Boisterous and rude personality

...Easily excitable. Overly troublesome

...Questionable moral principles

...Improper behavior and conduct

...Practices deceit and trickery

...Concerned with own self-interests

...Behavior and attitude problem

...Abusive and offensive language

...Spreads ill-will and disharmony

...Instigates and provokes disharmony

...Overreacts to minor situations

...Insulting and arrogant personality

...Low level of self-confidence

...Argumentative with irritating persistence

Unfavorable Personality & Work Relationships (Levels 4-1)

...Belligerent and hostile personality

...Unsophisticated behavior and attitude

...Exaggerated self-opinion and self-importance

...Overly submissive in nature

...Deceptive and deceitful character

...Creates ill-will and discontent

...Not a strong personality

...Overly apologetic and humble

...Overconfident. Abnormally high self-opinion

...A prankster. Not serious minded

...Often degrades and humiliates others

...Abrasive personality and abrupt manner

...Speaks and acts on impulse

...Overly challenging and aggressive personality

...Displays irrational and erratic behavior

...Conduct beyond bounds of decency

...Displays open contempt for authority

...Insulting and abusive to others

...Unyielding to reason or rationale

...Without personal restraint or calmness

...Not open, honest in manner

...Unable to overcome personal problems

...Manipulates others to own end

Unfavorable Personality & Work Relationships (Levels 4-1)

...Becomes easily agitated and excited

...Lacks personal sincerity and believability

...Uncaring in reason or sympathy

...Abusive in language and action

...Bad in manner and disposition

...Will not go out of way to help others

...Personal behavior incompatible with good discipline

...Deliberately goes out of way to irritate others

...Subject to mood changes without warning

...Blunt and rude in speech and manner

...Thoughtless in considering feelings of others

...Personal problems demand excessive time of others

...Lacking in social grace and courtesy

...Careless of the feelings of others

...Unable to restrain or control emotions

...Behavior goes beyond the bounds of good taste

...Has personality clash with almost all co-workers

...Disagreeing personality dims spirit of others

...Discussions frequently turn into heated disputes

...Displays carefree and reckless abandon attitude

...Has great difficulty getting along with others

...Argumentative. Opposes all views other than own

Unfavorable Personality & Work Relationships (Levels 4-1)

...Stirs up discontent and resentment among others

...Inconsistent behavior, subject to sudden bursts of anger

...Takes uncompromising stand in even minor matters

...Does not always think through situations

...Lacks quality and depth of character

...Personal conduct prejudicial to good order

Want some new answers?
Ask someone else, not yourself.
From the book: **Successful Leadership Today**

It is human nature to want to be
recognized and rewarded for
special effort or achievement.
From the book: **Successful Leadership Today**

CHAPTER 14

PROBLEM SOLVING, MENTAL FACULTY, & JUDGMENT

(LEVELS 4-1)

Unfavorable Problem Solving, Mental Faculty, Judgement (Levels 4-1)

UNFAVORABLE PROBLEM SOLVING, MENTAL FACULTY & JUDGMENT

WORD BANK

NOTE: The words in this word bank, USED ALONE, describe UNFAVORABLE PERFORMANCE. When combined with other "qualifying" words, many of these words can be used to describe FAVORABLE PERFORMANCE.

EXAMPLE: DULL (UNFAVORABLE)
NEVER DULL (FAVORABLE)

Words listed in other word banks can similarly be used to describe FAVORABLE PERFORMANCE.

ABSENTMINDED	ARTLESS	CLEVERLESS
CONFUSE	CONFUSION	CONNIVE
CRASS	DENSE	DULL
FATHOMLESS	FEEBLEMINDED	FOOLISH
HALF-LEARNED	HALF-SCHOLAR	IGNORANCE
IGNORANT	ILLITERATE	ILLOGIC
ILLOGICAL	IMMATURE	IMMETHODICAL
IMPRACTICAL	IMPRUDENCE	IMPRUDENT
INANE	INCAPACITY	INCOGNIZANT
INCOHERENCE	INCOHERENT	
INCOMPREHENDABLE		INCOMPREHENSION
INCONCEIVABLE	INCONSEQUENT	INEDUCABLE
INEPT	INEPTITUDE	INEXPERIENCE
INEXPERTISE	INSENSIBILITY	INSENSIBLE
INSIGNIFICANT	INTELLECTUAL WEAKNESS	
IRRATIONAL	IRRATIONALITY	MEANINGLESS
MENTAL DEFICIENCY	MENTAL HANDICAP	MENTAL VOID
MENTAL WEAKNESS	MINDLESS	MISCALCULATE
MISCALCULATION	MISCONCEIVE	MISCONCEPTION
MISINTERPRET	MISJUDGE	MISJUDGMENT
MISTAKE	MISTAKEN	MISUNDERSTAND

MISUNDERSTANDING		MISUNDERSTOOD
NESCIENT	OBSCURE	OBTUSE
ONE-TRACK-MIND	ORDINARY	OVERSIGHT
PEDANT	RIDICULOUS	SENILE
SENILITY	SENSELESS	SHALLOW
SHALLOWNESS	SHORTSIGHTED	SIMPLE
SIMPLE-MINDED	SPECULATIVE	STUPID
STUPIDITY	SUPERFICIAL	SUPERFICIALITY
THICK	TRIFLING	UNACQUAINTED
UNAWARE	UNCERTAIN	UNCERTAINTY
UNCOMPREHENSIVE		UNCOMPREHENSIBLE
UNCONVERSANT	UNDISCERNING	UNEDUCABLE
UNENLIGHTENED	UNERUDITE	UNFAMILIAR
UNFATHOMABLE	UNINVENTIVE	UNIMAGINATIVE
UNINFORMATIVE	UNINFORMED	UNINQUISITIVE
UNINTELLIGENT	UNINTELLIGIBLE	UNKNOWING
UNKNOWLEDGEABLE	UNKNOWN	UNLEARNED
UNLETTERED	UNMINDFUL	UNPERCEPTIVE
UNREAD	UNREASONING	UNRECEPTIVE
UNRECOGNIZABLE	UNREFINED	UNSCHOLARLY
UNSCHOOLED	UNTAUGHT	UNTUTORED
UNVERSED	UNWISE	UNWITTING
UNWITTINGNESS	VACUOUS	WITLESS

Unfavorable Problem Solving, Mental Faculty, Judgement (Levels 4-1)

BULLET PHRASE STATEMENTS

Select a word in COLUMN 1 and add a word from COLUMN 2.

EXAMPLE: POOR JUDGMENT

COLUMN #1	**COLUMN #2**
	ARTISTIC IMAGINATION
BAD	CREATIVE ABILITY
DEFICIENT	CREATIVENESS
INADEQUATE	CREATIVE POWER
INFERIOR	DEDUCTIVE POWER
LACKING IN	IMAGINATION
LACK OF	INTEGRATIVE POWER
POOR	INTELLIGENCE
	JUDGMENT
	KNOWLEDGE
	MENTAL ALERTNESS
	MENTAL CAPACITY

"No great man ever complains of want
of opportunity." RALPH WALDO EMERSON
From the book: **Successful Leadership Today**

"By far the most valuable possession
is skill." HIPPARCHUS
From the book: **Successful Leadership Today**

Unfavorable Problem Solving, Mental Faculty, Judgement (Levels 4-1)

BULLET PHRASE STATEMENTS

...Intellectually deficient ...Unsound judgment

...Limited knowledge ...Little ingenuity

...Uninquisitive mind ...Mentally slow

...Bad judgment ...Shallow thinker

...Immature judgment ...Without foresight

...Immature mind ...Mentally malnourished

...Lacking in knowledge ...Serious judgment error

...Lack of curiosity ...Dull, unimaginative thinker

...Limited learning capacity ...Unreasoned thought process

...Not mentally alert ...Slow to act

...Lacks original thought process

...Cannot grasp all essentials

...Undisciplined sense of judgment

...Lacking in good judgment

...Limited problem solving abilities

...Not well organized mentally

...Lacks knowledge and ability

...Without orderly mental continuity

...Aimless, errant decision making facilities

...Lacks mental depth and soundness

...Unsophisticated reasoning and judgment equipment

...Negative mental attitude and outlook

304

Unfavorable Problem Solving, Mental Faculty, Judgement (Levels 4-1)

...Uninventive, relies on old ideas

...Does not explore new possibilities

...Fails to properly weigh facts

...Unable to grasp pertinent details quickly

...Finds it hard to retain detailed information

...Lacks good judgment and common sense

...Plans lack breadth, originality and substance

...Not clear in thought or reasoning

...Rigid thinking restricts ability to learn

...Slow to learn and develop professionally

Unfavorable Problem Solving, Mental Faculty, Judgement (Levels 4-1)

COMPLETE THE PHRASE

...Absentminded when it comes to (...)

...Gets confused when (...)

...Unable to comprehend (...)

...Has impractical ideas on (...)

...Incapable of (...)

...Inexperienced in (...)

...Subject to misjudgment when/if (...)

...Shortsighted in (...)

...Unaware of (...)

...Remains unfamiliar in (...)

...Unmindful in area(s) of (...)

...Unreceptive to (...)

...Below average ability to (...)

...Has mental void when (...)

...Routinely miscalculates (...)

...Has one-track-mind when (...)

...Too many cases of oversight when/if (...)

...Unacquainted in (...)

...Unknowledgeable of (...)

...Unable to understand (...)

...Below-par knowledge of (...)

Unfavorable Problem Solving, Mental Faculty, Judgement (Levels 4-1)

...Becomes confused when (...)

...Unversed in (...)

...Slow to comprehend (...)

...Uncertain in area(s) of (...)

...Frequently misinterprets (...)

...Makes routine mistakes when/in (...)

...Superficial knowledge of/in (...)

...Uninformed in (...)

...Unable to recognize (...)

Unfavorable Problem Solving, Mental Faculty, Judgement (Levels 4-1)

CHAPTER 15

LEADERSHIP, SUPERVISION, & MANAGEMENT

(LEVELS 4-1)

LEADERSHIP LEVELS

LEVELS 10-9
* Delegates responsibility successfully
* Promotes individual involvement and development
* Inspires self-improvement and high morale
* Inspires complete respect and confidence
* Maintains SUPERIOR rapport with others

LEVELS 8-7
* Delegates responsibility effectively
* Sincere concern for others
* Enjoys respect and confidence of others
* Maintains GOOD morale and rapport with others

LEVELS 6-5
* Influences others to work consistently and accurately
* USUALLY delegates responsibility effectively
* Maintains SATISFACTORY rapport with others

LEVELS 4-3
* DOES NOT delegate responsibility effectively
* Dictates activities to others
* Cannot maintain good morale
* Shows little concern for welfare of others

LEVELS 2-1
* RESTRICTS self-improvement of others
* FAILS to delegate responsibility properly
* AVOIDS others

Unfavorable Leadership, Supervision, & Management (Levels 4-1)

UNFAVORABLE LEADERSHIP, SUPERVISION & MANAGEMENT

WORD BANK

ADMINISTER
COMMAND
CONTROL
DICTATE
DIRECTION
GUIDANCE
IN CHARGE
LEADER
MANAGEMENT
OVERSEE
RULE
SUPERVISION

AUTHORITY
CONDUCT
CONTROLLER
DIRECT
GOVERN
HEAD
LEAD
MANAGE
OVERLOOK
PRESIDE
SUPERVISE

"Leadership is action
not position." DONALD McGANNON
From the book: **Successful Leadership Today**

TEAMWORK: Partnership in harmony.
From the book: **Successful Leadership Today**

BULLET PHRASE STATEMENTS

Select a word in COLUMN 1 and add the appropriate ending from COLUMN 2.

EXAMPLE: IMPERSONAL LEADER

COLUMN #1	COLUMN #2	
ABRASIVE	OVERBEARING	
ABRUPT	PESSIMISTIC	
ARROGANT	PRUDISH	
BIASED	RUDE	
CALLOUS	RUTHLESS	
COLORLESS	SELF-SERVING	
COMPLACENT	SHORTSIGHTED	LEADER
DISAGREEABLE	SHORT-TEMPERED	
DISCONTENT	SPIRITLESS	
DISCOURTEOUS	TACTLESS	
DISRESPECTFUL	TEMPERAMENTAL	
FAULTFINDING	THOUGHTLESS	LEADERSHIP
FINICKY	TIMID	
HARD-NOSED	UNASSERTIVE	
HEARTLESS	UNCONCERNED	
HIGH HANDED	UNCOOPERATIVE	
HIGH-STRUNG	UNDEPENDABLE	
HOT-TEMPERED	UNDISCIPLINED	MANAGER
IMPATIENT	UNFRIENDLY	
IMPERSONAL	UNGRACIOUS	
IMPOLITE	UNINSPIRED	
INARTICULATE	UNMINDFUL	SUPERVISOR
INATTENTIVE	UNPOLISHED	
INCONSIDERATE	UNPOPULAR	
INDECISIVE	UNPREDICTABLE	
INSINCERE	UNPRINCIPLED	
IRRATIONAL	UNREALISTIC	
JOYLESS	UNREASONABLE	
KNOW-IT-ALL	UNSCRUPULOUS	
MANNERLESS	UNSOCIAL	
NAIVE	UNSTABLE	
OFFENSIVE		

Unfavorable Leadership, Supervision, & Management (Levels 4-1)

Select a word in COLUMN 1 and add the appropriate ending from COLUMN 2.

EXAMPLE: THOUGHTLESS LEADER

COLUMN #1   **COLUMN #2**

AIMLESS   LAX
CARELESS   LIFELESS
CRUDE   NEGLECTFUL
DEFECTIVE   NONPRODUCTIVE
DISAPPOINTING   OUT-OF-DATE
DISGRACEFUL   PROBLEM
DISORDERLY   SLUGGISH
ERRATIC   SUBSTANDARD   LEADER
FAULTY   THOUGHTLESS
FLAWED   UNCONCERNED   LEADERSHIP
FRUITLESS   UNCOOPERATIVE
HELPLESS   UNDEPENDABLE   MANAGER
IDLE   UNOBSERVANT
IMPOTENT   UNORGANIZED   SUPERVISOR
INADEQUATE   UNPREDICTABLE
INCOMPETENT   UNPROFESSIONAL
INCONSIDERATE   UNRESOURCEFUL
INCONSISTENT   UNRESPONSIVE
INEFFECTIVE   UNRELIABLE
INEFFICIENT   UNSKILLED
INEXPERIENCED   UNSUCCESSFUL
INFERIOR   WEAK
LACKLUSTER

Good thoughts about an individual
do no good unless expressed.
From the book: **Successful Leadership Today**

Unfavorable Leadership, Supervision, & Management (Levels 4-1)

BULLET PHRASE STATEMENTS

...Unsound management practices

...Unforgiving leadership traits

...Improper counseling techniques

...Inflexible, unimaginative leadership

...Non-compassionate, harsh leader

...Plagued by indecisiveness

...Mechanical, non-inventive leadership

...Weak, inadequate leader

...Indecisive and evasive

...Dull, uninspiring leader

...Weak, ineffective manager

...Spiritless, lifeless supervisor

...Weak, vacillating leadership

...Ineffective leadership skills

...Inflexible, rigid taskmaster

...Doubtful, confusing leadership

...Mundane, methodical leadership

...Gives misguided directions

...Uses questionable leadership

...Impersonal, detached leader

...Poor planner. Great hindsight

...Has difficulty managing paperwork

...Overly demanding and self-assertive

...Sometimes impatient with subordinates

...Insensitive and callous leadership

...Incapable of compassionate leadership

...Not an inspiring leader

...Not a potent, effective leader

...Gets less than desired results

...Oppressive in character and action

...Organization lacks order and cohesiveness

...Excessively lenient in handling others

...Neglects personal welfare of others

...Too easily influenced by others

...Produces less than desired results

...Leadership style leaves uneasy feeling

...Fails to properly supervise others

...Decisions are open to question

...Frequently reverses point of view or attitude

...Does not always consider gravity of situation at hand

...Does not seek, and reluctantly accepts, any responsibility

Unfavorable Leadership, Supervision, & Management (Levels 4-1)

...Frequently displays immaturity and bad judgment

...Not aggressive in meeting established goals

...Accommodating to others' desires to a fault

...Condemns or shuns thoughts and ideas of others

...Unable to cope with difficult situations without assistance

...Becomes bogged down in petty, insignificant details

...Helpless in meeting new situations without direct guidance

...Inclined to berate others when they fail to meet perfectionist standards

...Preoccupation with minor details impairs soundness of judgment

...Requires routine guidance in determining that which is major and that which is minor in importance

...Reluctant to make decisions in major matters within scope of responsibility

...Relies too heavily on others for guidance and direction

...Accepts recommendations of others with little or no analysis

...Makes decisions that are not sensible or prudent

...Acts out of emotion, not reason

...Wasteful and extravagant use of resources

...Unforeseen and unplanned problems routinely arise

...Displays no rational or orderly planning process

...Proposed plans and actions riddled with paradox

...Exerts undue influence and pressure on others

...Rubs a mistake in, not out

...Organization out of kilter and does not have sense of direction

...Does not provide a personal touch to leadership

...Can't make proper decisions under pressure

...Sometimes overbearing and overly intolerant of mistakes

...Not firm and resolute with others

...Treatment of others less than desired and expected

...Unconventional and unorthodox style of leadership

...Harsh and abrasive in leadership style and language

...Abusive language and improper treatment routinely evidenced

...Leadership and guidance lacks substance and purpose

...Improper leadership taking its toll on effectiveness

...Plagued by lack of self-confidence and positive leadership

...Assigns work but does not follow-up

...Leadership ability is questionable at best

...Fails to achieve minimum acceptable performance

...Unfair and inequitable in treatment of others

...Too submissive to be an effective leader

...A bad leader and a worse follower

...Overly harsh and critical of minor mistakes

...Not a strong leader. Too permissive and lenient

Unfavorable Leadership, Supervision, & Management (Levels 4-1)

...Lacks necessary personal traits to be a successful leader

...Fails to maintain harmony and cohesiveness

...Policies are not uniform and consistent

...Able to receive only half-effort of others

...Does not exhibit a knack for making positive things happen

...Fails to monitor work of others

Frequent verbal support from
seniors is a great motivator.
From the book: **Successful Leadership Today**

CHAPTER 16

SELF-EXPRESSION & COMMUNICATION SKILLS

(LEVELS 4-1)

SELF-EXPRESSION

LEVELS 10-9
* Commands large vocabulary
* Submits flawless written products
* Projects ideas in most straightforward, comprehensive manner

LEVELS 8-7
* Good command of English language
* ABLE to translate thoughts into clear, understandable sentences
* Submits written work in timely manner

LEVELS 6-5
* Average command of English language
* Neat, accurate correspondence
* Gets point across
* Able to prepare routine reports

LEVELS 4-3
* Limited vocabulary
* CANNOT get meaning across in concise, organized means on paper

LEVELS 2-1
* POOR USE of English grammar and composition
* VERY LIMITED vocabulary

Unfavorable Self-Expression & Communication Skills (Levels 4-1)

UNFAVORABLE SELF-EXPRESSION AND COMMUNICATION SKILLS

DEFINITIONS

ACCENTUATE	To highlight or emphasize something.
ARTICULATE	Express oneself effectively.
CLARITY	Being clear.
CLEAR	Easily understood.
COHERENT	Logically consistent.
COMMUNICATE	Convey something to another.
CONCISE	Brief and to the point.
CONVERSATIONALIST	One who excels in conversation.
CONVERSE	Exchange thoughts through speech.
CONVEY	To communicate to another.
DICTION	Verbally express in clear, correct manner.
EDIT	Adhere to written acceptance or standard.
ELOQUENT	Fluent expression.
ENUNCIATE	Speak articulate words.
EXPOUND	Cover something in detail.
EXPRESS	To make something known in words.
FLUENT	Speak or write with ease.
GRAPHIC	Clear and lively description.
IMPART	Communicate to another.
LINGUAL	Articulated speech.
LINGUIST	One who speaks more than one language.
LINGUISTIC	Language.
ORATOR	A skilled public speaker.
PRONOUNCE	To articulate words.
SUCCINCT	Express without useless words.
SELF-EXPRESSION	Express oneself.
TERSE	Brief, smooth and elegant expression.
VERBAL	Speech or talk.
VIVID	Sharp, clear impression.
VOCABULARY	Total words used or known.

A leader inspires and motivates
people toward a common purpose.
From the book: **Successful Leadership Today**

318

BULLET PHRASE STATEMENTS

Select a phrase in COLUMN 1 that matches the desired words in COLUMN 2 and COLUMN 3.

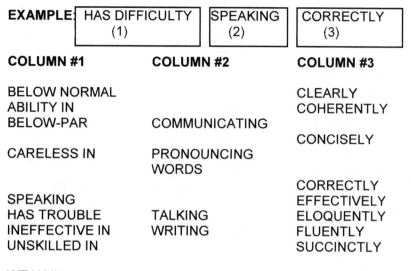

EXAMPLE: | HAS DIFFICULTY (1) | SPEAKING (2) | CORRECTLY (3) |

COLUMN #1 **COLUMN #2** **COLUMN #3**

COLUMN #1	COLUMN #2	COLUMN #3
BELOW NORMAL ABILITY IN BELOW-PAR	COMMUNICATING	CLEARLY COHERENTLY CONCISELY
CARELESS IN	PRONOUNCING WORDS	
SPEAKING HAS TROUBLE INEFFECTIVE IN UNSKILLED IN	TALKING WRITING	CORRECTLY EFFECTIVELY ELOQUENTLY FLUENTLY SUCCINCTLY
WEAK IN		

Select a word in COLUMN 2 and COLUMN 4 that fits in with the words in COLUMN 1 and COLUMN 3.

EXAMPLE: | NOT (1) | ARTICULATE (2) | IN (3) | SPEECH (4) |

COLUMN #1	COLUMN #2	COLUMN #3	COLUMN #4
NOT		IN	
	ARTICULATE		THE ENGLISH LANGUAGE
	CLEAR		GRAMMAR
	COHERENT		ORAL EXPRESSION
	CONCISE		SELF-EXPRESSION
	ELOQUENT		SPEAKING
	FLUENT		SPEECH
	GRAPHIC		THE SPOKEN WORD
	SUCCINCT		THE WRITTEN WORD
	TERSE		WRITING
			WRITTEN FORM

Unfavorable Self-Expression & Communication Skills (Levels 4-1)

Select one or two words in COLUMN 1 and add the appropriate ending with a word from COLUMN 2.

EXAMPLE: INADEQUATE SPEAKER

COLUMN #1   COLUMN #2

BASHFUL	INEXPERIENCED
ABRASIVE	INSENSITIVE
AMBIGUOUS	LACKADAISICAL
ARROGANT	LIFELESS
BELOW AVERAGE	MANNERLESS
BELOW-PAR	OBNOXIOUS
CARELESS	OFFENSIVE
COLORLESS	REDUNDANT CONVERSATIONALIST
CRUDE	SARCASTIC
DISTASTEFUL	SECOND-RATE ORATOR
FLAWED	SLUGGISH
HUMORLESS	SPIRITLESS PUBLIC SPEAKER
ILL-MANNERED	SUBSTANDARD
IMPERFECT	TACTLESS
IMPOLITE	UNCERTAIN
IMPOTENT	UNDISTINGUISHED SPEAKER
INADEQUATE	UNPROFESSIONAL
INARTICULATE	UNRESPONSIBLE
INCOMPETENT	UNSEASONED
INEFFECTIVE	UNSKILLED

"No matter what may be the ability of
the officer, if he loses the confidence
of his troops, disaster must sooner
or later ensue." GENERAL ROBERT E. LEE
From the book: **Successful Leadership Today**

Unfavorable Self-Expression & Communication Skills (Levels 4-1)

CHAPTER 17

UNFAVORABLE THESAURUS

(LEVELS 4-1)

UNFAVORABLE THESAURUS

A

ABASE	ABERRANT	ABHORRENT
ABNORMAL	ABRASIVE	ABRUPT
ABSENTMINDED	ABSURD	ABUSE
ABUSIVE	ACCOST	ADVERSARY
ADVERSE	ADVERSITY	AGITATE
AGITATOR	AGONY	ALOOF
ALTERCATION	AMISS	AMOK
ANTAGONIST	ANTAGONISTIC	ANTAGONIZE
ANTISOCIAL	APLOMB	APPALL
APPALLING	ARGUMENTATIVE	ARROGANCE
ARROGANT	ARTLESS	ASKEW
AUDACIOUS	AUDACITY	AWKWARD
AWRY		

B

BACKWARD	BAD-TEMPERED	BEGRUDGE
BELLIGERENCE	BELLIGERENT	BERATE
BERSERK	BETRAY	BIAS
BIASED	BLUNDER	BLUNT
BOASTFUL	BOISTEROUS	BOTCH
BRAG	BRAGGER	BRASH
BRASSY	BREAKDOWN	BROW BEAT
BRUSQUE	BUNGLE	BUNGLING

321

C

CAPTIOUS
CENSURE
CHAOTIC
CHEAT
CLEVERNESS
COCKSURE
COLD
COMPLAINING
CONCEIT
CONDESCEND
CONDESCENDING
CONFRONT
CONFUSION
CONSPIRE
CONTRADICTORY
CONTROVERT
CORRUPTION
CRAFTY
CRISIS
CRUEL
CUNNING

CATASTROPHE
CHAGRIN
CHARADE
CHEATER
CONFUSE(D)
COCKY
COLLAPSE
COMPULSIVE
CONCEITED
CONDESCENDENCE
CONFLICT
CONFUSE
CONFUTE
CONTEMPT
CONTRITE
CORRUPT
COVER-UP
CRANKY
CRITICISM
CRUELTY
CURT

CAUSTIC
CHAOS
CHASTISE
CIRCUMVENT
CONFUSION
COERCE
COLORLESS
CONCEAL
CONDEMN

CONFLICTING
CONFUSED
CONNIVE
CONTEMPTIBLE
CONTROVERSY
CORRUPTIBLE
CRAFTINESS
CRASS
CRITICIZE
CRUSTY
CYNICAL

D

DAUNT
DECEITFUL
DECEPTION
DEFRAUD
DEFIANT
DEGRADE
DELUGE
DEMERIT
DENOUNCE
DEPENDENT
DEPRESSED
DERELICT
DESPAIR
DESPISE

DAUNTLESS
DECEIVE
DEFEATIST
DEFECTIVE
DEFICIENCY
DEGRADATION
DELUSION
DEMISE
DENSE
DEPERSONALIZE
DEPRESSING
DERELICTION
DESPAIRING
DESPITE

DECEIT
DECEIVER
DEFECTIVE
DEFIANCE
DEFICIENT
DELUDE
DEMEAN
DEMORALIZE
DEPENDENCE
DEPLORE
DEPRIVE
DEROGATORY
DESPERATE
DESPITEFUL

Unfavorable Thesaurus (Levels 4-1)

DESPOND	DESPONDENCY	DEPLORABLE
DESPONDENT	DESTROY	DESTRUCT
DESTRUCTION	DESTRUCTIVE	DETRIMENTAL
DEVIANT	DEVIATE	DEVIOUS
DIEHARD	DIRE	DISACCORD
DISADVANTAGE	DISAGREE	DISAGREEMENT
DISAPPOINT	DISAPPOINTING	DISAPPOINTMENT
DISASTER	DISASTROUS	DISBELIEF
DISCORD	DISCREDIT	DISDAIN
DISDAINFUL	DISGRACE	DISGRACEFUL
DISGRUNTLE	DISGUST	DISHEARTEN
DISHONEST	DISHONESTY	DISHONOR
DISLOYAL	DISLOYALTY	DISMAY
DISOBEDIENCE	DISOBEDIENT	DISOBEY
DISPASSIONATE	DISPUTE	DISREGARD
DISREPUTABLE	DISREPUTE	DISRESPECT
DISRESPECTFUL	DISRUPTIVE	DISSENSION
DOGMATIC	DOWNFALL	DREADFUL
DULL	DURESS	

E

EBB	EFFETE	EGOCENTRIC
EGOISM	EGOIST	EGOTISM
EGOTISTIC	EGREGIOUS	EMBITTER
EMPTY	ENERVATE	ENIGMA
ENMITY	ENRAGE	EQUIVOCATE
ERADICATE	ERR	ERROR
EXACERBATE	EXAGGERATE	EXANIMATE
EXCESSIVE	EXCITABLE	EXCUSE
EXORBITANCE	EXORBITANT	EXTRANEOUS
EXTRAVAGANT	EXTREME	EYESORE

F

FACETIOUS	FAIL	FAILED
FAILURE	FAKE	FALLIBLE
FALSE	FALSEHOOD	FALSIFY
FALSITY	FARCICAL	FASTIDIOUS
FATHOMLESS	FAULT	FAULTFINDING

323

FAULTY	FAVORITISM	FEARFUL
FEEBLE	FEEBLEMINDED	FEUD
FIASCO	FICTION	FICTITIOUS
FINAGLE	FLAGRANT	FLAUNT
FLAUNTY	FLAWED	FLIPPANT
FLOP	FLOPPISH	FLOUT
FLUNK	FOPPISH	FORBIDDING
FORESTALL	FORFEIT	FOUL-UP
FLOUNDER	FRACAS	FRACTIOUS
FRANTIC	FRAUD	FRAUDULENT
FRENZY	FRUITLESS	FUMBLE
FURIOUS	FUROR	FURY
FUTILE	FUTILITY	

G

GALL	GALLING	GAMESMANSHIP
GAUCHE	GIMMICK	GLARING
GLOOM	GLOOMY	GOOD-FOR-NOTHING
GRANDEUR	GRANDIOSE	GRAVE
GRIEVOUS	GRIEVE	GRIM
GRIMACE	GRIPE	GROSS
GROUSE	GRUDGE	GUILELESS
GUISE		

H

HABITUAL	HALF-LEARNED	HARASS
HARD-AND-FAST	HARDHANDED	HARDHEADED
HARD-HEARTED	HARD-NOSED	HARMFUL
HARD PUT	HARD-SET	HARD-SHELL
HARDSHIP	HARM	HARSH
HATRED	HAZARDOUS	HEARTLESS
HEAVY-HANDED	HEEDLESS	HELPLESS
HIDEOUS	HIGH HANDED	HIGH-STRUNG
HIGH-TONED	HOPELESS	HORRENDOUS
HOSTILE	HOSTILITY	HOT-TEMPERED
HUMILIATE	HUMILIATING	HURRIED
HURTFUL	HYPER	HYPERCRITICAL
HYSTERIA	HYSTERICAL	

324

I

IGNORANCE IGNORANT ILL-BEHAVED
ILL-DISPOSED ILLEGAL ILLEGIBLE
ILL-FATED ILL-GOTTEN ILLICIT
ILLITERACY ILLITERATE ILL-NATURED
ILL-TEMPERED IMMORAL IMPERIL
IMPERIOUS IMPETUOUS IMPIOUS
IMPOSSIBLE IMPOSSIBILITY IMPROPER
IMPROPRIETY IMPUDENT INANE
INAPT INEPTNESS INCAPABLE
INCAPACITATE INCAPACITY INCOGNIZANT
INCOHERENCE INCOHERENT INCOMPARABLE
INCOMPATIBILITY INCOMPATIBLE INCOMPETENCE
INCOMPETENT INCOMPREHENDABLE
INCOMPREHENSIBLE INCOMPREHENSION
INCONCEIVABLE INCONSIDERATE INCORRECT
INCORRECTLY INCORRIGIBLE INCORRUPTION
INDEFENSIBLE INDEFINABLE INEXPERTISE
INDIGNANT INDIGNATION INDIGNITY
INDISCIPLINE INDURATE INEDUCABLE
INTELLIGIBLE INEPT INEPTITUDE
INEQUALITY INEXCUSABLE INEXPERIENCED
INFLAME INFLEXIBLE INFURIATE
INGRATITUDE INHOSPITABLE INHUMANE
INIMICAL INEQUITY INJUDICIOUS
INJURE INJUSTICE INORDINATE
INSENSIBILITY INSENSIBLE INSENSITIVE
INSIDIOUS INSINCERE INSINCERITY
INSOLENCE INSOLENT INSUBORDINATE
INSUFFERABLE INSULT INSUPERABLE
INSURGENT INSURMOUNTABLE
INTELLECTUAL WEAKNESS INTERCEDE
INTIMIDATE INTIMIDATING INTOLERABLE
INTOLERANCE INTOLERANT INTRACTABLE
INTRANSIGENT INVALID INVALIDITY
INVECTIVE INVEIGH INVOLUNTARY
IRATE IRE IRRATIONAL
IRRATIONALITY IRREDEEMABLE IRREFORMABLE
IRRELATIVE IRRELEVANT IRREPRESSIBLE
IRRESPONSIBLE IRRESPONSIVE IRREVERENCE
IRRITABLE IRRITATE IRRITATING

Unfavorable Thesaurus (Levels 4-1)

J

JABBER   JEALOUS   JEALOUSY
JOYLESS

K

KINDLESS   KLUTZ   KNOW-IT-ALL
KNUCKLE UNDER

L

LAST	LAST-DITCH	LAZY
LIFELESS	LOATH	LOATHE
LOATHING	LOATHSOME	LOFTY
LOOK DOWN	LOQUACIOUS	LOSER
LOSS	LOST	LUDICROUS

M

MALADJUSTED	MALADROIT	MALEVOLENCE
MALEVOLENT	MALFEASANCE	MALFUNCTION
MALICE	MALICIOUS	MANNERLESS
MEANINGLESS	MENACE	MENTAL DEFICIENCY
MENTAL HANDICAP	MENTAL VOID	MERCILESS
MINDLESS	MISAPPLY	MISBECOME
MISBEHAVIOR	MISCHIEF	MISCALCULATE
MISCALCULATION	MISCONCEIVE	MISCONCEPTION
MISCONDUCT	MISERABLE	MISFIT
MISHANDLE	MISINFORM	MISINTERPRET
MISJUDGE	MISJUDGMENT	MISLEAD
MISMANAGE	MISPRONOUNCE	MISQUOTE
MISREAD	MISTAKE	MISTAKEN
MISTRUST	MISUSE	MOROSE
MUDDLE	MUMBLE	

Unfavorable Thesaurus (Levels 4-1)

N

NEGATE   NEGATIVE   NEGLECT
NEGLECTFUL   NEGLIGENCE   NEGLIGENT
NEGLIGIBLE   NERVELESS   NOISY
NONPRODUCTIVE   NONSENSE   NAUGHT

O

OBNOXIOUS   OBSCURITY   OBSESSION
OBSOLETE   OBSTACLE   OBSTINATE
OBSTRUCTION   ODD   ODDITY
OFFEND   OFFENSIVE   ONE-TRACK-MIND
ONE-UPMANSHIP   ONE-WAY   OBSEQUIOUS
OBSTRUCTIVE   OPINIONATED   OPPOSED
OPPOSITION   OPPRESS   OPPRESSIVE
OSTRACIZE   OUST   OUTBURST
OUTCAST   OUTLANDISH   OUTRAGE
OUTRAGEOUS   OUTSPOKEN   OVERBEARING
OVERLOOK

P

PALL   PANIC   PARANOID
PARLOUS   PATHETIC   PATRONIZE
PECCANT   PENDANT   PENITENT
PENSIVE   PERFUNCTORY   PERSECUTE
PERT   PERTINACIOUS   PERTINACITY
PERTURB   PETULANT   PILFER
PITFALL   PITIFUL   PITILESS
PITY   POLEMIC   POMPOSITY
POMPOUS   POOR   PORTENTOUS
PRECARIOUS   PREJUDICE   PREJUDICED
PREJUDICIAL   PROBLEM   PROVOCATIVE
PROVOKE   PROVOKING   PRUDE
PRUDISH   PRY   PRYING
PUGNACIOUS   PUNDIT   PURPOSELESS

327

Q

QUARREL	QUARRELSOME	QUIT
QUITTER		

R

RAGE	RAMPAGE	REASONLESS
REBELLIOUS	REBUFF	REBUKE
REBUT	REFUSAL	REFUSE
REFUTE	REGRET	REGRETFUL
REJECT	RELAPSE	REMISS
REMORSE	REMORSEFUL	REMORSELESS
RENOUNCE	REPREHEND	REPREHENSIBLE
REPRIMAND	REPROACH	REPROBATE
REPUDIATE	REPUGN	REPUGNANCE
REPULSE	REPULSION	REPULSIVE
RESENT	RESENTFUL	RESENTMENT
RESTRAIN	RESTRAINT	RETARD
REVOLTING	RIDICULOUS	RISKY
RIVAL	RIVALRY	RUDE
RUIN	RUN-DOWN	RUTHLESS

S

SACRIFICE	SARCASM	SARCASTIC
SAUCY	SCANDALOUS	SCAPEGOAT
SCOFF	SCORN	SCORNFUL
SCRUPLE	SCRUTABLE	SECOND-GUESS
SECOND-RATE	SELF-CENTERED	SELF-CONSCIOUS
SELF-DEFEATING	SELF-IMPORTANT	
SELF-INDULGENCE	SELFISH	
SELF-OPINIONATED	SELF-RIGHTEOUS	
SELF-SEEKING	SENILE	SENILITY
SENSELESS	SEVERE	SEVERITY
SHAM	SHAMEFUL	SHAMELESS

328

SHARP-TONGUED	SHIFTLESS	SHIFTY
SHODDY	SHORT-TEMPERED	SIMPLE
SIMPLENESS	SIMPLISTIC	SLOPPY
SLOPWORK	SLOVEN	SLOVENLY
SLUGGISH	SLY	SMALL
SMEAR	SMIRK	SMUG
SNIDE	SNUB	SNUFFY
SOFTHEARTED	SKEW	SORROW
SORROWFUL	SPEECHLESS	SPITE
SPITEFUL	SPURIOUS	SPURN
SQUANDER	STODGY	STRICT
STRINGENT	STUPEFY	STUPID
STUPIDITY	STUPOR	SUBNORMAL
SUBSTANDARD	SUFFER	SULLEN
SUPERCILIOUS	SURLY	SURVIVE
SWAY		

T

TACTLESS	TASKMASTER	TEDIUM
TEMERITY	TEMPTATION	TEPID
THANKLESS	THICK	THOUGHTLESS
THRIFTLESS	THWART	TORMENT
TRANSGRESS	TRAVESTY	TRICKY
TRITE	TROUBLE	TROUBLEMAKER
TROUBLESOME	TRUANT	TURBULENT
TURMOIL	TRUSTLESS	

U

UNABLE	UNACCOMPLISHED	
UNACQUAINTED	UNADVISED	UNAMBITIOUS
UNAPT	UNARTISTIC	UNASPIRING
UNASSERTIVE	UNAWARE	UNBENDING
UNCHARITABLE	UNCIVIL	UNCOMPLETED
UNCOMPROMISING	UNCOMPREHENSIBLE	
UNCOMPREHENSIVE	UNCONTROLLABLE	
UNCONVERSANT	UNCOOPERATIVE	UNCOURTEOUS
UNCULTURED	UNDENIABLE	UNDEPENDABLE
UNDERHANDED	UNDERMINE	UNDERSTUDY

UNDIGNIFIED	UNDESIRABLE	UNDISCERNING
UNDISCIPLINED	UNDISTINGUISHED	UNEDUCABLE
UNEDUCATED	UNENLIGHTENED	UNERUDITE
UNFAIR	UNFAITHFUL	UNFATHOMABLE
UNFAVORABLE	UNFEELING	UNFINISHED
UNFIT	UNFORTUNATE	UNFRIENDLY
UNGRACEFUL	UNGRACIOUS	UNHAPPY
UNINFORMATIVE	UNINFORMED	UNINSPIRED
UNINTELLIGENT	UNINQUISITIVE	UNINVENTIVE
UNINTELLECT	UNINTELLECTUAL	UNINTELLIGIBLE
UNKIND	UNKINDLY	UNKNOWING
UNKNOWLEDGEABLE	UNKNOWN	UNLAWFUL
UNLEARNED	UNLETTERED	UNMANAGEABLE
UNMERCIFUL	UNNERVE	UNOBSERVANT
UNPERCEPTIVE	UNPERCEPTIVENESS	
UNPLEASANT	UNPOLISHED	UNPOPULAR
UNPREDICTABLE	UNPRINCIPLED	UNPROFESSIONAL
UNREAD	UNREADY	UNREASON
UNREASONABLE	UNREASONING	UNRECEPTIVE
UNRECOGNIZABLE	UNSCHOOLED	UNSKILLED
UNSKILLFUL	UNSOCIABLE	UNSOCIAL
UNSOUND	UNSTUDIED	UNTRUSTWORTHY
UNSUCCESSFUL	UNSUITABLE	UNTAUGHT
UNTIDY	UNTRUE	UNTRUTH
UNTRUTHFUL	UNTUTORED	UNVERSED
UNWILLING	UNWISE	UNWITTING
UNWITTINGNESS	UNYIELDING	USELESS
USURP		

V

VACUOUS	VAIN	VALUELESS
VENDETTA	VENGEANCE	VENGEFUL
VERBALISM	VEX	VICE
VICTIMIZE	VINDICTIVE	VIOLATE
VIOLATION	VIOLENCE	VIOLENT
VITIATE		

330

WANGLE	WANTING	WANTON
WASHED-UP	WASTE	WASTED
WASTEFUL	WEAR OUT	WILE
WILL-LESS	WISHY-WASHY	WITLESS
WORRISOME	WORRY	WORSE
WORSEN	WORST	WORTHLESS
WRECK	WRETCH	WRETCHED
WRONG	WRONGDOER	WRONGDOING
WRONGFUL	WROTH	WRY

"The wise are instructed by reason;
ordinary minds by experience;
the stupid, by necessity;
and brutes by instinct." CICERO
From the book: **Successful Leadership Today**

"Before everything else,
getting ready is the
secret of success." HENRY FORD
From the book: **Successful Leadership Today**

CHAPTER 18

PHRASE, THOUGHT, IDEA, OR IDIOM

The material in this section is intended for use in a
variety of communication methods

Abandoned normal path

Abandoned traditional

Aberration

Able to size up

Able-bodied

About-face

Above and beyond

Above board

Abrasive

Abreast of the times

Abrupt

Absolute confidence

Absolute dedication

Absolute faith in

Absolutely committed to

Absolutely essential

Absorbed in

Abundance of

Accelerated change

Accepted challenge

Accepted responsibility

According to circumstances

Ace in hole

Achieved greatness

Acquainted with success

Across the board

Acted in concert

Acted prudently

Acted swiftly

Action not reaction

Active role

Active support(er)

Actively engaged in

Actively promoted

Acute sense of

Acutely aware

Acutely sensitive to	Adamant in stand
Add fuel to the flame	Added extra dimension
Added value(s)	Address needs of
Addressed issue(s)	Addressed the question
Admired character	Adolescent
Adopt a course	Advanced idea
Advanced state of	Adversity
Advocate for	Afflicted with
Against all odds	Against backdrop of
Against the grain	Aggravated already bad
Aggressive agenda	Aggressively enforced
Agonizing decision	Ahead of times
Alert to possibilities	Alienated others
Alive with	All-out effort
Altercation with	Always eager to
Always gives 110 percent	Amassed abundance of
Amazing speed	Ambitious campaign
Ambitious initiatives/progress	Amid changing scene of
Among the best	Analyzed various elements
Anemic	Angry tone
Answerable to/for	Antagonistic

333

Phrase, Thought, Idea, or Idiom

Anti-establishment

Apathy

Appease(s) others

Applaud efforts of

Appreciates hard work

Arm in arm

Around-the-clock

Articulate(d) new image

Ascended to

Asleep at the switch

Aspiring newcomer

At arm's length

At face value

At forefront

At pinnacle

At-all-cost

Atmosphere not conducive

Attracts followers

Avalanche of evidence

Award-winning

Awful consequences

Any number of

Apparent hostility

Appetite for

Appreciate uniqueness of'

Architect of

Arm-twisting

Arouses

As general rule

Asks too little

Aspire to excellence

Assessment of situation

At crossroads

At fingertips

At odds with

At risk

Atmosphere conducive to

Attention to detail

Attuned to needs

Awakened spirit(s) of

Away from mainstream

Awkward position

Phrase, Thought, Idea, or Idiom

Awkward situation	Ax to grind
Back away from	Back to the wall
Backbone	Backlash
Backward	Bad dream/side
Bad timing	Bad to worse
Badly damaged	Bail out
Ball of fire	Bang up job
Bank on it	Barely missed a beat
Barren waste land of	Beacon of hope
Bear down	Bear out
Bear responsibility	Bear the burden
Beat all odds	Beat the drum
Became focal point	Became symbol for/to
Bedrock	Beef up
Beehive of activity	Began to take form/shape
Begin to unravel	Beginning to end
Behind closed doors	Behind the scene(s)
Believability	Belligerent action
Benchmark	Bend over backwards
Beneficial to	Benefit of doubt
Benefits from understanding	Best foot forward

Phrase, Thought, Idea, or Idiom

Best interest of	Best kept secret
Best tradition	Better late than never
Better prepared	Between the lines
Bewildered	Beyond a doubt
Beyond comprehension	Beyond remedy/repair
Bicker(ing)	Big time
Bigger than life	Bit by bit
Bit of drama arose	Bits and pieces
Bitter end	Bitter failure
Bitter pill	Bitter struggle
Bitter-sweet	Black balled
Black day	Blacklist
Blatant violation	Blazed new trail
Bleak, uncertain future	Blemished record
Blessed with	Blissful ignorance
Blistering pace	Blue-chip
Blue-ribbon	Body of evidence/work
Bogged down in	Bold arrogance
Bold new/move	Bomb shell
Boosted spirits	Borderline
Bottleneck	Bottom line

Phrase, Thought, Idea, or Idiom

Bottom of the barrel

Boundaries of fairness

Bowed to pressure(s)

Brain trust

Brainstorm

Break down in

Break new ground

Breaking point

Breakneck speed

Breath of fresh air

Breeding ground for

Bright and perceptive

Bright future

Bring into focus

Bring up the rear

Broad consensus

Broad stroke

Broke back of

Broken will

Brought forces to bear

Brought under control

Bought into focus

Bouts of depression

Boyish excitement

Brainchild

Brazen attitude

Break faith

Break through

Break-neck pace

Breakthrough

Breathed new life

Bridged the gap

Bright chapter/future

Brighten the day

Bring into line

Brink of success/collapse

Broad expectations

Broader understanding

Broke resolve

Brought about/out

Brought to life

Brush up on

337

Phrase, Thought, Idea, or Idiom

Brush with disaster

Build a fire under

Build(t) a fire under

Bulldog determination

Burn out

Burst of creativity

Business at hand

Business-like

Calculated risk

Call(ed) the signal(s)

Callused

Came crashing down

Came of age

Came to aid of

Came to fruition

Came to terms with

Can't miss

Captivated by

Captured mood

Career defined by

Carefully engineered

Brutal shock

Build bridges

Building blocks

Buried in depression

Burning desire

Bursting with

Business end of

By the book

Calculated risk/response

Called upon to

Calm authority

Came full circle

Came prepared

Came to an understanding

Came to regret

Came up short

Capitalized on

Captured imagination

Captured the advantage

Carefree

Carefully planned

Phrase, Thought, Idea, or Idiom

Careless act	Cares deeply
Cares little for	Carried forward
Carrot and stick	Carry through
Carry(ied) the ball	Carry(ies) weight
Cast a bond	Cast a doubt
Cast adrift	Cast aside
Cast doubt on	Cast light upon
Cast shadow of doubt	Cast shadow over
Catalyst of/for	Catastrophe
Catastrophic blow	Catch fire
Caught flat-footed	Caught red-handed
Caused a backlash	Cautiously optimistic
Cemented relationships	Centerpiece
Certain curiosity	Chain of events
Chain reaction	Chalk up success(es)
Challenge of change	Challenges conventional ideas
Challenges(d) status quo	Challenging opportunity(ies)
Challenging task(s)	Champion(s) cause(s)
Championed efforts to	Championing innovation
Chance to carry on	Change of the guard
Changed course of	Changed face of

Phrase, Thought, Idea, or Idiom

Changing climate of	Changing times
Chaotic	Character and grace
Characteristic enthusiasm	Characterized by
Charged ahead	Charisma
Charismatic	Charted course
Checkered performance	Cherished idea of
Choice of values	Choked growth
Choked off inspiration	Choose to ignore
Circumvent	Clamp down on
Clarity of purpose	Class act
Classic example	Clean and quick
Clean slate	Clean sweep
Cleaned up problems	Cleaned up real mess
Clear agenda	Clear as day
Clear picture	Clear vision
Cleared the path	Clearly articulated
Clever idea(s)	Climate of
Climbed to top	Close brush with
Close cooperation	Close knit group
Close scrutiny	Close(d) ranks
Closed the door	Clouded by/issue

Phrase, Thought, Idea, or Idiom

Coalition building	Cocky optimism
Cohesive group	Cold analysis
Cold feet	Collective influence
Collision course	Colorful style
Colossal mess	Come alive
Come full circle	Come to a head
Come to grips with	Comfort level
Commands attention	Commit to memory
Commitment to course of action	Commitment to future
Committed to	Common cause
Common effort	Common enemy
Compassionate response	Compelling evidence
Compelling reasons	Competitive spirit/edge
Complacency set in	Complete disarray
Complete failure/success	Complete turnaround
Compounded by	Compounded situation
Con artist	Concept became reality
Concrete benefits	Concrete form
Concrete ideas	Concrete support
Confidence builder	Confidence restored
Confidence shattered	Confining barrier(s)
Conflict of interest	Confronted challenge(s)

341

Phrase, Thought, Idea, or Idiom

Confuse issue

Connects with others

Conscious effort

Consistent pattern of

Constant state of

Consummate

Contaminated by

Contested every step

Continued success

Continued to advance

Continuous improvement

Contributed to

Contributed to success of

Controversial

Conveniently forgot

Conventional wisdom

Convinced others

Cooler heads prevail(ed)

Cooperative spirit

Corruption

Confusion reigned

Conquered

Consensus builder

Conspicuous absence

Constructive attitude

Consummate craftsman

Content of character

Continued quest for

Continued to adapt

Continuing cycle of

Contrary personality

Contributed to demise

Controlled response

Controversial issue

Conventional barrier(s)

Conveys style

Cook the books

Cooler heads prevailed

Cornerstone of

Cost too high

342

Phrase, Thought, Idea, or Idiom

Countless hours/numbers	Countless number
Courage to face	Courageous act(s)
Course of action	Cover up
Cover(ed) all eventualities	Covered all bases
Coveted award	Crack down
Crack under pressure	Cream of the crop
Cream rose to top	Created (new) process of
Created atmosphere/climate	Created havoc
Created tension	Creative approach to
Creative genius	Creative masterpiece
Creditability gap	Creditability undermined
Crippling blow	Crisis situation
Critical	Critical shortage/juncture
Critical test	Critical time/juncture
Critically acclaimed	Criticized for
Crossed the line	Crown jewel
Crowning achievement(s)	Crucial issue(s)
Crucial to success	Crusader for
Crusader's zeal	Crystal clear
Culmination of	Cultural development
Curious to a fault	Cushion of safety

343

Phrase, Thought, Idea, or Idiom

Customary confidence

Cut and run

Cut the mustard

Cynical

Damage control work

Damn with faint praise

Dark chapter/cloud

Dark side of

Darkened spirit(s)

Daunting problem(s)

Dazzling performance

Debt of gratitude

Decisive action(s)

Decisive time(s)

Dedicated efforts

Deep respect

Deeply moved

Deep-seated

Defenseless position

Defiant opposition

Defined character/essence

Cut above

Cut teeth on

Cutting edge

Daily challenges of

Damaged creditability

Danger(s) overlooked

Dark cloud over

Dark undercurrent(s)

Dashed the hopes

Days numbered

Dealt heavy blow

Deceptively simple

Decisive action(s)/step

Decline in

Deep feelings/respect

Deepening rift

Deeply rooted

Defender of

Defensive posture

Defies logic

Definition of character

Degenerated into	Degraded position
Degree of certainty	Delicate balance
Delinquent	Delivered as expected
Demeaning	Demise
Demise of	Depleted resources
Deprived	Designed to address
Desired effect	Desperate attempt
Desperate gamble	Desperate measures
Desperately needs(ed)	Despite deep cuts
Despite precautions	Destroyed
Destructive influence	Devastating blow
Develop full potential	Devious
Devoid of	Devoted resources to
Devoted to	Diamond in the rough
Dictatorial	Did not fare well
Die is cast	Diehard
Difficult business of	Difficult event/circumstances
Difficult times	Difficult transition
Difficulties encountered	Diligent practice
Diluted effectiveness	Diminishing number
Direct/Indirect pressure	Directly influenced

Phrase, Thought, Idea, or Idiom

Directly responsible for

Disappointing results

Disaster

Disastrous consequences

Disbelieving eyes

Discarded without reason

Discord

Disillusioned with

Disinformation

Dismal performance

Dispassionate judgment

Disruptive influence

Distasteful

Distinctively different

Distinguished tradition

Distorted sense of

Diverse background

Do a good turn

Do justice to

Dogmatic

Dominated area of

Disadvantage of

Disappointment to

Disaster looms(d) ahead

Disbelief

Discarded

Disciplined passion

Discovered

Disinclined to

Disjointed operation

Disorganized efforts

Disrupted delicate balance

Dissident voice

Distinct advantage

Distinguished

Distinguishing characteristic(s)

Disturbing conclusion(s)

Diverse point(s) of view

Do great things

Doesn't measure up

Dominant force

Dominated field

Phrase, Thought, Idea, or Idiom

Door always open	Do-or-die
Double-talk	Down hearted
Down side	Down the drain
Down to earth	Down to the wire
Downfall	Downplayed
Down-turn in	Draining confidence
Dramatic change/time	Dramatic swing in
Dramatic turn of events	Dramatically illustrated
Drastic measures/steps	Draw back
Draw the line	Dream come true
Drew heavily on/upon	Driving force
Drop in the bucket	Dubious honor
Due course	Dulled initiative
Dumbfounded	Dwindling
Dynamic	Dynamic force
Eager anticipation	Eager to
Ear marked for	Early state of
Earned place in	Ease effect(s)
Eased burden	Easily sidetracked
Easy to understand	Eccentric
Eclipsed previous record	Electrified

Phrase, Thought, Idea, or Idiom

Element of risk

Elevated to level of

Eliminated all

Elite

Embarked upon

Embodied central idea

Embodies unique

Embraced concept

Emerging

Employing strategy of

Encourages the heart

End in sight

Endangered outcome

Enduring place in

Energy devoted to

Enflamed the passion

Engaged in

Enhanced image

Enlist emotion(s)

Enriched the lives

Enthusiasm ran high

Elevated level of

Eleventh hour

Eliminated need for

Eloquent

Embattled

Embodies qualities of

Embodies values of

Embraced with enthusiasm

Emotional baggage/scars

Empty argument

Encumbered by

End of the line

Endless possibilities

Enduring qualities

Enflamed tensions

Engaged imagination

Engineered path of future

Enjoys(ed) increase(d)

Enrich

Entertaining thought

Enthusiastic support

348

Phrase, Thought, Idea, or Idiom

Entirely new perspective

Entrusted with

Envisions the future

Equal to challenge

Equitable distribution

Escalating tensions

Especially significant

Essential element/trait(s)

Established legacy/stability

Even less prepared

Ever-expanding obligations

Every possible avenue

Every way possible

Example of

Excellence grew

Exciting development

Exciting time(s)

Exercise(d) the option

Exerted due influence

Expeditious

Experienced viewpoint

Entrenched position

Environment of openness

Epitome of

Equal to task

Eroded morale

Escalation of

Essential element(s)

Established foothold

Ethical lapse

Ever ready to

Ever-present/growing

Every step of the way

Examined all aspects

Exceeded expectations

Exciting accomplishment(s)

Exciting possibilities

Exercise(d) best judgment

Exercised influence

Exerted influence

Expended great energy

Exploited

Exploits noteworthy

Explore(d) new methods

Expressed concern

Extended range

Extensive damage

Extraordinary challenge(s)

Extravagant

Extreme view(s)

Exuberant

Eye on future

Eye-opening

Face challenge(s)

Face value

Face(d) the challenge

Faced prospect of

Faced tall odds

Failed to comprehend

Failed to materialize/detect

Failed venture

Fall flat on face

Fall short

Explore new direction(s)

Explosive emotions

Expresses conviction

Extensive analysis

Extra motivation

Extraordinary measure(s)

Extreme measures

Extremely delicate

Eye of the storm

Eye-catching

Fabrication of truth

Face up to

Face(d) issue(s) head on

Faced many challenges

Faced real challenge

Faded away

Failed to keep pace

Failed to realize

Failure to take initiative

Fall from grace

Fall to pieces

Phrase, Thought, Idea, or Idiom

Fall(s) short

False promises

Falsehood

Far and wide

Far-fetched

Farsighted

Fast-moving

Feeble act

Feel the energy

Feeling for what is right

Fell behind

Fell in with

Fell out of favor

Fell victim to

Fertile soil for

Few and far between

Fierce competitor

Fiercely loyal

Filled the air

Filled with apprehension

Final decision

False assumption

False sense of security

Far and away

Far more reliable

Far-reaching

Fascinated by/with

Faultless

Feel tension

Feel the pulse

Feet on the ground

Fell by the wayside

Fell into disarray

Fell prey to

Fertile imagination

Feverish activity

Fiasco

Fierce determination

Fill the bill

Filled vacuum

Filled with excitement

Final touch(es)

351

Phrase, Thought, Idea, or Idiom

Fine detail	Fine line
Finest	Finest tradition
Firestorm of criticism	Firm constructive element
Firm conviction	Firm position/resolve
Firm resolve	Firmly committed
Firmly rejected	First and foremost
First ever	First in long line of
First rank importance	First stabilized, then reversed
First step down road to	First step(s)
Firsthand experience	Fitting climax
Fix responsibility	Fizzle out
Flag bearer	Flag-waving
Flair for	Flamboyant style
Flare(d) up	Flaunt authority
Flawed	Flawless
Flawlessly executed	Flight from reality
Flirting with danger	Flood of support
Floundered	Flourish in face of
Flourishes in environment of	Flushed with victory
Flying blind	Focal point
Focus attention on	Focus(es) on

Phrase, Thought, Idea, or Idiom

Focused and re-doubled efforts

Foiled efforts

Followed footsteps

Foot in the door

For good measure

For the better

Force in

Forced to

Forged ahead

Formed diverse

Formidable tool

Forte

Fortune(s) changed

Foster(s) sense of

Fought diligently

Fought losing battle

Foul up

Found satisfaction

Foundation of/for

Fragile situation

Fragmented

Focused determination

Follow(ed) the crowd

Foot dragging

Foothold in

For others to emulate

For the most part

Forced the issue

Forever changed

Forged united effort

Formed the foundation

Formula for success

Forthcoming

Forward-looking

Fostered improved

Fought long and hard

Fought tooth and nail

Found excuse

Foundation built on

Founder of

Fragmentary

Frame of mind

353

Phrase, Thought, Idea, or Idiom

Frank assessment

Frantic pace

Free of incident

Free-spirited

Fresh new

Fresh start

Frightfully inadequate

From the onset

Fruits of labor

Fueled ambition(s) of

Full cooperation

Full extent/measure

Full of hope

Full range of

Full steam ahead

Full-court press

Full-time job

Fully prepared to/for

Fundamental value(s)

Fundamentally inconsistent

Furthered cause

Frank observation(s)

Free from stigma of

Free rein

Frequent contributor

Fresh page in

Friend and supporter

From bad to worse

Fruitful

Fuel the imagination

Fueled creative spirit

Full court press

Full force

Full of possibilities

Full speed ahead

Full swing

Full-grown

Fully committed to

Fundamental principal/values

Fundamentally different

Fundamentally sound

Future begins now

Phrase, Thought, Idea, or Idiom

Future-oriented	Gain(ed) ground
Gained admiration	Gained favor
Gained foothold	Gained notoriety
Game of catch-up	Garbage behavior
Gateway to	Gave a hard time
Gave birth to	Gave free rein
Gave rise to	Gave wide berth
General order of things	Generated resentment
Generous assistance	Generously gave
Genuine act of/article	Genuine desire
Get a fix on	Get a grip on
Get off on wrong foot	Get to heart of
Get(s) behind	Giant step forward
Give(n) blank check	Give-and-take
Glaring reality	Glimmer of hope
Glorious effort(s)	Glued to facts
Go against the grain	Go all out
Go along with	Go astray
Go back on	Go extra mile
Go hand-in-hand	Go overboard
Go to bat for	Go to extreme(s)

Phrase, Thought, Idea, or Idiom

Go to limit(s)	Go-for-broke attitude
Golden opportunity	Good first step
Good fortune/measure	Good-for-nothing
Got in way	Got jump on
Grace under fire	Gracefully accepted
Graduated to level	Grand scale
Grass roots	Gratifying
Gravitate toward(s)	Gravity of situation
Great chapter in history	Great deal of
Grew in intensity	Grew in sophistication
Grew in wisdom and stature	Grim outlook
Grind to a halt	Gripping reality
Groomed to/for	Gross negligence
Ground breaking	Ground floor
Ground to a halt	Ground-breaking
Growing concern	Growing crisis/pains
Growing disillusionment	Growing sense of frustration
Guardian angel	Guide the way
Guided change	Guiding hand
Guiding light/vision	Guilty of
Had a hand in	Had advantage of

Phrase, Thought, Idea, or Idiom

Had free rein

Half-baked idea(s)

Hallmark

Hand picked

Handicapped by

Handled delicate issue(s)

Hands full

Hand-tied

Hard case

Hard pressed

Hard-earned

Hard-nosed

Hardy attitude

Harmonious relationship(s)

Harsh reality

Have upper hand

Head on defiance

Head(ed) off

Head-strong

Healthy source of

Heart of gold

Hair-raising experience

Half-hearted

Hammer away

Hand(s) full

Hand-in-hand

Handled with respect

Hands-on person

Hard as nails

Hard nut to crack

Hard to fathom

Hard-fisted

Hard-pressed

Harm's way

Harness(ed) power

Hats off to

Head above water

Head over heals

Headed in right direction

Healed wounds

Heart and soul

Heart-to-heart

357

Phrase, Thought, Idea, or Idiom

Heated debate	Heavy burden
Heavy price to pay	Heavy-handed
Hectic schedule	Heightened activity
Held firm	Helped build
Helped inspire	Helped solidify
Helping hand	Herculean effort
Hidden qualities	High and dry
High frequency of	High gear
High hope(s)	High stress environment
High time	High/Low profile
Higher goal(s)	High-flying
High-handed	Highly developed
Historic event	History of
Hit bottom	Hit the books
Hit the mark	Hit the skids
Hit-and-miss	Hold fast
Honed to perfection	Honest feedback
Hope faded	Hope for future
Hopeless situation	Hopelessly involved
Hopelessly lost	Host of challenges
Host of problems	Hot seat

Phrase, Thought, Idea, or Idiom

Hot spot

Hours on end

Hypercritical

Ideal conditions

If present trend continues

Ignored advice

Ill fated

Ill-afford to

Illuminates spirit of

Immediate impact/success

Immersed in

Impatient for new challenge(s)

Impeccable timing

Impending disaster

Implemented blueprint

Important first step

Important source of

Impressed with

Improperly

Improved quality of

In a bad way

Hotly debated/contested

Hunger for

Hysteria

Ideal for

Ignited fire in/to

Ill at ease

Ill will

Ill-fated

Illustrious career

Immediate turnaround

Impassioned

Impeccable taste

Impeccably prepared

Impetus to/for

Implemented comprehensive

Important point(s)

Impractical

Impressive

Improved lives

Impulsive troublemaker

In a nutshell

Phrase, Thought, Idea, or Idiom

In aftermath

In due course/time

In face of

In great measure

In line with

In short supply

In step with

In the face of

In the prime

In touch with

In wake of

Inclined to

Increased tension

Increasingly clear

Incredible level/sense of

Indecisive action

Indescribably

Indifferent to

Inequity

Inexhaustible energy

In-fighting

In collusion with

In eye of controversy

In full stride

In high gear

In mainstream

In spotlight

In the driver's seat

In the mind's eye

In the works

In vain

Inactivity

Increased appetite for

Increasing number of

Increasingly unhappy

Indebted to

Independent thinking

Indifference

Indispensable to

Inescapable reality

Inextricably connected

Inflated ego

360

Phrase, Thought, Idea, or Idiom

Inflicted heavy loses

Influential presence

Infused with spirit

Inherent dislike/danger

Inherently risky

Injects life

Inner strength

Inquisitive

Insatiable appetite

Insensitive to

Inside track

Insignificant issue(s)

Inspiration to all

Inspired by

Instinct for

Instituted measures

Integrity

Intense dedication/work

Intense pressure

Intentionally deceive

Internal struggle/turmoil

Influence on

Infuse(d) fresh ideas

Ingenuity

Inherent problem/danger

Inherited unsuccessful

Injustice to

Innovative new way/solutions

Ins and outs

Insecure

Inside information

Insignificant

Inspiration

Inspire shared vision

Inspiring breakthrough

Instinctive feel

Integral part of

Intense dedication

Intense personality

Intense routine

Internal fire

Intimate knowledge

361

Phrase, Thought, Idea, or Idiom

Intimidated	Intricately involved
Intriguing concept/idea	Intrinsic values
Intrinsically superior	Introduce(d) new life
Introduced new	Intuitive
Invaluable contribution(s)	Invested talent/time
Investment in future	Invigorating program
Iron discipline/fist	Iron out differences
Iron will	Ironically destined to
Irrational exuberance	Irrefutable evidence
Irregularities	Irreplaceable
Irreplaceable service	Irreversible damage
Isolated in wake of	Joined in effort
Jolt of adrenaline	Judicious effort
Jump the gun	Jump to conclusions
Jumped on bandwagon	Jump-start
Just in time	Keen awareness
Keen grasp of	Keen observation
Keep an eye on	Keep head above water
Keep pace	Kept cool head
Kept on toes	Key element/ingredient(s)
Key juncture	Key part of

Phrase, Thought, Idea, or Idiom

Key role in	Key to success
Keyed up	Keystone
Kicked door open	Kindled spirit(s)
Knack for	Knock(ed) on the door
Know-how	Know-it-all
Knows value of	Labor in vain
Labor of love	Labor under disadvantage
Labored hard	Lack of
Lacked expertise	Lacking
Ladder of success	Lagging behind
Laid an egg	Laid back
Laid blame	Laid foundation/groundwork
Laid groundwork	Laid to rest
Laid waste	Landmark
Landmark decision	Lapse in
Larger than life	Last ditch effort
Lasting contribution(s)	Lasting impact
Latent with	Laughable consequences
Launched new	Launched new program(s)
Lavished praise	Lay claim to
Lay down the law	Lay to rest

363

Phrase, Thought, Idea, or Idiom

Lay waste

Leader's vision

Lean over backwards

Learn the hard way

Learned hard lesson

Leave no stone unturned

Left legacy

Left ugly mark

Lend a hand

Lenient to a fault

Let down

Level playing field

Life-long passion for

Lifted heavy weight

Light the way

Lightening quick

Limitations evident

Lip service

Litany of violations

Little to show for

Lively spirit

Lead the way

Leading the way

Leaps into action

Learned first-hand

Least number of

Left a mark

Left permanent scar

Legacy of service

Lengthy process

Less than optimistic

Level best

Lifeblood

Lift(s) people's spirit(s)

Light at end of tunnel

Lighten the burden

Like clockwork

Lingering problems

Lit fire under

Little by little

Lively exchange.

Locked horns with

Phrase, Thought, Idea, or Idiom

Long and arduous

Long haul/journey

Long shot

Long-lasting/-standing

Long-term commitment

Look down upon

Looked up to

Loose cannon

Lose ground

Loses perception/sight of

Lost advantage

Lost ground/respect

Lost will to

Low tolerance

Lowest common denominator

Lukewarm reception

Made a difference

Made good use of

Made it easy for

Made short work of

Made to order

Long be remembered

Long periods of

Long, hard road

Long-term approach

Long-term relationship

Look(s) other way

Looks beyond

Loosened shackles

Lose touch

Losing battle

Lost grip on reality

Lost valuable time

Low profile

Lower the boom

Lowest form of

Lump together

Made good on

Made inroads

Made point of

Made the best of

Made way through

Phrase, Thought, Idea, or Idiom

Magnitude of situation	Main ingredient(s)
Mainstream	Maintained composure
Maintained course	Major challenge(s)
Major contributor	Major crack in
Major obstacle	Major threat
Major transition	Make a point
Make allowance(s) for	Make best of
Make good (on)	Make over
Make short work of	Make the grade
Make waves	Makes things work
Manipulated to own ends	Margin of safety
Marked coming	Marred by
Marvelous	Massive undertaking
Master stroke	Master the situation
Mastered details of	Mastermind(ed)
Masterpiece	Masterwork
Matter of course	Matter of degrees
Matter of fact	Matter of principle
Maverick	Maximum capacity
Measure of success	Measure of success/failure
Meet challenges	Meet demands

Phrase, Thought, Idea, or Idiom

Meet halfway	Meet new challenges
Meet the needs	Memorable event/work
Menace	Mental powers
Mere words fail to	Merit(s) special praise
Met criteria	Meticulous
Meticulous attention to	Middle of the road
Milestone(s)	Mind-set
Mired in	Miscalculated
Misfortune	Misguided
Misguided use of	Misjudged
Misled	Miss(ed) the mark/point
Missed opportunity(ies)	Mission accomplished
Mixed blessing(s)	Mixed reputation
Mixed signals	Mobilizes others
Modeled after	Moderating effect
Moment of truth	Monumental
Moral base	Moral dilemma
Moral involvement	Moral outrage
More important aspect	More questions than answers
Mortal blow	Mountain of talent
Mounted major challenge	Move(d) forward

Phrase, Thought, Idea, or Idiom

Moved expeditiously

Moved in positive direction

Multi-faceted/talented

Nail down

Narrow(ed) the gap

Natural enthusiasm

Nearsighted approach

Needed lift

Negated by

Neglected

Nervous anticipation

Never gave up

New and challenging

New approach

New horizons

New wrinkle surfaced

Nice going

Nip in the bud

No holds barred

No stranger to

Noble intentions/undertaking

Moved forward

Muddle through

Muster up courage/strength

Narrow minded

Natural choice for

Near perfection

Necessary for future of

Needed shot in the arm

Negative response

Nerves of steel

Never forgot

Never wavered/faltered

New and exciting

New breed of

New way of thinking

Newfound

Nick of time

No end in sight

No longer a force

Noble gesture

Non-conformist

368

Phrase, Thought, Idea, or Idiom

Nose to the grindstone

Notable exception

Nothing of significance

Nourished

Nullified earlier

Number one superstar

Nurtured

Obsessed with 1

Off and on

Off deep end

Off the wall

Often in trouble

Ominous

On cutting edge

On hot seat

On the ropes

Once and for all

One and all

On-going process/problem

Open and aboveboard

Open confrontation

Not to be forgotten

Nothing left to chance

Nothing short of

Nourishes spirits

Number of near misses

Numerous defects

Oblivious to

Obvious weakness

Off base

Off the cuff/mark

Off to fast start

Old fashioned

On business end of

On guard for/against

On the ball

On the spot

Once-over

On-going battle

Onward and upward

Open arms

Opened door/gate

369

Phrase, Thought, Idea, or Idiom

Opened flood gates

Open-handed

Opportunity presented itself

Oppressed

Orchestrated

Out of bounds/control/date

Out of place/step

Out of touch

Out on a limb

Outdated ideas

Outside mainstream

Outward calm

Over and above

Over looked problem(s)

Overabundance of

Overcame all obstacles

Overcame problem(s)

Overkill

Overly cautious

Overshadowed

Overtones of

Opened new horizon

Openly defied

Opportunity to create

Optimistic appraisal/outlook

Out in the cold

Out of element

Out of thin air

Out of touch with reality

Outcome never in doubt

Outpouring of

Outspoken

Over a barrel

Over extended

Over the top

Overall strategy

Overcame difficulties

Overestimate(d)

Overload(ed) system

Overnight success

Overtaken by events

Overwhelming evidence

Phrase, Thought, Idea, or Idiom

Overwhelmingly positive

Paid no attention

Painfully obvious

Paragon of virtue

Part and parcel

Particularly good at

Pass the buck

Passed the torch

Passing of the guard

Passionate defender of

Path of growth

Pave(d) the way

Peace of mind

Peak of

Perfect blend/choice

Perfect opportunity

Persona

Personal crusade

Personality clash

Phenomenal change

Pick the brain(s)

Pace of change

Paid the price

Painstakingly work

Paralyzed by

Particularly effective

Particularly productive

Pass(ed) muster

Passed with flying colors

Passionate advocate

Pat on the back

Pathetic

Pay attention

Peacemaker

Peck away

Perfect example

Persisted in

Personal agenda

Personal test of courage

Pessimistic outlook

Physical courage

Pick up the pieces

Phrase, Thought, Idea, or Idiom

Pick(ed) holes in	Picture perfect
Pillar of	Pillar of strength
Pinnacle	Pinpoint accuracy
Pioneer in field/spirit	Pioneering spirit
Pitch(ed) in	Pitfall(s)
Pivotal situation	Placed emphasis on
Places blame	Places high premium
Plagued by	Plain and simple facts
Planted the seed	Play hard ball
Played down	Played full part
Played important role	Played out on giant scale
Played positive role	Playing with fire
Pleasantly surprised	Pleased with
Point of contention	Point(ed) the finger
Point-blank	Poised for
Poised on edge of	Poisoned the water
Policy maker	Political climate
Political landscape	Politically incorrect
Pomp and circumstances	Poor display
Poorly handled	Popular belief
Posed a threat	Position weak

Phrase, Thought, Idea, or Idiom

Positive influence on	Positive movement
Positive response	Positive thinking
Positive/Negative Feedback	Potent
Potential crisis	Potential risk(s)
Potentially dangerous	Potentially significant
Pounced upon	Powder keg ready to explode
Power base	Power of presence .
Power play	Power vacuum
Powerful tool	Power-packed
Powers of observation	Practical application
Pragmatic	Precious little/few
Precious source of	Precision
Pre-disposed	Premature
Preoccupied with	Preponderance of evidence
Presence of mind	Press luck
Press(ed) hard	Press(ing) ahead
Pressed forward	Pressing matters
Pressure-cooker situation	Prevail upon
Price too high	Priceless
Pride of accomplishment	Primary objective
Prime mover	Prime reason

Phrase, Thought, Idea, or Idiom

Primitive ideas	Principles sacrificed
Prized position	Problem prevalent to
Problem solver	Problems surfaced
Process of discovery	Productive pursuit
Productivity increased	Professional suicide
Professional triumph	Professional vigor
Profited by/from	Profound influence/impact
Profound respect	Profoundly affected
Progressive new	Prominent
Promise of things to come	Prone to
Proof positive	Proper balance of
Properly handled/prepared	Protective arm of
Proud to serve	Proved fruitful
Proved mettle	Provided chemistry necessary
Provided insight into	Provided outlet for
Proving ground	Provoke(d)
Prudent	Prudent balance of
Public integrity	Public relations problem
Public trust	Pull strings
Pull(ed) plug on	Pull(ed) punch(es)
Pulled out all stops	Pulled together

Phrase, Thought, Idea, or Idiom

Pure bedlam

Pursued with tenacity

Push(ed) forward

Pushed envelope

Pushed to limit(s)

Put (back) on track

Put finger on

Put in a good word

Put lid on

Put strain on

Putter around aimlessly

Quagmire

Quest for

Questionable techniques

Quick on the uptake

Quickly soared to top

Radical change

Radically different/new

Raised doubt

Raised spirit(s) of

Raised the question(s)

Pursue all avenues

Push came to shove

Push(ed) panic button

Pushed idea of

Pushing the limit(s)

Put an end to

Put good face on

Put in order

Put measures in place

Put to the test

Puzzling

Quantum leap

Questionable decision

Quick on the trigger

Quick to

Radiates

Radical departure

Ragged attempt

Raised new issues

Raised state of the art

Ran counter to

375

Phrase, Thought, Idea, or Idiom

Ran into difficulties	Ran out of time/ideas
Random act(s) of kindness	Range of performance
Rapid decline	Rapid evolution
Rapid increase in	Rare insight
Rare privilege	Rarefied atmosphere
Rational expectation(s)	Ray of hope
Razor-sharp mind	Reached milestone
Reached new heights/summit	Reached peak of
Reacted quickly	Read between the lines
Readily available	Ready-made
Real change	Real division in
Real powder keg	Realized full potential
Reap consequences	Reasonable solution
Rebel	Rebounded from
Rebuilt confidence	Recipe for success
Reckless abandon	Reckless abandon/disregard
Reckless nonconformance	Recognized stewardship
Record breaking/shattering	Record of
Redeeming qualities	Redefined
Redefined concept	Re-energized efforts
Refined	Reflected changes

Phrase, Thought, Idea, or Idiom

Reform oriented	Refreshing thought(s)
Refused to accept	Regrettable circumstance(s)
Rehash old issues	Reinforced action(s)
Reinvigorated sagging	Rejuvenated
Rekindled flame	Relaxed confidence
Relegated to	Relentless pressure(s)
Relentless pursuit	Relinquished control
Relish with zest	Reluctance to
Rendered obsolete	Renowned for
Repeated success/failure	Repeatedly urged to
Repugnant	Reputation
Reservoir of experience	Reshaped
Residual damage	Resilient
Resounding success	Respectable showing
Respected figure	Responded full measure
Responded in full measure	Rest(ed) on laurels
Restored confidence	Revamped a sagging
Revered for	Revitalized
Revolutionary (new) idea(s)	Revolutionary method(s)
Revolutionized	Rhyme or reason
Rich in vitality	Rich past experience(s)

Phrase, Thought, Idea, or Idiom

Rich tradition/variety	Richly deserved
Riddled with	Right set of values
Right thing to do	Rigorous schedule
Rigorous standards	Rise to the occasion
Risk factor	Risk taker
Road to recovery	Road undercurrents
Rock hard	Rock-hard evidence
Rocky road	Root of problem
Rooted in history	Rose from depths of
Rose to the occasion	Rough edges
Run a risk	Run circles around
Run down	Run into the ground
Run of the mill	Run the gauntlet
Rush of adrenaline	Ruthless approach
Sacred cow	Sad day
Safeguard	Safely weathered
Sap the foundation(s) of	Sapped energy/vitality
Save face	Save(d) the day
Saw future/light	Scapegoat
Scare tactic(s)	Scot-free
Scrambled to	Scraped together

Phrase, Thought, Idea, or Idiom

Search of excellence

Seasoned veteran

Second nature

Second to none

Seize the opportunity

Seized upon idea of

Self-styled

Sense of

Sensitive issue(s)

Sent clear message/signal

Series of tragic events

Serious blow to

Serious contender

Serious situation

Seriously weakened/strengthened

Served to

Set apart/free

Set course for future

Set new precedent

Set the stage

Set world on fire

Searches for opportunities

Second guess

Second thought(s)

Seed(s) of success

Seized the moment

Selective field

Sensation(al)

Sense of purpose

Sensitive to

Sent shock waves

Serious action(s)

Serious consequences

Serious crisis/situation

Seriously disrupted/hampered

Served the purpose

Set (record) straight

Set back

Set in motion/place

Set sights on

Set up and take notice

Setback

379

Phrase, Thought, Idea, or Idiom

Severe blow/hardship(s)

Severely strained

Shabby practices

Shadow of former self

Shady methods

Shake a leg

Sham

Shape(d) the

Shaped events

Shaping the future

Sharp increase

Sharp tongue

Sharply divided

Sharply focused

Sheer energy

Sheer willpower/force of

Shore up weak points

Short and sweet

Short-sighted

Shot in the arm

Shouldered responsibility

Show off

Shrink from responsibilities

Shrink in face of

Shut the door on

Shy away from

Side-step the issue

Sight set on

Sign of hope

Sign of the times

Significant changes/gains

Significant inroads

Significant milestone

Significant number of

Significant progress

Simple and straight-forward

Simply the best

Sincere honor

Singled out for

Single-minded

Single-minded energy

Single-minded purpose

Phrase, Thought, Idea, or Idiom

Singular purpose	Sinister
Sink teeth into	Sit on side line
Sit up & take notice	Situation of extreme(s)
Size up situation	Skeptical of
Slap in the face	Slip away
Slowed rate of	Smoke and mirrors
Smoke and mirrors	Smooth process
Smother creativity	Snail's pace
Social architect	Social fabric
Soft-pedal decision	Solely responsible
Solid base/foundation	Solid contributor
Solid resolve	Solidified
Someone special	Song and dance
Sophisticated role	Sorely needed
Sought after by	Soul of organization
Soul-searching	Sound(ed) the alarm
Sounding board	Source of knowledge/light
Sparked innovation	Spawned new
Spawned rise of	Spearhead
Spearheaded effort(s) to	Special feel for
Special gift for	Special quality(ies)

Phrase, Thought, Idea, or Idiom

Special rapport with

Spelled success

Spirit of cooperation

Spirits dwindled

Split hairs

Spotless

Springboard of/for

Spurred action/growth

Squandered opportunities

Square-shooter

Staggering blow/losses

Staggering toll

Stalemate

Stand tall

Stands alone

Stark contrast

Started slow climb

State of disarray

Stated objective(s)

Status symbol

Stay(ed) in background

Spell of good luck

Spirit of

Spirited debate

Splendid record

Split-second

Spotlight

Springboard to

Squander away

Square away

Squeaky clean

Staggering range of talent

Stainless record

Stand on own two feet

Stand up and be counted

Standstill

Started from scratch

State of despair

State of the art

Stately appearance

Staunch supporter

Steady stream of

382

Phrase, Thought, Idea, or Idiom

Steal the spotlight	Steered course of
Stem rising tide	Stem the tide
Step ahead of	Step aside
Step/Level above	Stepped forward
Stern measures	Stick it out
Stiff opposition	Stigma
Stir up discontent	Storm on horizon
Stormy relationship(s)	Story of dedication
Straight as an arrow	Straight shooter
Straighten up	Straightforward response
Strain put on	Strategy aimed at
Straw broke camel's back	Strength through unity
Strengthened resolve	Strengthens others
Strenuous schedule	Stretched boundaries/limits
Stretches the imagination	Strict conformance/standards
Strict control	Strident support
Strike a blow	Striking results
String along	Strings attached
Stroke of genius	Stroke of luck/genius
Stroke of the pen	Strong advocate
Strong background	Strong influence

383

Phrase, Thought, Idea, or Idiom

Strong voice for	Strong will
Struck by fact	Structural change/reform
Struggled (un)successfully	Struggled to stay afloat
Stubborn determination	Studied works of
Stumbled through/upon	Stumbling block
Stunning results	Stunt growth
Substantial impact/number	Substantially improved
Success story	Successes mounted
Successfully challenged	Successfully created
Suffered downward slide	Summon(ed) up the courage
Sunny disposition	Superficial
Supporting cast	Supportive fashion
Surge in activity	Surge of
Surpassed all expectations	Surrounded by uncertainty
Survival of the fittest	Sustained commitment
Sustained effort	Sustained progress
Sweep out/aside	Sweep under the rug
Sweeping changes/reform	Sweet victory
Symbol of	Sympathetic ear
Systematic	Systematic approach
Tackle(s) any	Tainted in controversy

Phrase, Thought, Idea, or Idiom

Take a back seat

Take by storm

Take hold of

Take interest in

Take offense

Take stock

Take to heart

Take/Took full advantage of

Task at hand

Taste of

Temper(ed) the spirit

Temporary setback

Tenacious

Tense time(s)

Tenuous position

Test of will/character

Tested to limit(s)

Tests new ideas

Thirst for

Thought-provoking

Thrives in/on

Take a dim view of

Take heart

Take in hand

Take into account

Take part in

Take the lead

Take to task

Tarnished

Task master

Tedious steps

Temperamentally suited

Tempt faith

Tendency to

Tensions high

Terminal damage

Test willpower/water(s)

Testimony to

Theatrical nature

Thoughtful analysis

Threshold of

Through thick and thin

385

Phrase, Thought, Idea, or Idiom

Throw down the gauntlet	Throw the book at
Throw up hands	Throws weight around
Thumbs up/down	Tight knit group
Time beginning to tell	Time is ripe
Time of transition	Timeless
Time-tested	Timid
Tireless efforts	To make matters worse
To put it mildly	To the bitter end
Toe the line	Tone down
Too little, too late	Took a stand
Took advantage of	Took back seat
Took for granted	Took fresh look
Took full advantage	Took inventory of facilities
Took issue with	Took liberty to
Took lightly fact of/that	Took nose-dive
Took on added responsibility	Took special interest in
Took the helm	Took toll on
Top speed	Top to bottom
Top-level performance	Top-notch
Tore down barrier(s)	Tormented
Total and complete failure	Total confidence

Phrase, Thought, Idea, or Idiom

Total dimension of	Total focus
Totally clear	Tough act to follow
Tough nut to crack	Tough taskmaster
Toward the future	Tower of strength
Track record	Traditional concept
Traditional values	Tragic consequences
Transcends	Transformed
Transparent motive(s)	Treat with discourtesy/courtesy
Trial and error	Tricky business
Tried and failed	Tried and true
Tried in vain	Triggered a
Triggered response	Triumph
Trivial matters	Trivialize importance
Trouble adapting	Troubled history/past
Troubled waters	True pioneer/visionary
True to form	True transformation
True visionary	Trumped up charge(s)
Trusted advisor	Trusted completely
Tug-of-war	Turbulent
Turmoil arose	Turn(ed) cold shoulder
Turn (thumbs) down	Turn for better/worse

Phrase, Thought, Idea, or Idiom

Turn inside out

Turn over new leaf

Turn the tables

Turn(ed) a deaf ear

Turn(ed) the tide

Turnaround

Turned back on

Turned blind eye to

Turned on the heat

Turned the corner

Turning point

Ultimate success

Ultimate test

Unable to grasp

Unacceptable

Unanswered questions

Unassailable performance

Unattained goals

Unaware

Unbearable

Unbeatable combination

Unbecoming

Unbreakable spirit

Uncharacteristic display

Uncharted territory

Uncluttered thought

Uncompromising principles

Undaunted

Undaunted courage

Undeniable appeal

Under a cloud

Under any circumstances

Under best of circumstances

Under fire

Under perform(ance/er)

Under pressure

Under the wire

Underdog

Underestimated

Underhanded dealings

Underlines importance

Underlying cause

Phrase, Thought, Idea, or Idiom

Underscore(d) importance	Undertaking
Underwent process of	Unencumbered
Unenviable position	Unexpected
Unexpected loss(es)	Unexpected obstacle(s)
Unexpected turn to/for	Unexplored avenues
Unfilled promises	Unfinished business
Unfolding event(s)	Unforeseen events
Unfortunate accident/incident	Unglamorous task(s)
Unification of	Unifying force
Uninhabited	Uninvolved
Unique achievement(s)	Uniquely diverse/suited
United behind	Universal support
Unleashed	Unlikely to
Unlocked door of opportunity	Unmatched skill
Unmistakable	Unnecessary barriers
Unorthodox	Unprecedented
Unprecedented skill/talent	Unpredictable
Unreachable goal(s)	Unreasonable delay
Unrelenting	Unrest
Unrestrained passion for	Unshakable character
Unstoppable momentum	Unstoppable resolve

Phrase, Thought, Idea, or Idiom

Unsuitable

Untapped resource(s)

Untrained eye

Unwanted attention

Unwanted entanglements

Up hill

Up to the task

Upgraded

Ups and downs

Urgent business

Ushered in new

Vacillating

Vain effort

Valid option

Vast numbers

Verbal support

Versed in

Very special

Victim of own success

Vigilant

Vigorous pursuit

Unsuspecting

Untenable position

Unusual circumstances

Unwanted entanglements

Up and coming

Up in arms

Up-beat/scale

Uplifting experience

Urged caution

Uses own rules

Utter failure

Vain attempt

Valiant gesture

Valuable insight

Vastly different

Verge of

Very impressive

Viable option(s)

Victimized by

Vigorous effort(s)

Vigorous response

Phrase, Thought, Idea, or Idiom

Vile act	Vindicated by
Vindictive	Vintage
Violent	Virtual standstill
Virtually eliminate(d)	Virtually unchecked
Virtue of hard work	Virtuoso
Vision of future	Vision of substance
Visionary	Vital (first) step
Vital importance	Vital interest/aspect
Vital role	Vitality
Voice of	Voiced dissatisfaction
Voiced opposition	Volatile
Voyage of discovery	Vulnerable part
Vulnerable position	Waged relentless
Walk a tightrope	Walked out on
Warmly received	Wash hands of
Waste away	Wasted time/motion
Wasteful methods	Water(ed) down
Watershed	Wax and wane
Way it should be	Weak response
Wear and tear	Wear down
Weather(ed) the storm	Weed out

Phrase, Thought, Idea, or Idiom

Weigh the options	Weigh the words
Weight of responsibility	Welcomed addition
Well received	Well suited for
Well versed	Well-founded
Went all out	Went fare beyond
Went head-long into	Went overboard
Whatever it takes	Whitewash
Whole-hearted	Wholehearted endorsement
Wide range of	Widely accepted/embraced
Widely recognized	Wide-spread
Wild goose chase	Wild scheme(s)
Wildly different	Will power
Willing to sacrifice	Win laurels
Window dressing	Window of opportunity
Wing and a prayer	Winning game plan
Winning ways	Wipe the slate clean
With (a) passion	With honor(s)
With particular clarity	Within reach
Without a clue	Without difficulty
Without reservation	Without second thought
Withstand test of time	Withstood onslaught

Phrase, Thought, Idea, or Idiom

Won hearts and minds

Wonder work

Work ethic

Workable solution

Worked closely with

Worked long hours

Worked tirelessly to

Workhorse

World of good

Worst case scenario

Worthwhile goals

Wreak havoc

Yielded in face of

Zest for challenge

Won respect of

Words cannot express

Work under adversity

Workaholic

Worked frantically

Worked perfectly

Worked to end

World class

Worn down

Worst circumstances

Worthy of mention/blame

Wrong doing

Zero in on

Phrase, Thought, Idea, or Idiom

CHAPTER 19

CONDUCTING COUNSELING SESSIONS

TYPICAL 2-WAY CONVERSATION

Before conducting a counseling session it is important to realize how difficult a simple 2-way conversation can become. Keep the below information in mind when attempting to communicate your thoughts to someone. When sending an important message, elicit some kind of response or feedback from the listener to ensure the message was received and correctly understood.

STEP 1 - SPEAKER'S THOUGHTS
            (WHAT SPEAKER WANTS TO SAY)

STEP 2 - SPEAKER SENDS MESSAGE (TALKS)
            * (See Note 1 Below)

STEP 3 - SPEAKER'S VISUAL ELEMENT ADDED TO
            MESSAGE
                        (GESTURES, FACIAL EXPRESSIONS,
                        VOICE TONE & INTENSITY, ETC.)

STEP 4 - LISTENER'S RECEPTION OF MESSAGE (HEARS)
            ** (See Note 2 Below)

STEP 5 - LISTENER'S UNDERSTANDING
            (WHAT LISTENER HEARD & SAW)

STEP 6 - LISTENER'S THOUGHTS

STEP 7 - LISTENER SENDS MESSAGE RESPONSE (TALKS)
            * (See Note 1 Below)]

STEP 8 - LISTENER'S VISUAL ELEMENT ADDED TO
            MESSAGE
                        (GESTURES, FACIAL EXPRESSIONS,
                        VOICE TONE & INTENSITY, ETC.)

STEP 9 - ORIGINAL SPEAKER'S RECEPTION OF
        RESPONSE (HEARS) ** (See Note 2 Below)

STEP 10 - ORIGINAL SPEAKER'S UNDERSTANDING
        (WHAT SPEAKER HEARD & SAW)

The most potent part of this 2-way exchange of information is the VISUAL element, not the spoken word.

* NOTE 1:
Incorporated into a speaker's message is that speaker's:
- personality type (including talking direct/indirect & autocratic, diplomatic, etc.)
- past experiences
- education
- understanding of subject matter
- phraseology of subject matter
- emotional involvement & state of mind
- how to correctly convey message to particular listener

** NOTE 2:
Incorporated into a listener's reception of the message is that listener's:
- personality type
- past experiences
- education
- understanding of subject matter
- emotional involvement & state of mind
- perception of the speaker
- attention or inattention to speaker

Research has shown that at the end of a day at work the average person has correctly retained only about 25 percent of the verbal input received. The other 75 percent was misunderstood or forgotten.

ACTIVE LISTENER

One of the most important skills that anyone can have, especially a counselor, is to be a good listener. Being a good listener means to be an ACTIVE LISTENER. Being an active listener means keeping the mind focused on the person

395

speaking. Focus your attention on the speaker and only on the speaker. That is more difficult than you might think. The average person talks at the rate of about 150 words a minute. The brain can "listen" at the rate of about 450 words a minute. This means that the brain has a lot of idle time even when listening to someone talk. If you are not an active listener your mind can jump to other matters. If you start thinking about a response to another person when that person is still talking, you are not actively listening. If your mind drifts off to other matters, you are not actively listening. If you interrupt a person who is speaking, you are not actively listening.

COUNSELING

BEFORE COUNSELING BEGINS

Before counseling someone about their performance, take a few minutes to prepare yourself and your surroundings.

People are more comfortable & relaxed in a familiar environment. These conditions afford you the luxury of feeling more confident & in control of a conversation. If possible, arrange counseling sessions in your own office and at your own desk.

SETTING

- In private, 1-on-1 talk
- Comfortable temperature
- No outside noise distractions
- No interruptions

SEATING ARRANGEMENTS

- SITTING ON OPPOSITE SIDES OF DESK:
MORE COMBATIVE, SUBORDINATE FEELS **LESS AT EASE**.

- CORNER-TO-CORNER SEATING:
LESS COMBATIVE, SUBORDINATE FEELS **MORE AT EASE**.

- DO write down all performance areas you want to discuss.
- DO mentally go over WHAT information you are going to cover.
- DO mentally go over HOW you are going to present the information.
- DO think of what the person to be counseled might say in response to the information you present and formulate your response.

DURING COUNSELING

One way to start a counseling session might be to read aloud the job description of the individual being counseled. Then, take it from there. All too often a person thinks he/she is doing a good job while the superior may have other thoughts. When possible, start with the positive aspects of the individual. Give the person a "well done" where deserved. This will help to put the individual at ease and reduce the chances of getting started on a negative note.

Remember, one of the most important things you can do for a subordinate is to state your goals and objectives, and your expectations of him/her.

- DO NOT conduct an I TALK, YOU LISTEN counseling session.
- DO NOT raise your voice during counseling.
- DO NOT become threatening during counseling.
- DO NOT allow a confrontation to surface.
- DO NOT be ambiguous about the information you present.

- DO be friendly, cheerful & upbeat.
- DO make frequent eye contact.
- Do keep the entire counseling session on a POSITIVE note. This means don't say things like, "Your performance in area of ... was less than expected." Instead, say something like, "Can you think of any area(s) where you might improve yourself." Or, "Maybe you can become more effective if ..."
- DO try to reduce tension & increase trust & understanding.
- DO express your confidence in the individual.
- DO present the most important information direct & simple.

398

- DO get the person being counseled to state what
    improvements or changes that he/she will attempt to
    make.
- DO elicit & listen to feedback.
- DO try to understand what the other person is saying.
- DO set goals, objectives & commitments.
- DO determine, if there is a problem, if additional training
    is needed.
- DO remember the main theme of the counseling session is to
    motivate and challenge the individual.
- DO keep meeting focused on main subject(s).
- DO remember the person being counseled needs to become
    involved in the counseling process.
- DO remember that leadership is something you do WITH
    people, not TO people.
- DO remember that leadership is a function of relationships.
- DO remember, usually the more involved a person is in a
    task or project, the more motivated that person will
    become.

ENDING COUNSELING SESSION

- DO end counseling session with high enthusiasm on both
    sides.
- DO end counseling session by restating highlights of the
    meeting and all proposed actions. And, put the proposed
    actions in writing.
- DO get a commitment from the individual on proposed
    action(s).
- DO end session on a positive note.
- DO follow up on goals, objectives & commitments.
- DO NOT promise improved marks based on ASSUMED
    improvement.

CHAPTER 20

BRAG SHEET

This short chapter is perhaps the most important part of this book for you personally.

If you don't know how to write a quality performance appraisal, you don't know how to read one--your own included.

Unfortunately, most people being evaluated don't learn the real difference between a good, strong write-up and one that only "sounds" good until it is too late in their career to do much good. Because of rank, position or education many people falsely believe that they are automatically good performance appraisal writers. As a result of this false assumption, they hurt themselves and the good performers who work for them. A "sounds-good only" narrative on you is as much your fault as it is the person who writes it--you let the person do it to you. A good write-up must have some substance, some job accomplishment specifics.

Everyone should have an opportunity to submit information they would like to have considered when performance appraisal time comes around. For example, if you submitted an input that contained hard facts on your specific accomplishments, your superiors would be hard-pressed to not use the information in your narrative.

The list could go almost indefinitely. The point is **THERE IS A LIST**. Commit yourself to maintaining a "brag sheet" file throughout each reporting period. If you don't come up with two or three items a week to place in the file, you aren't trying--or you aren't doing your job. When it is time to provide an input to your performance appraisal, break out everything you have, compile it and then decide what you want to use.

Keep in mind, your superiors probably don't have time to record all of the accomplishments of everyone who works for

400

Brag Sheet

them. For a top performer, they would be happy to include any important information you submit. Plus, providing this information makes a superior's job of constructing a narrative much easier.

The more information you have in your brag file the better. Include dates, hours worked, and any other information needed to give specific accomplishments and tasks.

Brag Sheet